FORBIDDEN

FORBIDDEN

A 3,000-YEAR HISTORY OF JEWS AND THE PIG

JORDAN D. ROSENBLUM

NEW YORK UNIVERSITY PRESS
New York

NEW YORK UNIVERSITY PRESS
New York
www.nyupress.org

© 2024 by New York University
Paperback edition published 2026
All rights reserved

Library of Congress Cataloging-in-Publication Data
Names: Rosenblum, Jordan, 1979– author.
Title: Forbidden : a 3,000-year history of Jews and the pig / Jordan D. Rosenblum.
Description: New York : New York University Press, 2024. |
Includes bibliographical references and index.
Identifiers: LCCN 2023049395 (print) | LCCN 2023049396 (ebook) |
ISBN 9781479831494 (hardback) | ISBN 9781479847518 (paperback) |
ISBN 9781479831500 (ebook) | ISBN 9781479831517 (ebook other)
Subjects: LCSH: Jews—Identity. | Human-animal relationships—
Religious aspects—Judaism. | Swine—Religious aspects—Judaism. |
Swine—Symbolic aspects.
Classification: LCC GN547 .R67 2024 (print) | LCC GN547 (ebook) | DDC
296.7/3—dc23/eng/20240414
LC record available at https://lccn.loc.gov/2023049395
LC ebook record available at https://lccn.loc.gov/2023049396

This book is printed on acid-free paper, and its binding materials are chosen for strength and durability. We strive to use environmentally responsible suppliers and materials to the greatest extent possible in publishing our books.

The manufacturer's authorized representative in the EU for product safety is Mare Nostrum Group B.V., Mauritskade 21D, 1091 GC Amsterdam, The Netherlands. Email: gpsr@mare-nostrum.co.uk.

Manufactured in the United States of America

10 9 8 7 6 5 4 3 2

Also available as an ebook

In memory of Harold Blau,
who read every word I ever wrote

CONTENTS

List of Illustrations   ix

Introduction: "My Mother Made Great Pork Chops": The More-than-3,000-Year History of Jews and the Pig   1

1 "All Who Eat It Agree": The Signifying Swine in the Second Temple Period   15

2 "A Jew May Not Raise Pigs Anywhere": Euphemism and Stigma in the Classical Rabbinic Period   35

3 "The Piggish Talmud": From Metaphor to Mockery in the Medieval Period   59

4 "Sav'd His Bacon": Pig and Persecution in the Early Modern Period   83

5 "Pigs Represent for Us a New Problem": Pig Polemics across the Globe in the Modern Period   105

6 "No Jew Ever Died Refusing to Eat Shrimp": Pig Polemics in the United States in the Modern Period   141

Conclusion: "Thank You Very Much. I Am a 🐷": Arriving at the Tail of Our Tale   175

Acknowledgments   183
Notes   189
References   233
Index   249
About the Author   261

ILLUSTRATIONS

FIGURE I.1.	Hebrew and Italian children's wooden blocks	13
FIGURE 1.1.	*New Yorker* cartoon by Paul Roth	23
FIGURE 1.2.	Illuminated manuscript of 1 Maccabees 1:62–63	27
FIGURES 2.1. and 2.2	Silver denarius minted in Rome, 77–78 CE	45
FIGURE 3.1.	Illuminated manuscript of Apocryphal Childhood of Christ	67
FIGURE 3.2.	Jew swearing an oath	69
FIGURE 3.3.	Fifteenth-century German woodcut depicting a *Judensau*	73
FIGURE 4.1.	"The Conversion of Nathan"	91
FIGURE 4.2.	"The Jew Naturalized"	95
FIGURE 5.1.	"Suitors to the Pig Faced Lady"	107
FIGURE 5.2.	Poster from circa 1930.	114
FIGURE 5.3.	Soviet Yiddish propaganda poster from 1931	129
FIGURE 5.4.	Postcard by Isaac Bashevis Singer to Melech Ravitch	130
FIGURE 6.1.	A "Hebrew Volunteer" during the Civil War	153

INTRODUCTION

"My Mother Made Great Pork Chops":
The More-than-3,000-Year History of Jews and the Pig

I N August 2006, US Senator George Allen (R-Virginia) was in the midst of a controversial bid for reelection. His campaign, which would prove unsuccessful, was on its heels after several missteps, including his reported ownership of stock in Barr Labs, a company that sold the Plan B emergency contraceptive, a.k.a. the "morning after pill"—a problematic investment for a candidate running on the Republican ticket in the South—and his use of a racial slur. Later that same month, another potential scandal came to light: namely, the fact that his mother probably had Jewish lineage. According to the matrilineal principle of Jewish law, Jewish identity is imparted by one's biological mother.[1] If one's biological mother is Jewish, then one is Jewish. Though a member of the Presbyterian Church, Senator Allen now had to explain this revelation about his religious and ethnic identity to his constituency.[2] Less than a month later, the *New York Times* reported the following exchange: "'I still had a ham sandwich for lunch,' Mr. Allen told The Richmond Times-Dispatch, referring to rules against eating pork, 'and my mother made great pork chops.'"[3] In denying the relevance of his distant Jewish past—one that he had only learned about days before uttering those words—Senator Allen turned to the food on his plate. And this food came from one animal in particular: the pig. It is telling that he also highlighted his mother's culinary prowess with regard to pork chops. Since it was her lineage that had come into question, he clearly used the pig to marginalize and even erase her Jewish identity. After all, how "Jewish" could his mother be if she "made great pork chops"? Though Senator Allen probably was not aware of it, he was engaging in a millennia-old practice of using the pig to locate himself as either inside or outside the territory marked as "Jewish."[4]

This book explores the more-than-three-thousand-year history of using the pig as a litmus test for Jewish/non-Jewish identity and practice. In order to do so, it crosses a vast expanse of space and time, from ancient Israel to the modern United States, with stops physically across the globe and temporally across the millennia. In taking the reader on this journey, the big question this book seeks to answer is, Why did the pig become a such popular means—indeed, *the* means—by which people signal their Jewishness, non-Jewishness, or rebellion from Judaism? Or, in short, Why does the pig matter? To answer this question requires an entire book.

While this journey is not exhaustive—this book cannot cover every discussion about Jews and pigs in every time, place, and context—it will map out enough of the contours to uncover that the answer to the "why" question is not singular but plural. I am trained as a scholar of ancient Judaism, with a particular focus on the Classical Rabbinic Period. In order to tell this sweeping history, I must venture far outside the temporal and geographical borders of the ancient Mediterranean—an adventure that, I must confess, is thrilling, in the double sense of both *exciting* and *terrifying*. It is important also to highlight two of the guiding principles I adhered to during the writing process. First, writing a narrative that explains a development over more than three thousand years necessarily requires that the author be selective. Sifting and winnowing through the data, I had to decide what stories to include in the main text, which ones to comment on in notes, and (hardest of all) which ones to leave out of the story. Obviously, other authors might have made different choices. Throughout, my approach has been to focus on building a narrative that makes the most sense (and is the most interesting). Because my aim is to answer the "why" question, I have sought to highlight the material that seems to provide the clearest answers and the least convoluted path toward those answers. For those who want to dig deeper, I encourage you to read the notes, which contain additional evidence, nuance, and the occasional Easter egg.[5]

Second, I not only stand on the shoulders of giants but also leap from one shoulder to the next. What I mean by this is that numerous scholars have written about Jews and the pig in isolation, considering a single incident or location in time and space. Over the nearly twenty years of research that went into writing this book, I found amazing evidence in entire books devoted to the subject, in individual chapters or articles, in random sentences, buried in footnotes, and beyond. One of the main contributions of this book is to collect these individual nuggets of knowledge and to piece them together to assemble the larger puzzle. Oftentimes, when scholars considered a piece of the pig puzzle in isolation, they missed a nuance, a novel development, or a sense of how their bit of information fits into the larger porcine trajectory. A central argument of this book is that, taken together, the many interactions between Jews and the pig have created a complex and interconnected narrative. I endeavor to carefully note what debts I owe to the numerous scholars on whom I rely and what insights I offer based on how I have assembled the more-than-three-thousand-year-old pig puzzle.

"AN ANIMAL ON THE HUMAN SIDE": WHY "PIG" AND NOT "PORK"

In order to understand the frame in which I construct this puzzle, I must call attention to an important note on nomenclature. Throughout, I refer to the animal in question as "the pig," rarely referring to it as "pork" or "bacon" or "ham." In doing so, I want to remind us that the pig is so much more than just food: it is also both an embodied and metaphorical nonhuman animal, which is being used to stake various claims about the identities of human animals.

Pig, as I deploy the term, contains multiple meanings. Here, I am in agreement with the historian Jamie Kreiner, who in her book on pigs in the early medieval West, persuasively asserts, "Pigs were difficult to fully domesticate, both physically and conceptually. They called attention to themselves and required some engagement with their complex lives. As a result, in these centuries pigs had both singular and plural meanings. 'The' pig was a category of human understanding. It was shorthand for thinking about a species that humans manipulated and evaluated. But early medieval societies also engaged with pluralized pigs, with specific and various individual pigs that had some control over the worlds they inhabited. In short, the history of the pig or pigs is a contrapuntal one."[6] By preferring to use the term "pig" or "the pig," I seek to constantly remind us that we are talking about both embodied pigs and embodied humans, as well as both metaphorical pigs and metaphorical humans.[7]

Focusing on "pig" and not "pork" further serves to highlight the animality of the pig. I was first introduced to this concept by the scholar of religion and rabbinics Beth A. Berkowitz. In her brilliant book *Animals and Animality in the Babylonian Talmud*, Berkowitz succinctly summarizes, and then goes on to concretely demonstrate, the utility of critical animal studies for the study of ancient Judaism. Berkowitz finds the notion of animality beneficial for two reasons. The first is "to point to this expanded way of seeing other species in relation to our own."[8] This allows us to attend to the agency of nonhuman animals, for example.[9] Berkowitz compares "animality" to "personality," which we routinely consider as personal and individual to human animals; and now we can expand that concept to include nonhuman animals, especially the pig. "The second aim of 'animality' is to make anthropocentrism more visible."[10] This reminds us what is at stake in constructions that erect rigid boundaries between human and nonhuman animals. Important for what unfolds in subsequent chapters, Berkowitz argues, "The use of the adjective 'animalistic' to criticize certain human behaviors as overly aggressive or hyper-sexual demonstrates the manipulability of the notion of the animal and the flexibility of the binary of human/animal. In the discourse of animality, a person can easily end up on the animal side, and an animal on the human side."[11] We shall discover that the pig proves to be especially flexible, with its physical and/or symbolic limbs contorting to move this embodied and/or metaphorical animal through time and space. Used to criticize or correct, to laugh or to learn, to hate or to love, among myriad other actions and emotions, the pig and its animality bring into relief the more-than-three-thousand-year-old story of Jews and non-Jews negotiating definitions of Jewish identity and practice.

Further, while we will continuously explore the real and perceived relationships between real and perceived pigs, we must remember that, for any era discussed, *we should not presume that all Jews avoided pig*. In fact, evidence across time and space suggests that at least some—and, in certain periods and places, even a significant percentage—of Jews partook of the pig. In these moments, the animality of the pig remains central. Sometimes these Jews ate the pig; other times they simply interacted with pigs; and other times they deliberately deployed these real and metaphorical nonhuman animals for a variety of rhetorical and/or culinary purposes. In remembering that the pig contains multiple meanings, we must not flatten out all of Jewish experience to that of a complete abstention from pig. Concomitantly, we must not forget that, for many Jews, avoiding the pig was essential to Jewish identity and practice. Across this diverse range of practices, embodied and metaphorical pigs roam, rooting in the dirt in order to help us forage fascinating moments of insight, like truffles hidden below the surface, where only pigs can find them.

"IT IS IMPURE FOR YOU":
THE BEGINNING OF THE PIG TABOO

Our story begins in the Iron Age. Tracing footprints on the sands of time, we tread upon the sands of ancient Israel. It is here where we first encounter the association between the pig and the people who will later be called Jews. But they are not "Jews" yet. The transformation of ancient Israelites into modern Jews—from Judeans to Jews—is a long story that unfolds in subsequent chapters.[12] In fact, to tell the tale of how "Judeans" transform into "Jews," one simply cannot omit the pig. From beginning to end—from snout to tail—the pig plays a prominent role in these dramatic events.

Our epic story has a rather inauspicious start. For if all we had was the Hebrew Bible, we would have been unable to predict the fascinating adventure that follows. The majority of biblical food laws appear in Leviticus 11 and Deuteronomy 14.[13] Contained within these two chapters are lists of animals permitted and prohibited for consumption by the ancient Israelites. Sometimes criterion for inclusion and/or exclusion are provided, and sometimes they are not. For example, we are told that fish must possess both fins and scales in order to be deemed edible, but we are not told why various fowl are prohibited.[14]

The first category of animals that appears in each chapter is quadrupeds (Hebrew: *behemah*). The biblical text commands that every animal in this category, in order to be acceptable for consumption, must *both* have split hooves and chew the cud (meaning that if they lack one or both, then they are prohibited).[15] It then offers specific examples of animals that have one, but not both, of the criteria. The camel, the rock badger, and the hare chew the cud but do not have split hooves, so they are forbidden.[16] And then the central protagonist of our story appears:

> **And the pig, though it has hoofs, with the hoofs cleft through, it does not chew the cud; it is impure for you. (Leviticus 11:7)**

> **And the pig, though it has hoofs, it does not chew the cud—it is impure to you; from their flesh, you shall not eat, and their carcasses you shall not touch. (Deuteronomy 14:8)**

I present both the version that appears in Leviticus 11:7 and the one that appears in Deuteronomy 14:8 so that the reader has the entirety of the evidence before them. In both verses, we are told that the pig lacks one important criterion—it does not chew the cud. In Leviticus 11:7, we learn that the pig "is impure to you"—which is the exact same language previously used to refer to the camel, the rock badger, and the hare.[17] In Deuteronomy 14:8, we discover both that the pig "is impure to you" and that one can neither eat its flesh nor touch its carcass. While the text commands that one not eat the camel, the rock badger, or the hare, we hear nothing about avoiding their carcasses.[18]

What do we learn from this evidence? First, we learn that the pig is biblically tabooed. But so are the camel, the rock badger, and the hare—and those are just the quadrupeds the Bible mentions as examples. Moreover, many other animals—bats, mice, geckos, owls, eagles, and so on—are also biblically tabooed. Second, perhaps the wording of Deuteronomy 14:8 implies that the pig is slightly more tabooed than the other quadrupeds. After all, it is set apart from the other three, and it is the only one whose carcass is specifically prohibited to be touched. But this is far from explicit in the text. And one could also read this final statement as bookending the two verses about all four quadrupeds. Third, while the ingestion of pigs is prohibited, there is nothing that explicitly prevents engaging in the pig—or, for that matter, camel or hare—business (breeding, buying, selling, etc.).[19]

Taken together, what we learn from Leviticus 11:7 and Deuteronomy 14:8 is that the pig is but one of many biblically prohibited animals. There is no reason to presume that it will take on a significance greater than any other prohibited animal down the road.

"A GOLD RING IN A PIG'S SNOUT": PIG AND METAPHOR

The pig appears only five other times in the Hebrew Bible. In each instance, the pig—and those who eat it—serves as a metaphor for idolatrous practices or other general bad life choices. Given the small number of references to the pig, it is worth taking a moment to briefly review each text.

Of the five other appearances of the pig, three of them are found in the final two chapters of the prophetic book of Isaiah.[20] In each instance, ingestion of the pig marks people as outsiders to the in-group. We do not eat the pig, Isaiah implicitly states, and when You eat the pig, You are not Us. Therefore, when Isaiah laments preaching in vain to "a rebellious people, who walk in a way that is not good," he notes, "They eat the flesh of pigs, and the broth of unclean things is in their pots."[21] Clearly, Isaiah believes that those who eat pig's flesh are not members of the righteous. However, note that there are other "unclean things" (Hebrew: *piggulim*) in these violators' diets. The pig is a metaphor for transgression, but it is not the only transgressive food.

In the next chapter of Isaiah, an oracle is revealed in which God lists a variety of idolatrous actions that are "evil in [his] sight" and, hence, cause divine displeasure.[22] One such evil act is "one who makes a cereal offering [and offers] the blood of a pig."[23] While the original Hebrew of this verse is difficult to understand, the context strongly implies cultic practices that violate biblical norms.[24] The divine oracle disapproves of practices that involve offering pig's blood. Here, the previous text from Isaiah is also relevant, as the context there "is most likely to a sacrificial meal in which pork was consumed."[25] Pig meat and pig blood index transgressive meals and cultic practices.

The last appearance of pig in Isaiah furthers this conclusion. Later on in the final chapter of the book of Isaiah, we are told that "those who eat pig meat, abominable things, and the mouse, together they shall come to an end."[26] While the transgressors who eat pig will come to an end, their inglorious shuffling off this mortal coil will not be a lonely one—alongside them will be those who eat abominable things and mice.[27] Though the pig gets first billing, it shares center stage with other biblically detestable creatures. Thus, one's relationship with the pig clearly indexes one's status to the normative community of non-pig-eaters, but so do many other foods and actions. Mice-eaters and pig-eaters are one and the same.

What we see here is that the pig and pig-related practices are metaphors for transgressive behaviors; but so are many other foods and actions. The pig has taken on symbolic importance, but so too have other tabooed protein sources. Even when the pig is singled out, we still must contend with the sparse appearances of this animal. After all, how much significance can one place on the pig if it plays but a bit part in the biblical drama? For example, the pig appears only once in the thirty-one chapters of the book of Proverbs: "A gold ring in a pig's snout: a beautiful woman lacking good sense."[28] Though translations of this verse usually equate the woman with the pig (e.g., "[As] a ring in a pig's snout, [so is] a beautiful woman lacking good sense"), the biblical studies scholar Michael V. Fox argues that this reading does not take the proverb's structure into account.[29] The woman is parallel with the ring, her beauty with the gold, and the pig with the husband. Therefore, while the wife's disapproved-of actions are front and center, it is her husband—and not the wife—who is the pig here. As Fox summarizes, "If, however, one's wife is empty-headed, he may think he has a trophy-bride, but he is really strutting about with a preposterous creature. He makes himself preposterous and piggish."[30] Regardless of which translation one prefers, "the saying warns men not to take such a wife."[31] Once we understand what this proverb is trying to communicate, we can see that the pig is a metaphor for disapproved-of practices.[32] Men may value beauty but not at the expense of good sense.

How much does this verse communicate regarding the pig? This metaphor is used but once. And elsewhere, when a roughly similar message appears, the pig is nowhere to be found. Thus, in the next chapter of Proverbs, we learn, "The woman of strength is her husband's crown, while the disgraceful one is like a rot in his bones."[33] Therefore, it would seem that the pig can serve as a biblical metaphor for transgressive or disapproved practices, but it is but one option of many to convey such meanings. While this will change over time—moving from *a* metaphor to *the* metaphor—clearly we are not there yet.

The final biblical pig appears in the book of Psalms.[34] Asaph, the Levite who reputedly authored this Psalm, recounts the devastation of Judah (northern Israel) that God allowed to occur. At one point, the Psalm painfully asks, "Why did you breach its wall, so that all who pass by pluck its fruit, wild boars gnaw at it, creatures of the field feed on it?"[35] While all other biblical references to the pig imply the domesticated variety, this is the wild boar (here, literally, "the pig of the forest"). Clearly, the boar destroying Judah is an insult, but other creatures (more literally, "those that move of the field") are also taking part in this destruction. Once again, the pig does not stand alone.

While we note the metaphorical function of the pig, these five references are not enough to distinguish it from numerous other biblically tabooed animals that serve as metaphors for disapproved-of actions and actors. For example, the eagle (Hebrew: *nesher*) is explicitly forbidden in Leviticus 11:13 and Deuteronomy 14:12. Yet, it appears often as a metaphor for the actions of hated other nations, which swoop in from their high perches and devour Israel like prey.[36] The totality of the evidence unambiguously indicates that the pig was but one, and not necessarily even the most prominent one, of many metaphors for forbidden practices and people. It does not hog the spotlight ... yet.

BUILDING SKELETAL ARGUMENTS FROM (SOMETIMES LITERAL) BONES

There are two related issues that require us to hold the biblical text in one hand and to turn from text to context with the other.

First, there is the well-trod territory of exactly what is the origin of the biblical pig taboo. While there are numerous theories, none sufficiently account for the data. Many of these theories are well known: the pig is matter out of place, the pig is a bad ecological fit, the pig is unhygienic, and so on.[37] All of these theories are flawed for various reasons, not least of which is that they are all monocausal.[38] As I will argue throughout our story, the pig prohibition takes on various layers and nuances across time and space. Reducing it to a single cause or rationale misses the richer, more complex picture. Though we cannot establish *the* reason why pig is tabooed, we will see numerous instances wherein this taboo is debated. Thus, we continuously will return to this question with the expectation that we will find multiple answers rather than a singular one. Further, the biblical text itself does not provide enough clues. And neither does the historical context. Though many readers of the biblical texts—professional scholars and amateur detectives alike—have offered a variety of theories, they must remain that: unproven theories. That being said, postbiblical figures—both Jewish and non-Jewish—will take this taboo seriously. Therefore, while the absolute origin remains unprovable, the legacy of this prohibition is quite easy to prove.

Second, there is the question of literal pig bones. Archaeologists have dug up many animal bones and then, with the help of zooarchaeologists who specialize in the study of skeletal remains, have posited theories about Jewish/non-Jewish identity based on the absence/presence of pig bones. There is a long and complex history of these endeavors, which sometimes overemphasize certain pieces of evidence and ignore others.[39] Far too often, the animal bones at a given site are not analyzed, either until much later than other extant evidence or simply not at all. Like many of the skeletal remains, theories about the historical dynamics being uncovered are incomplete. For example, does an absence of pig bones indicate an absence from the diet or an incomplete excavation? What about the evidence that many groups in surrounding areas also did not consume pig? What if one finds fewer pig bones but many other biblically nonkosher remains? If there are pig bones, does that mean that the people were not Jewish, or could they have been Jewish and still eaten pig? Just as dumpster diving through the remains of a modern apartment building will tell much—but not necessarily the complete picture—about its residents, the study of pig bones provides some, though not all, pieces of the puzzle. We will occasionally refer to some zooarchaeological findings. They will constitute some of the bones of our argument but still will not complete the skeleton.

BUILDING BLOCKS OF OUR TALE: CONCLUSIONS

We have seen both the first mentions of the pig taboo and of pig metaphors being used to signify the Otherness of practices and people. But these scattered references are insufficient to foreshadow the fascinating story that we are about to discover. In fact, they do not offer enough information to explain an experience that I had shortly after my son was born.

When my son was a few months old, a package arrived for him from my mother. Inside, we found a lovely collection of wooden alphabet blocks, with Hebrew letters and words on them. On one side of the blocks, there were pictures of different animals with their Hebrew names written below them. Since my wife grew up in Italy, we decided to order a second set of these blocks, made by the same company, which featured Italian words. When they arrived, I compared both sets and, to my amazement, discovered that these represented the building blocks of my argument. While the Italian blocks featured many of the same animals as the Hebrew blocks, there was one noticeable difference: the Italian blocks included a pig (Italian: *maiale*), but the Hebrew blocks did not (see figure 1.1). Importantly, the Hebrew blocks did not shy away from animals explicitly forbidden in the Hebrew Bible, as they featured the owl (Hebrew: *yanshuf*), the eagle (Hebrew: *nesher*), and even the camel (Hebrew: *gamal*).[40] The latter is especially telling, because, as noted earlier, *the biblical prohibition of the camel appears alongside that of the pig*. But the block company had decided that it would be culturally inappropriate to feature the pig on the Hebrew blocks.[41] Conversely, the pig has very positive resonances in Italian culture, and therefore it (and not the camel) appears in that block collection.

Figure 1.1. Picture of Hebrew and Italian children's wooden blocks. Reproduced by permission from Kevin Myers.

The irony here is worth repeating: in the Hebrew set of the children's blocks, the biblically forbidden pig is replaced with the biblically forbidden camel. If all we had was the Hebrew Bible, this would make absolutely no sense. How do we get from the Bible to these blocks? In chapter 1, the story of why the pig would not appear on children's building blocks in Hebrew but would in Italian begins to unfold.

1

"ALL WHO EAT IT AGREE"

The Signifying Swine in the Second Temple Period

BIBLICAL cultic practice centered around the offering of sacrifice in a central location: the Temple in Jerusalem.[1] Sacrificial offerings could consist of grains, wine, or animals. In the latter case, sacrificial animals had to be biblically suitable for ingestion; thus, goats, sheep, and cows were acceptable, but camels, hares, and pigs were not.

In 586 BCE, this sacrificial system came to a screeching halt when the Babylonians, as part of their territorial expansion, invaded Jerusalem and destroyed the Temple. For a cultic practice centered around a single cultic location (Jerusalem), contained within a particular territory (Israel) that foundational doctrines declared is an inalienable divine inheritance, this event was catastrophic. You can still hear the heartbreak and sorrow in a lament written shortly after the Jerusalem Temple fell: "How shall we sing the Lord's song on foreign soil?"[2]

Skip ahead to the year 539 BCE, and the cloud over the Israelites' heads began to lift. In that year, the Persians seized control over the region, expelling the Babylonians, and—importantly for our narrative—the Persian King Cyrus allowed the Israelites to return to their ancestral land. Eventually, they rebuilt the Temple in Jerusalem. The rededication of the Temple in 515 BCE inaugurated the era that scholars now refer to as the Second Temple Period. This institution defines this era, which lasted until 70 CE, when the Romans destroyed the Second Temple. The Second Temple Period therefore is neatly bookended by the dedication and destruction of the Second Temple.

In the latter half of the Second Temple Period, the pig begins to rise in rhetorical and symbolic prominence. As we shall see, the pig plays a role in narratives of the reestablishment of self-rule in this region and then in the sudden and catastrophic defeat and loss of self-rule at the end of this era. It is also at this very time that the understanding of what it means to be a member of this group is changing. Though the precise conceptual frameworks and categories are the subject of much scholarly debate, what remains certain is that the rise of the symbolic and rhetorical function of the pig not only coincides with this contestation and evolution of identity but also appears in the same texts and even in the same narratives within those texts.[3] Therefore, to tell the story of how biblical Israel moves from Judean tribe to Jewish religion, one cannot ignore the pig. Or, put differently, since ancient authors used the pig to signify new changes in group identification and embodied practices, we can tell the broader history of Jews and Judaism in the latter half of the Second Temple Period by means of the pig.

THE SIGNIFYING SWINE

Before we turn to the ancient evidence, I want to introduce a concept that frames the data presented both here and throughout our story. I playfully refer to this concept as "The Signifying Swine."[4] For those who are familiar with the field of semiotics, the pun is apparent. Semiotics explores "signs," which are the sum total of the relationship between the "signifier" and the "signified"—that is, between the representation of something and the something itself. As we shall see, the swine becomes a sign, which tells us as much about the representation of that animal (the signifier) and the pig itself (the signified). Hence, I refer to this as "The Signifying Swine" to remind us that the swine is indeed a sign.

While we will explore this development, the precise reason why the pig becomes a sign during this period remains unclear. Both Jewish and non-Jewish sources from this era devote more time to discussing the pig than to any other biblically tabooed quadruped. But why the pig is placed front and center in these texts is not communicated to us. Was the pig abhorred more than any other nonkosher beast at this time? Or was the pig simply the most commonly encountered nonkosher quadruped? We do not know.[5] What we do know is that, starting in this period, the absence of the pig from the Jewish menu proved worthy of note by both Jews and non-Jews alike. Later I offer a provocative suggestion: namely, that it is the particular role that the pig plays in Second Temple martyrdom narratives that leads to its outsized historical influence, both internally and externally, in regard to Jewish identity. Starting with these martyrdom narratives, the pig is invested with greater signification for Jewish identity and practice, which both Jews and non-Jews build on over the more than two millennia that follow. In short, these pig-related martyrdom narratives introduce the concept of submission to foreign rule via forced ingestion of pig, which will reappear in subsequent eras when we explore the violent motif of forced ingestion of pig as a means of forced conversion. But before we get there, we will first learn what ancient non-Jews had to say about the Jewish avoidance of the pig.

"THEY ABSTAIN FROM PORK": NON-JEWISH OBSERVATIONS ABOUT JEWS AND THE PIG

Zooarchaeological remains suggest that pig consumption in this region significantly increased during the Hellenistic and Roman Periods.[6] This is especially noted in regard to the Roman Period (during which time the Romans renamed the region Syria Palaestina).[7] Given the greater prevalence of pig on the ancient plate in Palestine, the absence of pig from the Jewish diet proved worthy of note.[8] In fact, pig abstention is one of the three Jewish practices most often discussed in ancient non-Jewish sources (the other two are Sabbath observance and male circumcision).[9] Yet, precisely how non-Jews became aware of this Jewish dietary taboo remains unclear. As noted earlier, whether this was noticeable because pig was the most commonly available biblically prohibited quadruped or because Jews actually abhorred the pig more than they did any other biblically prohibited quadruped, all we know for certain is that this aversion first became prominent in non-Jewish thought during this era.

As we begin to survey the various ancient polemical rhetorics about Jewish pig avoidance, we should start by noting that many comments made by non-Jews about this Jewish dietary practice can be categorized, as the historian Peter Schäfer correctly observes, as "casual reference and ethnographic explanation."[10] For example, when noting proper medical treatment for epilepsy, Erotianus writes in the second half of the first century CE, "one should inquire to which type the sick man belongs, in order that if he is a Jew we should refrain from giving him pig's flesh."[11] Shortly thereafter, the famous Stoic philosopher Epictetus (ca. 50–130 CE) asserts, "This is the conflict between Jews and Syrians and Egyptians and Romans, not over the question whether holiness should be put before everything else and should be pursued in all circumstances, but whether the particular act of eating swine's flesh is holy or unholy."[12]

Ethnographic explanations by ancient non-Jews are particularly interesting, as they attempt to offer a logical basis for the Jewish dietary prohibition. Importantly—since it cuts both ways, as we shall see—these hypothetical rationales do not evidence any real dialogue between non-Jew and Jew; rather, they are based on (real or perceived) observation and (sometimes disciplined and often undisciplined) speculation on the part of the author. Seeking to answer the question of "whether the Jews abstain from pork based on reverence or aversion for the pig," Plutarch (ca. 46–120 CE) offers a lengthy ethnographic explanation for the rationale behind the Jewish pig taboo.[13] He then provides rationalizations based on both reverence and aversion in order to speculate on why Jews "abstained from precisely the most legitimate meat."[14] The historian Cristiano Grottanelli divides Plutarch's explanations into four themes:

(1) *Earth and seed*; (2) *Lepra and scabies*; (3) *Mud and shit*; and (4) *Downcast eyes*.[15]

The theme *Earth and seed* encompasses reverence-based rationalizations for the pig taboo: Jews honor the pig because "it was the first to cut the soil with its projecting snout, thus producing a furrow and teaching man the function of the ploughshare."[16] Out of respect for imparting this vital agricultural lesson, the pig-pedagogue is not consumed; and "we need not be surprised if some people do not eat pork for this reason."[17] Indeed, Jews must revere the pig because, if Jews really hated pigs, then they would kill them.[18] Ironically, in the second century CE, Celsus Philosophus argues that Jews "abstain from pigs because they loathe them."[19] Either way, *sus ipso loquitur* (the pig speaks for itself)!

The three other themes identified by Grottanelli in Plutarch encompass rationalizations based on a Jewish aversion to the pig. The second theme, *Lepra and scabies*, is based on the presumption that "every pig is covered on the under side by lepra and scaly eruptions."[20] Therefore, Jews detest the pig because Jews detest such skin ailments.[21] Elsewhere, Tacitus (ca. 56–ca. 117 CE) more directly connects skin disease with the Jewish pig prohibition: "They abstain from pork, in recollection of a plague, for the scab to which this animal is subject once afflicted them."[22] While Tacitus's claim would appear to buttress Plutarch here, the third-century philosopher Porphyry asserts that Jews (and Phoenicians) abstained from eating the pig "because in their places pigs were not to be found at all."[23] Without any pigs around, Jews could not have caught a plague from them. Extant historical evidence, however, attests to the presence of pigs, though not necessarily to the veracity of any plague. The third theme, *Mud and shit*, is based on the common presumption that pigs wallow in mud and excrement and thus are dirty.[24] Oddly, here Plutarch alleges that "the very filthiness of their habit produces an inferior quality of meat."[25] This assertion about what we have previously been told is "precisely the most legitimate meat" seems strange, as most ancient conversations about the pig in regard to Jews acknowledge that pig meat is, indeed, delicious.[26] According to the fourth and final theme, *Downcast eyes*, "the eyes of the swine are so twisted and drawn down that they can never catch sight of anything above them or see the sky unless they are carried upside down so that their eyes are given an unnatural tilt upward."[27] This assertion connects pigs to lowly matters and to death. While Plutarch offers multiple explanations, no single explanation (or theme) is preferred. They are all possible. The only clear-cut conclusion is that Jews avoid the pig and they have their reasons for doing so. Without a decisive answer to the question "Why do Jews taboo the pig?" the search for a resolution continues.

In contrast to casual references and ethnographic explanations, the Latin satirists "form a rather distinctive category with some common characteristics."[28] As their name implies, the satirists produce satire. In antiquity—and for millennia after, as we shall see in subsequent eras—the juxtaposition of Jews and the pig made for great comedy. And as is often the case with comedy, it is not much fun to be the butt of the joke.[29]

In the first century CE, Petronius suggests that Jews may worship a "pig-god."[30] This claim appears in a poem in which Petronius mocks other distinctive Jewish practices, including circumcision and Sabbath observance. Unlike the ethnographic observations of Plutarch, for example, Petronius here is not trying to rationalize this Jewish practice; he is simply poking fun at it.[31]

Mockery of the Jewish avoidance of the pig moves up a notch when Juvenal (ca. 60–130 CE) focuses his comedic gaze in its direction. Referring to the rumor that King Agrippa II and his sister Berenice had engaged in an incestuous relationship, Juvenal wryly comments that this occurred "in that country . . . where a long-established clemency suffers pigs to attain old age."[32] Juvenal mocks Jewish rulers who have no problem violating one biblical taboo (incest) but are fastidious about another (the pig prohibition). In a later wisecrack, Juvenal drolly asserts that Jews "see no difference between eating swine's flesh, from which their father abstained, and that of man."³³ After all, Jews eat neither pigs nor humans, so what difference is there between their flesh? The audience is meant to laugh at this but not learn why this practice exists.

Another biting remark is reported by Macrobius in the first half of the fifth century CE. While this source is relatively late, it claims to record the words of Augustus (63 BCE–14 CE). Reputedly, Augustus made a snarky remark about the first century BCE King Herod the Great. Herod was a ruler of great renown, earning a well-deserved reputation both for his monumental building projects and for ruthlessly murdering his enemies (both real and perceived). And while his lineage includes his great-grandson Agrippa II (who appeared in the previous paragraph), Herod is known more for killing his sons than for his successful parenting. He earned this reputation honestly, as he had three of his own sons executed. Thus, the audience is primed to understand the humor behind this quip attributed to Augustus: "I'd rather be Herod's pig than Herod's son."³⁴ This pun juxtaposes Herod's alleged piety regarding Jewish dietary practice (which he was not well known for) with his penchant for murdering his children (which he was well known for).³⁵ It would have us believe that Herod has no compunction violating biblical law against murder when his son's head is on the chopping block, but he becomes pious when the pig's head is on a butcher block.

While ethnographic explanations sought to understand the rationale behind the Jewish abstention from the pig, the Latin satirists are less interested in learning than they are in laughing at this practice. The concept of The Signifying Swine appears in either event. The Jewish predilection against the pig is taken as a sign in both; it is presumed to mean something. But what precisely that *something* is—that is, what exactly the pig signifies—is up for debate. As we shall see, this debate continues on for more than two thousand years.

"THERE IS NONE WHOSE FLESH IS SO DELICIOUS AS THE PIG'S": JEWISH OBSERVATIONS ABOUT JEWS AND THE PIG

In 2014, a cartoon appeared in the *New Yorker*. Two ancient shepherds look away from a herd of biblically permitted sheep in order to gaze at a biblically prohibited pig. One shepherd inquires, "If He didn't want us to eat it, why'd He wrap the whole thing in bacon?"[36] The joke's premise is that both shepherds are Jews who are questioning God for forbidding a creature tantalizingly wrapped in bacon. (One wonders, How do they know that bacon is delicious?!) The cartoon leaves unresolved whether this was a passing thought, whether the shepherds were justifying their already transgressive dietary practices, or whether this was the first step down a slippery slope away from biblical practice.

Two elements of this joke are at least two millennia old: first, the recognition by Jews that pig meat is delicious; and second, the act of questioning why this mouth-watering mammal is biblically prohibited. For example, the prolific ancient Jewish author Philo of Alexandria (ca. 20 BCE–50 CE) notes, "Now among the different kinds of land animals there is none whose flesh is so delicious as the pig's, as all who eat it agree."[37] This line clearly attests to knowledge of the gustatory quality of the pig. Indeed, it relies on this fact to further its overall point because Philo argues that biblical legislation is designed to prevent gluttony and cultivate self-control.[38] Therefore, to avoid this most delicious meat is to embody discipline and virtue. This, according to Philo, is the answer to the bacon-wrapped question posed in the *New Yorker* cartoon.

Elsewhere, Philo records a blander rationale for the pig taboo: "Different people have different customs and the use of some things is forbidden to us as others are to our opponents."[39] The difference in tone here is probably due to the fact that these words are part of a response that Philo records from a Jewish delegation to the Roman emperor Gaius. In particular, the delegation is responding to the

"If He didn't want us to eat it, why'd He wrap the whole thing in bacon?"

FIGURE 1.1. *New Yorker* cartoon by Paul Roth. Reprinted by permission from the *New Yorker* © Condé Nast, 2014.

emperor's "grave and momentous question, 'Why do you refuse to eat pork?'"[40] While the non-Jewish audience laughs at Gaius's question about the rationale for the famous Jewish food taboo, presuming it to be a joke, the Jewish delegation provides a serious response based on the differing customs of different people. We should expect a delegation in that circumstance to offer the mildest and least objectionable response possible. They are treading carefully in the arena of porcine politics.

While Jews in the Second Temple Period devoted significant attention to the rationale for the biblical dietary laws, the pig's most prominent role in texts from this era relate to martyrdom.[41] In this context, as we shall soon see, The Signifying Swine takes on a lethal new dimension.

"COMPELLED TO PARTAKE OF THE MEAT": THE PIG IN NARRATIVES OF JEWISH MARTYRDOM

Earlier, I offered the provocative suggestion that the particular role the pig plays in Second Temple martyrdom narratives directly leads to its outsized historical influence, both internally and externally, in regard to Jewish identity. The time has now come to begin to prove this assertion.[42]

The story of the pig and Jewish identity takes a dramatic turn in historical accounts of the origin of Hanukkah. According to legend, the Maccabees are the heroes of the Hanukkah story, and the Seleucid ruler Antiochus Epiphanes is the villain. The Maccabees are depicted as freedom fighters, on a divinely authorized mission to wrest control of Israel from foreign rule. The subsequent practices associated with the holiday of Hanukkah serve to commemorate the Maccabees' success in battle and the reported events surrounding their victory and rededication of the Jerusalem Temple, particularly the miracle of the oil used in the Temple's eternal lamp lasting eight days, until more oil could be procured. Here, we must highlight an important but extremely underappreciated fact: in the earliest narratives about Hanukkah, we learn far more about pigs than we do about olive oil.[43] The miracle of the oil is a much later Hanukkah story. Back in its day, the main topic was not the miracle of the oil but the tragedy of the pig.

Writing in the first century BCE, the ancient historian Diodorus the Sicilian provides us insight into why Antiochus Epiphanes was so reviled by the Maccabees. In addition to various other actions, Antiochus Epiphanes reputedly used the pig to implement his political and cultural agenda regarding Jews and Judaism:

> And since Epiphanes was shocked by such hatred directed against all mankind, he had set himself to break down their traditional practices. Accordingly, he sacrificed before the image of the founder and the open-air altar of the god a great sow, and poured its blood over them.[44]

> Then, having prepared its flesh, he ordered that their holy books, containing the xenophobic laws, should be sprinkled with the broth of the meat; that the lamp, which they call undying and which burns continually in the temple, should be extinguished; and that the high priest and the rest of the Jews should be compelled to partake of the meat.[45]

When Antiochus Epiphanes sprinkles pig broth literally on the biblical texts that prohibit ingestion of the pig, he uses the pig to symbolize his domination over the Jews. Further, by forcing Jews to ingest the pig, he is compelling them to symbolically submit to his rule and to renounce their "xenophobic laws."[46] The pig functions rhetorically, therefore, to alter the Jewish altar, the Jewish holy books, and the Jewish body.[47]

Absent from Diodorus the Sicilian's narrative of Antiochus Epiphanes's infamous actions is one significant detail: Jewish martyrdom. With the term originating from an ancient Greek root meaning "to bear witness," martyrs offer their own lives as a testimony of their faith.[48] The historian Tessa Rajak excellently summarizes the mechanics of pig-related Jewish martyrdom:

> This phenomenon can be explained in terms of the specific functions of Jewish martyrology, in which a central purpose is to "save the nation," to establish models for the preservation of Jewish identity under alien rule. The dietary laws are a vital symbolic distinguishing mark. . . . And it is the special contribution of Jewish-Greek martyrology to integrate what had become an everyday identity-marker of Judaism, its dietary rules, with a picture of Jewish identity and faith stretched to abnormal limits in a crisis of persecution. Whether this representation was generated by a dimly remembered historic moment, a real and traumatic attempt by Seleucid overseers to force forbidden food on certain Jews, or whether by subsequent social developments, we do not know. Nor does it matter very much. Either way, this reconstruction of the past, with its distinctive archetypes of martyrdom, was fixed both in literature and in popular memory.[49]

What matters more than the accuracy of these accounts is their tremendous cultural power. By choosing a principled death over a compromised life, martyrs bear witness to their faith. It is this Truth that counts, regardless of whether the facts are all true.

Beginning in the Second Temple Period, this choice is symbolically represented in the decision either to ingest the pig and live or to abstain from the pig and die. Pig-related martyrdom explicitly appears in 2 Maccabees 6:18–7:42 and 4 Maccabees 5–18, variant texts that both describe two accounts of martyrdom at the hands of Antiochus Epiphanes: (1) the martyrdom of an old man named Eleazar and (2) the martyrdom of a mother and her seven sons.[50] In order to demonstrate the mechanics of pig-related Jewish martyrdom narratives, I summarize the more expansive text of 4 Maccabees.

Over and again in 4 Maccabees 5–18, it is clear that Antiochus Epiphanes desires to force Jews to eat the pig as a symbolic act of both their submission to his authority and their renunciation of their cultural mores and acceptance of his own. On several occasions, he expresses bafflement at why Jews refuse to eat the pig.[51] For example, when Antiochus Epiphanes (generously, in his opinion) offers Eleazar the opportunity to ingest the pig rather than suffer an excruciating death, he wonders, "Why should you abhor eating the excellent meat of this animal which nature has freely bestowed on us?"[52] Antiochus Epiphanes expects Eleazar to be swayed by the logic of his philosophical and culinary argument. Instead, Eleazar's obstinate refusal to consume the pig and thus to persevere leads him to—from the perspective of Antiochus Epiphanes—an unnecessary, and violent, death. Though Eleazar provides an eloquent philosophical defense for his porcine position, Antiochus Epiphanes cannot wrap his head around why one would choose a gruesome death rather than simply indulge in the "harmless" pleasure of "eating the excellent meat of this animal."[53] Antiochus Epiphanes fails to give sufficient philosophical weight to the biblical commandment to abstain.[54] Instead, he argues that God would forgive Eleazar (whose name in Hebrew means "God has helped") for choosing the

FIGURE 1.2. Illuminated manuscript of 1 Maccabees 1:62–63, Bible with St. Jerome's prologue. Soldier of Antiochus slays a Jew, who is holding a pig's head on a platter and who refuses to eat pig. Oxford, Bodleian Library MS. Auct. D.5.9, thirteenth century CE. © Bodleian Libraries, University of Oxford, used with permission, https://digital.bodleian.ox.ac.uk.

pig rather than death, since, he says, "even if there is some power that watches over this religion of yours, it would pardon you for any transgression committed under compulsion."[55] Such a sentiment might have come across more persuasively had it not been uttered by the very person compelling Eleazar to transgress. After all, one can forgive Eleazar for not heeding instruction on the nuances of Jewish law and philosophy from Antiochus Epiphanes.

Out of respect for both Eleazar's old age and his courage, Antiochus Epiphanes's guards suggest a way for him to avoid both the pig *and* death: "Why, Eleazar, are you so unreasonably destroying yourself in this foul way? Let us bring you some cooked food, and you pretend to taste of the swine's flesh and save yourself."[56]

The guards offer Eleazar what they presume is a reasonable compromise to avoid an otherwise lethal problem: pretend and persevere. Eleazar is uncompromising in his rejection of this farce, however, because he correctly concludes that such a solution involves losing the opportunity to die as a martyr. Even to pretend is to submit to the pig and thus to live an unprincipled and compromised life. In Eleazar's refusing to partake of this charade, his informed and intentional submission to torture and a violent death serves as a witness to his faith. To be a martyr requires commitment, in this case, commitment to a pig-free life and principled death.

Following immediately after the narrative of Eleazar's pig-related martyrdom, the tale of the mother and her seven sons begins. Here, we learn of the gory and gruesome death that each family member suffers rather than ingest the pig. We are told that this family of pious martyrs abstains from the pig in order to remain faithful to their ancestral law and to display mastery over their passions. In exemplary Greek fashion, they demonstrate (ironically, as we shall see) their ability to subordinate emotion to right reason.[57] As 4 Maccabees 13:2 states, "For if being enslaved to the passions they had eaten unclean food, we would have said that they had been conquered by them." When their reason and self-control prevail, they bear witness to all. This virtuous act of disciplined abstention in the face of violence and death is even more pronounced for the mother, who—in addition to staring down the barrel of her own demise—conquers both her maternal instinct to save her seven sons and the contemporary cultural and philosophical perception of a weaker female mind.[58] Self-control was gendered as a masculine virtue (indeed, the word "virtue" derives from *vir*, the Latin word for "man"); so it would not be lost on the contemporary audience what it means for that mother to act with such self-control while enduring that level of adversity. The mother acts like a man; Antiochus Epiphanes, who comes across as out of control and angry, does not.[59] Surprised by the family's fortitude, Antiochus Epiphanes exhorts them, "I not only advise you not to display the same mad frenzy as that old man who has just been tortured, but I beg of you to yield to me and take advantage of my friendship."[60] All they need to do is "renounce the ancestral law of [their] polity," and he would offer them powerful positions and wealth.[61] They refuse his offer of cultural and economic capital as soon as Antiochus Epiphanes stops speaking.[62] In so doing, the mother and her seven sons each die a martyr's death, enduring "manifold torments unto death for piety's sake."[63]

While fully acknowledging the violent and graphic deaths described in these texts, I now want to take a step back in order to assess the narrative function of pig-related Jewish martyrdom.[64] Written to advance a particular political, philosophical, and theological agenda, 4 Maccabees deploys various discursive strategies in service of this agenda. For example, take note of how both Antiochus Epiphanes and his guards express confusion over pig-related Jewish martyrdom. Their befuddlement, however, is a discursive strategy. Antiochus Epiphanes and his guards feign ignorance as to why a Jew would choose death over diet. This pretension of incomprehension serves a particular semiotic purpose: that of The Signifying Swine. In forcing Jews to eat the pig, Antiochus Epiphanes uses the semiotic sign of the swine in order to signify Jewish subjugation to the Other, that is, to the Pig. Playing naïve, he pretends to ponder why Jews refuse this "harmless" and "excellent meat." But this is just a literary pretense. Antiochus Epiphanes knows full well that, by eating the pig, Eleazar and the mother and her seven sons would embody submission; and by abstaining from the pig, they embody rebellion. Concealing his complicity behind a false wall of ignorance, Antiochus Epiphanes leaves the Jews with only two options: eat the pig and partake of the identity politics endowed in that act of meat-eating or choose martyrdom. From the perspective of the text, it is the hard choice that is easy to make.

Important to remember here is Rajak's earlier point about the relative irrelevance of historical veracity. For the texts' discursive purposes, whether these events actually occurred (either at all or precisely as they are described) does not really matter.[65] It does not matter whether the meat on the plate is metaphorical or material. What matters is how that meat is deployed rhetorically. Further, as the scholar of religion Bruce Lincoln reminds us, force and discourse can work together to achieve "ideological persuasion."[66] The discourse surrounding Antiochus Epiphanes's (real or imagined) actions certainly proves persuasive in the two millennia that follow. Its ideological persuasion is achieved, both in antiquity and beyond, regardless of its veracity. Therefore, we need not quibble about whether these texts are more or (in my opinion) less accurate.

Though slightly different from the stories in Maccabees, there is one other pig-related Jewish martyrdom narrative from the Second Temple Period that requires comment. Describing an incident that is reputed to have occurred in the latter half of the first century BCE under the rule of the Roman governor Flaccus, Philo of Alexandria records the events surrounding what, perhaps anachronistically, can best be described as a pogrom. According to Philo,

> Jewish women were rounded up in public. Then, if they were recognized to be of another race, since many were arrested as Jewess without any careful investigation of the truth, they were released. But if they were found to be of our nation then these onlookers at a show turned into despotic tyrants and gave orders to fetch swine's flesh and

> give it to the women. Then all the women who in fear of punishment tasted the meat were dismissed and did not have to bear any further dire mistreatment. But the more resolute were delivered to the tormentors to suffer desperate ill-usage, which is the clearest proof of their entire innocence of wrongdoing.[67]

In this violent narrative, the pig serves once again as an index for Jewish identity and submission to foreign domination. Those Jewish women who submit to consuming the pig are released without any further harm (which clearly acknowledges the harm already done to them prior). But those women who, like the mother in 4 Maccabees, refuse to submit to the pig are subjected to even more physical and psychological violence. While the Greek phrase for these actions (*aikias anekestous*, rendered in the quote as "desperate ill-usage") is not specific, I agree with the scholar of ancient Mediterranean religion Ross Kraemer that this is "perhaps a euphemism for rape."[68]

The gendered lens of this text is obvious throughout. Women are specifically targeted; men are not rounded up, detained, and subjected to "dire mistreatment" and "desperate ill-usage." There is no comment when some of these women, "in fear of punishment," consume the pig rather than suffer physical and psychological violence. As noted earlier, this reflects the cultural expectation of the weaker female mind who cannot act with the virtue of self-control. Why comment on what is presumed to be obvious? It is in the last sentence that the exceptional occurs and thus merits comment. The "more resolute" Jewish women—who act like their ancestor, the mother in 4 Maccabees—refuse to ingest the pig and thus are brutally assaulted. Glossing over this violence, Philo seemingly pridefully notes that this "is the clearest proof of their entire innocence of wrongdoing."[69] In choosing sexual assault over swine, Philo views the violence inflicted on these Jewish women as proof that they did not transgress the Law. From a modern perspective, this choice is anathema. It ignores the brutality that these women—whether embodied or metaphorical—are described as enduring. Philo seems far less concerned that they were violated and more concerned that they themselves did not violate. In lauding the latter, the gendered violence of the former is ignored and erased.

The rhetoric of gendered physical and psychological violence against women should disturb us. While I want to be careful not to minimize in any way sexual violence against women—whether ancient or modern—in this case, we need not take a stance on the historical accuracy of the events described by Philo. Like the narratives in 2 and 4 Maccabees, neither the veracity nor the historicity of this narrative affects the influential afterlife of the (real, invented, and/or fictionalized-but-based-on-actual-events) instance of pig-related violence against Jews. What matters for our present purposes is the potent and enduring power of these narratives. When they laud the brutal deaths and gendered violence actively chosen by Jews, they elevate the role of the pig. It is in these narratives that The Signifying Swine develops its semiotic relationship. While biblical texts treat the pig as just one of several categorically nonkosher animals, now it is singled out and endowed with greater signification. With the development in the Second Temple Period of pig as a litmus test for Jewish identity and practice, the quadruped morphs from a pig into THE PIG. From this era on, to eat the hare, the rock badger, or the camel simply does not carry the same transgressive weight as does eating the pig. While these ancient accounts might be more rhetorical than actual, the threat of violence embodied in the pig now exists. This will be realized *both* rhetorically and actually numerous times over the course of the next two millennia. Pig is now worth dying for.

FROM PIG TO THE PIG: CONCLUSIONS

By the end of the Second Temple Period, much has changed in the history of Jews and Judaism. And, as we shall soon see, even greater changes are in store. Evolving attitudes toward the pig map neatly onto these changes. While at the beginning of the Second Temple Period, pig is just one of many biblically forbidden animals, the same cannot be said by the end of the period. This development, unexpected from what we learned previously, will be further developed in chapter 2, wherein we will learn how the pig comes to represent Rome, Romans, and the Roman destruction of the Second Temple. For now, however, we reflect on three themes that have emerged from our present discussion.

First, the development from a pig to *the pig* occurs at the same time that the category of Judaean develops into that of Jew. That is, as a tribal definition morphs into a religious one, the pig takes on symbolic importance. This is not coincidental. Rather, it is part of a larger process of redefinition and renegotiation of Jewish identity. In this evolution, we should not be surprised that new symbols and symbolic meanings emerge. Over the subsequent two millennia covered in the pages that follow, redefinition and renegotiation of both Jewish identity and the relationship between Jews and the pig will continue.

Second, the pig's development in this manner actually foreshadows its future as a malleable symbol. By taking on this metaphorical weight, it is endowed with greater importance vis-à-vis Jewish identity and practice. While The Signifying Swine originates in the Second Temple Period, it grows depth and nuance over the ensuing two millennia. When subsequent generations look for a symbol to represent their own contemporary reality, the pig becomes a common—and eventually obvious—choice. The pig accumulates historical baggage, becoming heavier as it is laden with more meaning. While the fact that the pig means something particular develops in this period, we shall discover in future eras that what precisely that porcine meaning is will change as we move through time and space.

Third, the pig appears in dialogues between Jews and non-Jews that are, in fact, monologues. Ancient ethnographers and Latin satirists comment on the Jewish pig taboo, but they do not reflect direct engagement with actual Jews. And though we spent much time discussing pig-related Jewish martyrdom, all of those accounts are written from the perspective of Jewish authors who have more interest in advancing their own polemical goals than in actively dialoguing with non-Jews on the subject. This is another theme that will continue throughout our story: narratives about Jews and the pig, whether written by Jews or non-Jews, tend to be monologues rather than dialogues. They advance the authors' perspectives and do not necessarily reflect actual events on the ground. The pig is a symbol, representing perception more than reality.

2

"A JEW MAY NOT RAISE PIGS ANYWHERE"

Euphemism and Stigma in the Classical Rabbinic Period

THE Second Temple Period concludes in 70 CE with a devastating and transformative tragedy: the destruction of the Second Temple at the hands of Romans. The loss of the Second Temple creates a vacuum. How could a religion centered around cultic ritual at a single cultic location survive the loss of its Temple? Careful readers will have a sense of déjà vu. After all, the very name Second Temple reminds us that there was once a First Temple. Destroyed by the Babylonians in 586 BCE, the Second Temple was (re)built and rededicated in 515 BCE. Some Jews gazed into the Second Temple's ashes and, through tears in their eyes, fervently kept watch, waiting for history to repeat itself. As years passed, however, it became clear that, unlike the phoenix, the Third Temple would not rise from the ashes (for the foreseeable future, at least).

If this historical moment were a movie trailer, the camera would slowly zoom in on the smoldering ruins of the Second Temple. Over a soundtrack of melodramatic orchestral music, a deep, somber voice would then intone, "In a world without the Temple, as ancient Jews struggle to make sense of devastation and loss, one small group rises from the ashes. Meet . . . the Rabbis." And so it is now time to introduce the Rabbis, a small group who will eventually represent the dominant expression of Judaism.[1] From this point onward, the Rabbis will be an ever-present part of our conversation—whether discussing the group itself, other Jewish groups that reject or ignore rabbinic authority, or non-Jewish authors reflecting on or interacting with (almost always) rabbinic Judaism. Therefore, unless otherwise noted, for the remainder of our story, presume the noun "Judaism" to refer to "rabbinic Judaism," that is, to refer to the Rabbis' conception of Jewish belief and practice.

The Rabbis emerge from a small group of disciple circles in the first century CE in the Galilee (northern Israel). As they gain followers over time, two major rabbinic centers develop: one in Roman Palestine (roughly modern-day Israel) and the other in Sasanian Babylonia (roughly modern-day Iraq). The group claims origins that predate the destruction not only of the Second Temple but also of the First Temple. In fact, they trace their lineage back to the Revelation of Torah at Mt. Sinai. According to rabbinic lore, God revealed not one but two Torahs to Moses on the top of Mt. Sinai: both the Written Torah (the Hebrew Bible) and the Oral Torah (rabbinic traditions). Therefore, when Rabbis interpret biblical texts and use them to make modern legal decisions, they understand themselves to be acting with divine authority.

We will focus here on the Classical Rabbinic Period, which dates from 70 to 640 CE.[2] Colonial conquests bookend this period: it begins with the destruction of the Second Temple by the Romans and concludes with the Muslim conquest of Palestine in 640 CE. For that reason, as well as based on what we have learned previously, we should not be surprised that the pig plays a prominent role in narratives describing the domination of Jews by non-Jewish rulers. In so doing, the historical baggage of the pig becomes even heavier, as yet another layer of meaning is packed inside. Whether embodied or metaphorical, the more the pig is fed, the more it weighs.

Before we begin, we should briefly ruminate on a key development that occurs during this period. As we shall see, the pig becomes a metonym for all nonkosher food. This metonymic development will prove important as our story continues to unfold, because it becomes a vital component—if you will forgive yet another pun, a *swine qua non*—of why the pig matters so much for Jewish/non-Jewish identity. Since pig represents all nonkosher food, it effectively serves as a byword for conversations about food and Jewish/non-Jewish identity. And since culinary conversations are such an important component of analysis of identity construction and maintenance, the pig matters.

"EATING 'THAT KIND'": EUPHEMISMS FOR THE PIG

The metaphorical weight of the pig is expressed linguistically in several rabbinic texts in which the authors cannot even bring themselves to utter the creature's name. Avoiding the word "pig," rabbinic texts often refer to "that thing" or "that kind." In doing so, they endow the pig with greater symbolic power. As the famous mythical wizard named Dumbledore once advised, "Always use the proper name for things. Fear of a name increases fear of the thing itself."[3] Classical rabbinic texts certainly evidence increased fear of the pig. By not naming that fear, they feed the fear; and, like an embodied pig, the more you feed it, the larger it grows.

An example of linguistic avoidance of the word "pig" is found in the following Talmudic report of a proverb: "Rav Pappa said: This is what people say: Hang a heart of palm on a pig and it will [continue] to do [its regular activities]."[4]

Rav Pappa (a famous rabbinic beer baron) introduces a folk saying that conveys the same message as another famous Latin proverb: *de gustibus non est disputandum*, commonly rendered in English as "there is no accounting for taste."[5] Even though a pig has a delicacy hung around its neck, it continues to do its own thing.[6] Everyone has their own tastes. This seems simple enough. But the word I translated as "pig" is actually two words in Hebrew: *davar aḥer* (דבר אחר), meaning "another thing" or, as I will render it throughout, "that thing." The power of the pig is expressed via linguistic substitution.

When the pig is glossed as "that thing"—or, occasionally, as "that kind"—the cultural and theological significance of the animal continues to grow, extending far beyond what one would expect based just on reading the biblical texts.[7] Further, avoidance of the word "pig" connects this animal with other categories that the Rabbis prefer to refer to euphemistically. Collectively, the "that thing" categories take on greater power, once again proving that "fear of a name increases fear of the thing itself." While the collective weight of these categories increases, unfortunately so too does the confusion of the reader. For example, one Talmudic text discusses the importance of eating immediately after the popular medical cure of bloodletting.[8] Failure to do so was believed to have dire repercussions. Thus, if a person departs from a bloodletting session without eating first and then "encounters a murderer, [the hungry bloodlettee] will die."[9] That cause and effect seems clear. But now "that thing" enters the picture: "If [the hungry bloodlettee] encounters 'that thing' it is harmful with regard to 'that thing.'"[10]

We have two "that thing" categories directly interacting here. But how are we to know what is what and which is which?[11] Commentators fill in the gap by pointing out that elsewhere in the Babylonian Talmud it is claimed that the dirty pig is responsible for nine-tenths of the world's plagues.[12] Therefore, the first "that thing" is understood to refer to "the pig" and the second "that thing" to "skin disease."[13] Pigs carry plagues, and in both biblical and rabbinic texts, skin disease is the plague par excellence.[14] Thus, a bloodletting patient who has left the clinic without eating beforehand is presumed to be in danger of contracting skin disease if, in their hungry and vulnerable state, they bump into a pig on their way home. The linguistic substitution of both terms serves to distance them from all other nonkosher animals and plagues. They stand out as exceptional and thus are endowed with additional power.

Reading over an early draft of this chapter, an anonymous reviewer asked an excellent question: How do we really know that "that thing" is the pig (or any of the other "that things" discussed both earlier and later)? Clearly, this is a case of linguistic avoidance. But if the authors are successful enough in avoiding the term, how do we ascertain what precisely is the topic of conversation? In my analysis of "that thing" throughout, I have followed the interpretative tradition of rabbinic literature. For example, in the bloodletting text just discussed, the renowned medieval exegete Rashi glosses the Babylonian Talmud's initial use of the phrase *davar aḥer* with a single word: "pig."[15] Whether or not this reflects the original authorial intent, it is clear that before long this particular "that thing" is widely understood as referring to the pig. Perhaps based on some other rabbinic texts where the porcine connection is more concrete or on other (perhaps no longer extant) factors, the association became commonplace. Regardless, the interpretive afterlife of "that thing" as pig testifies to the power of the pig in framing subsequent exegesis. The same goes for the other "that things," which taken together begin to emerge as a separate category: those things that are too scary to name.

Often, those things that are too scary to name refer to actions deemed beyond the rabbinic pale, especially to forbidden sexual relations and idolatry. A famous example is encountered in the Talmudic tractate on idolatry (Hebrew: *Avodah Zarah*). In the midst of a conversation about why various foodstuffs of idolaters are prohibited, the following statement appears: "And [the Sages decreed] against Their wine on account of Their daughters; and against Their daughters on account of 'that thing'; and against 'that thing' on account of 'that thing.'"[16] Without commentary, the text—especially the final line—is quite confusing. While it is beyond our purview to discuss this passage in detail, the Babylonian Talmud and its commentaries go on to explain that "Their daughters" refers to the fact that idolaters' wine is prohibited out of concern that it could lead to marriage (presuming a male, heteronormative audience), as those who drink together might cement their social relations via intermarriage; and "Their daughters" on account of "that thing" refers to avoiding intermarriage out of fear of it leading to idolatrous practice; and "that thing" on account of "that thing" refers to fears that, if idolatrous male children and Jewish male children hang out together, then that could lead to homoerotic intercourse.[17] "That thing" in this text then refers to forbidden religious and sexual practices.[18] And both are too scary to name.[19]

Like any category deemed too frightful to name, linguistic substitution marks the glossed word(s) as especially powerful. Euphemism can also lead to humor, as we shall see later.[20] But that humor often comes with an edge, or the joke does not go over well. For example, consider this encounter between a well-known Rabbi and his apparently bored students: "There were two students who were sitting before Rav. One [of the students] said: This study is making us like a tired 'that thing.' And [the other] one said: This study is making us like a tired kid. And Rav did not speak with that [first] one."[21] Perhaps the first student was trying to make a joke. Perhaps he was being too honest. Or perhaps he simply did not consider the weight of his words. Either way, his reference to the pig—despite his linguistic substitution of "that thing"—clearly upsets his teacher. The fact that the second student—who also expresses boredom but with reference to a baby goat—does not lose favor with his teacher suggests that "that thing" is the thing that irks Rav. While you can kid about kids, even if you do not use the word itself, the pig is no joking matter.[22]

"THIS EVIL EMPIRE": ROME, THE PIG, AND THE DESTRUCTION OF THE SECOND TEMPLE

While being unwilling to even utter the word "pig" adds to its metaphorical weight, perhaps the most consequential pig-related development in the Rabbinic Period is the explicit connection between the pig and "The Evil Empire," a.k.a. Rome. In imagining the pig as embodying Rome (and vice versa), the Rabbis turn the pig into a symbol for corruption, greed, oppression, and violence—all of which they associate with Rome. In order to understand how this porcine association works, we will look at two interrelated connections between the pig and Rome: first, establishing the link between the pig and Rome; and second, connecting the dots between Rome / The Pig and the destruction of the Second Temple.

The association between Rome and the pig comes through a series of connections.[23] It starts with the biblical figure Esau. In Genesis 25, we learn that Esau and his twin brother, Jacob, are the longed-for children of Isaac and Rebekah. The stage for their contested relationship is set within Rebekah's womb, in which the twins are explicitly described as fighting with each other.[24] Rebekah inquires of the Lord why the children whom she and Isaac so desperately yearned for are fighting vigorously against each other. In response, she is told, "Two nations are in your womb, two separate people shall issue from your body; one people shall be mightier than the other, and the older shall serve the younger."[25]

When Esau emerges first from Rebekah's womb, the reader is prepared for both a rocky relationship between the twins and for the eventual role reversal of Jacob, the younger twin, gaining prominence over Esau, the older twin.[26] And this is exactly what we find when we read the biblical account. Most important for our present purposes is that the two-separate-nations claim proves prophetic. Jacob remains in the land of Canaan, settling in Bethel. That location lives up to its name (*Bethel* literally means in Hebrew "House of God"), when God appears and renames Jacob "Israel."[27] Now the eponymous ancestor of Israel, Jacob/Israel is explicitly identified as the chosen ancestor to whom belongs all previous divine promises to his grandfather Abraham and his father, Isaac.[28] That leaves Esau on the outside looking in. Displaced socially, theologically, politically, and economically, Esau, along with all of his wives and children, took "all the property that he had acquired in the land of Canaan, and went to another land because of his brother Jacob. . . . So Esau settled in the hill country of Seir—Esau being Edom."[29] With that final line, not only does the prophecy of separate nations come true, but also we now have a clear identification of Esau with Edom.

Over the next millennium or so, Edom makes occasional appearances as an enemy and/or ally of Israel's enemies. For example, it is depicted as mocking Israel when Jerusalem falls to the Babylonians in 586 BCE.[30] And a couple of hundred years later, Judah Maccabee and his brothers wage war against the sons of Esau.[31] In rabbinic literature, Edom/Esau makes appearances as not just a generic enemy but a particular enemy: namely, Rome. For example, commenting on Genesis 27:22 ("the voice is the voice of Jacob, but the hands are the hands of Esau"), the Jerusalem Talmud records the following exegetical interpretation: "Jacob's voice cried out because of what Esau's hands did to him at Betar."[32] Betar was the last fortress to fall to Rome in 135 CE, thus marking the devastating end to the Bar Kokhba Revolt (132–135 CE).[33] Thus, Esau's hands are identified with the destructive hands of Rome. Further, Hadrian—the Roman emperor responsible for this military defeat and the harsh Roman policies that followed in its aftermath—is elsewhere in rabbinic literature referred to as "Hadrian, king of Edom."[34] All of these instances are seen as fulfillment of the biblical prophecy of brother against brother—Esau/Edom versus Jacob/Israel—with the fervent hope that the final piece of the prophetic puzzle ("the older shall serve the younger") gets set firmly, and definitively, in place.

In connecting Esau/Edom to Rome, all of the concerns about one get mapped onto the other. And the body on which these concerns are mapped is embodied in the pig. For example, *Genesis Rabbah* 65:1 asks, "Why is [Esau] compared to a pig? Just as this pig when it lays down, it puts forth its hooves as if to say 'I am pure,' so too does this Evil Empire commit robbery and violence [while] giving itself the appearance as if holding court."[35] The pig publicly displays its cloven hooves, as if to claim that it is pure. But do not judge a book by its cover, because the external, seemingly pure body of the pig conceals its impure innards. It does not chew the cud and therefore is not kosher. So too, The Pig puts on a grand show in public, claiming to run impartial law courts. But scratch the surface, and you will find a violent and corrupt Rome. This is why Esau/Edom/Rome is compared to the pig. Both masquerade as pure, but they are nonkosher wolves in kosher sheep's clothing.[36]

Elsewhere, in an extended exegesis on Leviticus 11:7 ("And the pig, though it has hoofs, with the hoofs cleft through, it does not chew the cud; it is impure for you"), *Leviticus Rabbah* 13:5 opens by asserting, "'And the pig': this is Edom." It then continues to unpack the verse, further embodying Edom as The Pig. "It does not chew the cud" is understood to teach a few things about Edom, including, "it does not praise God. Not only does it not praise [God], but it blasphemes and reviles [God]"; and "it does not raise righteous people. Not only does it not raise [righteous people], but it kills them."[37] Edom is The Pig; and both are presumed guilty of immoral and reprehensible behavior. As the saying goes, which we will encounter in a very different setting much later, "a pig is a pig is a pig."[38]

Now that we have established the connection between Esau, Edom, and Rome, we are prepared to understand how the pig / The Pig functions in narratives about the destruction of the Second Temple. As we learned previously, the pig had developed into a litmus test for Jewish identity and practice. Commenting on this, the archaeologist Max Price states, "One of the most significant developments in the Classical period was the weaponization of pork against the Jews."[39] While the pig was brandished as a weapon in Second Temple Period texts, it more literally embodies a weapon in a few rabbinic texts. The gun that appeared in act 1 is about to be fired now that we are in act 2.

As was the case in the previous discussion about the Second Temple Period, we should note that the narratives in which the pig is weaponized against the Jews are texts written by Jewish authors for particular rhetorical purposes. Therefore, neither the veracity nor the historicity of these narratives requires serious consideration. Whether or not they actually occurred, we know for certain that the cultural memory of their having occurred proves influential and inspiring long after the (real or supposed) events unfolded. What really matters, then, is the potent and enduring power of these narratives. More specifically, what matters is how and why the pig is literally weaponized.

In a handful of rabbinic texts, the pig appears like a cocked and loaded weapon in the hands of The Pig. Rome takes aim at the Second Temple and literally fires the pig in order to destroy its target. For example, "They brought to [Vespasian] a catapult and drew it up against the wall of Jerusalem. They brought him cedar boards, and he set [them] into the catapult, and he struck them against the wall until he made a breach [in the wall]. They brought a pig's head, and they set [the pig's head] into the catapult, and he hurled it toward the [sacrificial] limbs that were on the [Temple] altar. At that moment, Jerusalem was captured."[40]

Vespasian, later a Roman emperor, was the military commander of the Roman army during the Jewish Rebellion. Though his son, Titus, actually oversaw the destruction of the Second Temple in 70 CE, these details are often conflated.[41] Remember, veracity and historicity should not get in the way of an ancient text making a good point![42] What matters here is that the head of the Roman military forces—and ultimately the head of Rome itself—literally catapults a pig's head onto the Temple's sacrificial altar. And at the moment that the head of the pig, hurled by the head of Rome, lands on the Temple altar, "Jerusalem was captured." Having weaponized the pig, The Pig conquers Jerusalem.

In another set of traditions, the pig packs its own powerful punch. Looking back to the destruction of the Second Temple, we learn of porcine events that occurred "during the days of that Evil Empire [a.k.a. Rome]."[43] Trapped inside the walls of Jerusalem due to siege, Jews would lower baskets of gold to others outside the walls, who would take the payment and fill the baskets with kosher lambs to be hoisted up the walls and fed to those inside. One day, the baskets hoisted back up were filled not with lambs but with pigs. Halfway up the wall, "the pig stuck [its nails] in the wall and the wall shook." It is telling that here the text switches from plural ("two pigs" in the basket) to singular. The pig has transformed into The Pig. "At that moment," we are told that both sacrifice in the Temple ceased and that the porcine weapon had successfully hit its mark, leaving in its wake "the destruction of the Temple."[44] The Second Temple falls when The Pig deploys the pig as its literal and metaphoric weapon of mass destruction.

The connection between Rome, the pig, and the destruction of the Second Temple is preserved not only in texts. Vespasian and his son, Titus, minted coins whose imagery forever linked people, pigs, and

FIGURES 2.1 AND 2.2. Silver denarius minted in Rome, 77–78 CE. The obverse features Vespasian, and the reverse depicts a sow with three piglets. British Museum, R. 10436 (Asset Number 634594001). © The Trustees of the British Museum, used with permission.

place. Figures 2.1 and 2.2 show one such example of a silver denarius. Vespasian is depicted on the obverse (front) of the coin. On the reverse, a sow and three piglets appear. This porcine imagery connects Vespasian to both ancient and recent triumphs. Like a good Roman emperor, the ancient event is the founding of Rome. As the historian Jamie Kreiner summarizes, "The imagery was a traditional homage to the white sow and thirty piglets that Aeneas had discovered in fulfillment of a prophecy about the founding of Rome."[45] But it was also a reference to the recent snuffing out of the Judean Revolt.[46] One of the main units that participated in that Roman military victory was the Tenth Legion (the Legio X Fretensis, based in Jerusalem). Coincidentally, the Tenth Legion "displayed the wild boar as its favored avatar."[47] Thus, the symbol for the Roman military legion that destroyed the Second Temple was the wild boar. And this connection was immortalized in the coin of the realm. Gazing at that coin, one would remember both the founding of Rome and the destruction of the Second Temple. Pigs were there at the beginning and, more recently, were present when The Pig, utilizing weaponized pigs, quashed the Jewish Revolt and destroyed the Second Temple. Reflected in that coin one can see both the anger of ancient Jews and the pride of ancient Romans—opposite emotions inspired by the same porcine image, two sides of the same porcine coin.

"TURN TOWARD ME!": THE CURIOUS INCIDENT OF THE RABBI IN THE NIGHTTIME

Next we will explore how the association between the pig and Rome plays out in moments of potential pig-related Jewish martyrdom (or lack thereof) in rabbinic texts. But before we get there, we take a brief digression. I promise that this journey, which is less of a side trip and more of a stop along the way, will be worth the extra steps. First, we learn about an encounter between a famous Rabbi and two Roman women in which nothing happens. It is the reason *why* nothing happens that interests us. Allow me to explain.

In a well-known short story written by Sir Arthur Conan Doyle, Sherlock Holmes points a Scotland Yard detective toward a telling fact: a dog was quiet in the nighttime.[48] The fact that no noise occurred becomes the key that unlocks the mystery. The dog not barking is the curious incident of the dog in the nighttime, since (spoiler alert) the absence of barking suggests that the dog knew the criminal. Why do I bring this up here? Because we are about to read a story wherein the quiet inaction of a character is the key to unlock what is intended to be a humorous—and bawdy—mystery: why did Rabbi Aqiba refuse to have sex with two beautiful Roman women?

Without further ado, we turn to the story:

> When Rabbi Aqiba went to Rome, they slandered him before a certain general. [The general then] sent him two very beautiful women. They were bathed, anointed, and adorned like brides for their grooms.
>
> All night, they fell all over him. One said: Turn toward me! And the other said: Turn toward me! And he was sitting between them, spitting at them.

> In the morning, they went and met with the general and said to him: Death would be better for us than being given to this man!
>
> The general said to Rabbi Aqiba: Why did you not do with these women what men usually do? Are they not beautiful? Are they not children of Adam like you? Did not the One who created you create them?
>
> [Rabbi Aqiba] said to him: What could I do? Their body odor, like [the stench of] carrion meat or pig meat, overcame me.[49]

While we do not know the precise nature of the slander against the renowned Rabbi Aqiba, we have reason to fear.[50] Why? Because of the rabbinic tradition that Rabbi Aqiba died a gruesome martyr's death at the hands of Rome.[51] Whatever the nature of this slander, it causes the Roman general to send—as the text wants us to be clearly aware of—"two very beautiful women" into Rabbi Aqiba's bedroom. Why does the Roman general take this action? While we are not told explicitly, the scholar of rabbinic literature Jeffrey L. Rubenstein offers a plausible explanation: Rabbi Aqiba "is the target of some unspecified slanderous accusation, and the Roman governor, apparently seeking more concrete evidence of a wrongdoing, attempts to entrap the rabbi in a sex scandal."[52]

That night, Rabbi Aqiba must decide between giving into sexual temptation or embodying the rabbinic virtue of self-control. Rabbi Aqiba chooses the latter approach. However, he does so in a manner that also communicates disgust: he literally sits there all night spitting at them![53] The next morning, the Roman women are described as expressing anger to the general. While the embodied and psychological experience of sex work is much more complex, the text frames their remarks as if they are mainly conveying what they perceive as the insult of his sexual rejection. The general goes to speak with Rabbi Aqiba, as his actions make no sense to the general. Why did Rabbi Aqiba "not do with these women what men usually do?"—that is, why did he not have sex with them? And, moreover, are they not humans deserving of better treatment regardless?

In Rabbi Aqiba's answer, we learn why he felt such an expression of revulsion and disgust was necessary. And we also learn why this text is discussed in this book. Note that Rabbi Aqiba does not state that he did not want to "do with these women what men usually do." Rather, he asserts that he could not do so because their body odor overcame him.[54] And why was that? Because they smelled like non-kosher meat; in particular, they smelled like the pig.

The importance of the pig in this text is highlighted through a few key details. First of all, these are Roman women. The Pig smelling like pig is clearly meant to be humorous. Not only is it funny, but it is also serious: they are literally the embodiment of the pig, which their body odor proves. In case this was not obvious enough, remember that we are explicitly told that the Roman women prepared for the evening by bathing and anointing themselves; and yet, to Rabbi Aqiba, they still smell like pig.[55] Second, there is a Hebrew porcine pun that cues both this connection and injects further gendered humor. All night, the Roman women implore Rabbi Aqiba, "Turn toward me!" The Hebrew imperative of the verb "turn" is חזור (*ḥazor*). And the Hebrew noun for pig, used later in this text, is חזיר (*ḥazir*). You need not be able to read Hebrew to see that both words look similar (and, based on my transliterations, you can hear that also they sound similar).[56] This pun seems too obvious to be a coincidence—after all, each Roman woman is described as stating it all night long. Therefore, it is intended humor that the Roman women are described as linguistically marking themselves as non-kosher. The Pig is punning the pig to remind Rabbi Aqiba to trust his nose and avoid the pig / The Pig. Third, this pun also reminds Rabbi Aqiba about the perceived danger of engaging in sexual intercourse with Roman women—a slippery slope that elsewhere in rabbinic literature is perceived as leading in a downward spiral toward idolatry.[57] The words that rung in his ears all night long can actually be expressed aptly by retranslating "Turn toward me!" by using an American English vulgarism for coitus that highlights the pun; all night, the Roman women were imploring Rabbi Aqiba, "Pork me!"[58]

"[RABBI MEIR] DIPPED ONE OF HIS FINGERS IN PIG'S BLOOD": AVOIDING THE PIG BY EATING THE PIG

We have already seen how Rome is embodied in the pig, morphing in rabbinic literature from a foreign power into the paradigmatic colonial oppressor of The Pig. Faced with persecution by The Evil Empire, some Rabbis became martyrs, dying gruesome deaths and bearing witness to their faith.[59] On the basis of what we have learned previously, we would expect the pig to play a central role in such martyrdom accounts. But that is not what we find. Clearly, the power of the pig as a symbol of The Pig has grown, as we saw earlier; but for the Rabbis, it seems that the ingestion of pig is a binary: either one eats it or one does not. Pretending to ingest it—a farce that the old man Eleazar explicitly rejects in 4 Maccabees—is simply that: *pretending*.[60] It is not doing. In the binary eat / not eat, to pretend is not to eat. Therefore, one need not martyr themselves if they have the opportunity to act theatrically as if they did eat when, in reality, they did not ingest the pig.

We need to unpack this a bit more. The act of choosing a principled death is preferred over living a compromised life in both the Second Temple and Rabbinic Periods. However, what constitutes a compromised life vis-à-vis the pig changes from one era to the next.[61] In the Second Temple Period, to pretend to eat the pig is to forfeit the opportunity to bear witness through dying a martyr's death. This is why Eleazar refuses to go along with the charade offered by his captors. The Rabbis, on the other hand, develop another principle. Based on an interpretation of Leviticus 18:5, the Rabbis argue that the biblical verse "he shall live by them" (referring to "My statutes and My laws") means literally that: one should *live* by them and not die by them.[62] To martyr oneself rather than eat pig would be to *die* by them and not to live by them. There are only three exceptions to this principle: idolatry, forbidden sexual relations, and murder. Those—and only those—are the big three prohibitions that one should choose martyrdom over transgressing. But if the choice is between eating the pig or death, the Rabbis—unlike their Second Temple ancestors—would opt to eat pig.

The practical result of this principle in action renders incomprehensible the Maccabean stories of Eleazar, as well as the mother and her seven sons. For the Rabbis, they simply should have eaten the pig. Eleazar's actions are especially incongruous, as he was offered the chance to pretend to eat the pig. If, in the face of death, you are allowed to transgress the pig prohibition, all the more so you can *pretend* to transgress the pig prohibition! While choosing to eat—or even to pretend to eat—and thus to live was incomprehensible from a Second Temple perspective, this rabbinic principle flips the script. Thus, pig-related Jewish martyrdom stories are largely absent from rabbinic texts. That being said, it is worth examining a few instances when shifting rabbinic attitudes toward pig-related Jewish martyrdom change narrative possibilities and significations.

We begin first with putting the principle of "he shall live by them" into practice. But in this case, the "he" is a "she." The scenario under discussion is that of a pregnant woman who smells—and thus craves—food on Yom Kippur (the Day of Atonement).[63] As it is a fast day, generally it is forbidden to eat on Yom Kippur. But pregnancy is considered a potential threat to life, so the principle of "[s]he shall live by them" comes into play. Therefore, a pregnant woman craving food on Yom Kippur is fed until she feels better.[64]

The initial case proposed is that of a pregnant woman craving food on Yom Kippur. Then, a new wrinkle is added: What if the food that she craves is forbidden food? We learn, "[If] a pregnant woman smelled consecrated meat or pig meat, one inserts a hollow reed into the [meat's] juice and places it on her mouth. If that relieves her craving, it is well.[65] But if not, one feeds her the [meat's] juice itself. And if that relieves her craving, it is well. But if not, one feeds her the fat [of the meat] itself, for there is nothing that stands in the way of saving a life, except for [the prohibitions against] idolatry, forbidden sexual relations, and murder."[66] The question at hand is relevant on a daily basis (and not specifically on a fast day): Can a pregnant woman who desires prohibited food eat the food that she craves? The examples of prohibited foods are two categories of meat: consecrated meat (that is, meat consecrated for sacrifice in the Temple, which is generally prohibited for consumption) and pig meat.[67] The principle of "[s]he shall live by them" clearly applies here, as there is concern for life. But that does not mean that one should dive headfirst into the nonkosher waters. Rather, one should first gently dip their toe in the water. Thus, first they collect the prohibited meat's juice in a hollow reed and place it on her lips. This allows her to barely taste the essence of the meat. If that relieves her, then crisis averted. But if not, then they place their entire foot in the nonkosher waters and offer the juice from the prohibited meat. If that relieves her, then crisis averted. But if not, then she may dive in headfirst and eat the fat of the meat itself.[68] The rationale is explicit here: "for there is nothing that stands in the way of saving a life"—that is, except for those three prohibitions.

It is neither coincidental nor incidental that pig meat is one of the two examples of prohibited meat. As noted earlier, in this period the pig becomes a metonym for all nonkosher food. At the same time, the rabbinic principle of "[s]he shall live by them" means that—despite the growing cultural and theological baggage about the pig in particular—the pregnant woman should choose to eat the pig and live rather than abstain from the pig and, potentially, die.[69] After all, there is no reason to martyr yourself when pig is not one of those three prohibitions.

Our next two examples describe instances of rabbinic Jews living under Roman persecution. In rabbinic tradition, the time after the Bar Kokhba Revolt (132–135 CE) is known as a brief era wherein the Roman emperor Hadrian enacted a series of measures directed against the Jews. While the historical reality may not match the rabbinic memory of these events, once again we must keep in mind that it is the power of the narrative in subsequent retellings that shapes its impact on those who inherit these traditions.[70] Whether these events actually occurred, their narratives presume that Jews are in mortal danger as porcine events unfold; and it is for this reason that I include them in our conversation about pig-related Jewish martyrdom. In the two following examples, Jews disguise themselves as non-Jews in order to avoid disastrous detection by Roman authorities. And what completes their disguise? Pretending to eat pig.

The first anecdote appears during a discussion of rabbinic regulations requiring ritual hand washing prior to eating food:[71]

> It once happened during the time of [the Hadrianic] persecution that a certain Jewish shopkeeper would cook pure meat and pig meat and sell [them both], so that it would not be obvious that he was Jewish. As such, it was his practice that anyone who would enter his store [in order to eat and] did not wash his hands, he would know that he was an idolater and would place before him pig meat; but anyone who would wash his hands and recite a blessing, he would know that he was Jewish and would feed him pure meat.
>
> One time, a Jew entered in order to eat there and he did not wash his hands, so [the shopkeeper] thought he was an idolater [and] placed before him pig meat. He ate [pig] and did not recite the [Grace after Meals] blessing. When [the diner] came to settle his bill with him for his bread and meat, [the shopkeeper] said to him: You owe me such-and-such, for the meat that you ate costs ten *maneh* each piece.[72] [The diner] said to him: Yesterday, I ate it [and was charged] eight [*maneh*], but today you want to charge me ten?! [The shopkeeper] said to him: That which you ate is pig [which costs more]. When [the shopkeeper] told him this, [the diner's] hair stood on end, he was aghast, and said *sotto voce*: I am a Jew and you gave me pig meat?! [The shopkeeper] said to him: What the heck is wrong with you?! When I saw that you ate without washing your hands and without blessing [first], I thought that you were an idolater![73]

The Jewish shopkeeper and his Jewish customers develop a secret code.[74] The shopkeeper would openly serve pig meat to his customers, thereby throwing Roman authorities off his scent. After all, what kind of Jew would cook and sell pig meat?! But Jews knew that if they entered his shop and surreptitiously performed a rabbinic ritual hand-washing practice, they would signal their religious identity to the shopkeeper. He would then serve them nonpig meat. But—importantly—they would outwardly appear *as if they had consumed pig meat*. The Roman authorities would therefore presume that they were not Jews. After all, what kind of Jew would order and eat pig?! As an added bonus, their bill would be two *maneh* cheaper, so they were saving their life, their religious practice, and some money. The only problem occurs when one Jewish customer neglects to perform the secret code. The shopkeeper presumes that he is a non-Jew and serves him pig meat. Note that the text here is about the secret code and how rabbinic ritual hand-washing practices can secretly signal Jewish identity. But pig plays a key role in this story, as pretending to eat pig meat allows Jews to pass as non-Jews. Pig ingestion indexes non-Jewish identity, and thanks to the rabbinic principle that "he shall live by them," pretending to eat pig is an allowable means by which Jews can escape persecution by The Pig. Therefore, pig is the remedy to the potentially fatal malady of The Pig.

Our second, and final, anecdote involves a Rabbi on the lam from Rome:[75]

> Rabbi Meir was sought by the [Roman] government. He fled. Passing by the store of Romans, he found them sitting and eating "that kind." When they saw him, they said: "Is that him or not?" They said: "If that is him, let us call him over; if he comes and eats with us [then it cannot be him." They call him over]. [Rabbi Meir] dipped one of his fingers in pig's blood and put another finger in his mouth, dipping one and sucking another. They said to one another: "If that were Rabbi Meir, he would not have done so." They let him go and he fled. And this Scriptural verse applies to him: "the advantage of knowledge is that wisdom preserves the life of him who possesses it" [Ecclesiastes 7:12].[76]

As a wanted man, Rabbi Meir is traveling incognito when he is spotted by Roman authorities. Trying not to act suspicious, he does not run when they call him over to their table and subject him to a test of which we are by now familiar: the are-you-a-Jew pig test. Eat and you are not; abstain and you are. As readers, we are expected not to be surprised that The Pig is conveniently eating the pig. After all, that is what it does. We are also unsurprised that the narrator cannot utter the word "pig," first referring to it as "that kind." Wanted fugitive Rabbi Meir then casually does something that his Second Temple coreligionists would never have dared: he dips one of his fingers in pig's blood and places another finger in his mouth, appearing to suck the pig's blood off his finger. For the Romans, this "proves" that he was not the Rabbi they were looking for. As he has passed the pig test, they release him.

This literal act of prestidigitation allows Rabbi Meir to live another day.[77] He does not martyr himself as Eleazar or the mother and her seven sons would have because, rabbinically, he need not do so. In fact, the principle of "he shall live by them" would have allowed Rabbi Meir to dip a finger into pig's blood and to suck the actual pig's blood off that same finger. Doing so would have been allowed; and pretending is not doing, so all the more so pretending to do so is allowed. Further, the citation of Scripture completes the narrative. Summarizing Rabbi Meir's prestidigitation, Ecclesiastes 7:12 is invoked: "the advantage of knowledge is that wisdom preserves the life of him who possesses it." Not only did Rabbi Meir know that he would have been allowed to eat the pig to live, but he knew how to perform a sleight-of-hand trick, to make it appear to The Pig *as if* he ate the pig. Just because you can does not mean that you have to; and thus Rabbi Meir proves his true wisdom by managing simultaneously to "live by them" and to live them.

"CURSED IS THE ONE WHO RAISES PIGS": SWINE STIGMAS IN RABBINIC LITERATURE

Before concluding, we look at a variety of swine stigmas, that is, the ways in which the pig is marked in rabbinic literature as problematic at best and anathema at worst. Some of these swine stigmas are casual negative associations, and others are caustic and explicit condemnations of all things porcine.[78] The sum total of these many remarks broadens and deepens the gulf between rabbinic Jews and the pig.[79]

In general, pigs are considered dirty animals. This is a common cross-cultural misperception about pigs. Pigs get a bad reputation, even though many other animals equally can be considered dirty.[80] To offer one example, the sullied reputation of pigs underlies the rabbinic comparison between two- to three-year-old toddlers and pigs. How are toddlers and pigs similar? Because toddlers stick their hands in gutters where sewage drains.[81] This dirty reputation also has implications in the rabbinic purity system, wherein this physical dirt crosses the line into metaphorical dirtiness—that is, impurity. For example, when discussing the impermissibility of reciting certain prayers within a close proximity to excrement, the Babylonian Talmud notes that "the mouth of a pig"—even after it bathes in a river—"is like passing excrement."[82] Similarly, the Jerusalem Talmud does not mince its words when it simply declares, "Concerning the pig, it is a moving toilet."[83] Therefore, one should not pray near a pig, which is deemed tantamount to feces. And both are impure in regard to proximity for prayer.

Given all of the baggage that the pig accrues in the Second Temple and Rabbinic Periods, we should not be surprised to learn that the Mishnah categorically prohibits Jews from swineherding, stating, "A Jew may not raise pigs anywhere."[84] This famous proclamation strongly asserts that the pig stands alone, since all other animals discussed alongside the pig in this text (small cattle, chickens, dogs, pigeons) are not categorically prohibited but are only forbidden in certain locations or under certain circumstances.[85] This porcine prohibition is further reinforced when read alongside a subsequent tradition. As noted earlier, there was a popular story about the destruction of the Second Temple wherein, instead of provisions, pigs are placed in baskets that are hoisted up the walls of Jerusalem during the siege. These pigs (= The Pig) shake the walls of Jerusalem and destroy the Second Temple. Immediately after recounting this story, one version of the tale notes, "At that moment [the Rabbis] said: Cursed is the one who raises pigs!"[86] Swineherds are scapegoated (scapepigged?) for the catastrophic events of 70 CE.

The prohibition against raising pigs anywhere underlies another, less catastrophic, context. When discussing various Sabbath rules, we learn that one may provide sustenance to a dog on the Sabbath but not to a pig.[87] Dogs can be raised by Jews (with certain caveats), but pigs may not.[88] So offering pigs sustenance on the Sabbath would be deemed a Sabbath violation. While the Temple is not at stake here, honoring and keeping the Sabbath is.

Swine stigma further allows the pig to serve as a threat against disapproved behavior. One gruesome example relates to violations of mourning decorum: "A mourner is prohibited to engage in sexual activity during the days of his mourning. It once happened that a certain [mourner] engaged in sexual activity during the days of his mourning. [As a result, the mourner was punished] and pigs dragged his body away."[89] Mourning requires somber decorum. Among a myriad of rabbinic mourning customs is a prohibition against sexual activity. Swine stigmas suggest that the violation thereof is deemed especially heinous. There is an implicit conceptualization of this being a measure-for-measure penalty. By not controlling one's urges, they act like a pig; and thus, in the end, pigs will defile their body.[90] Subsequent interpretations further develop this association. The medieval exegete Rashi comments that "his body" has two possible interpretations: "his whole body; and some say, his penis."[91] In gendered poetic justice for his actions while he was a mourner, the body part engaged in sexual acts is removed by pigs during the days when others are mourning him. This is clearly a case of adding porcine insult to physical injury.

On several occasions, swine stigma pairs with other rhetoric of avoidance, to caution the presumed rabbinic, adult, male audience against getting too close to the forbidden flesh of humans (especially women) and nonhuman animals.[92] In these instances and all of the other cases noted earlier, swine stigma functions as a warning beacon: avoid the pig or risk peril to body and soul.

THE PIG STANDS ALONE: CONCLUSIONS

The Rabbinic Period begins with catastrophe: Judaism's central cultic location is in ruins. As rabbinic Judaism makes sense of these developments, it translates a Temple-based religion into a world devoid of a Temple. Looking back at that terrible moment, the Rabbis saw The Pig—the actions of Rome embodied in porcine form. That image, coupled with baggage inherited from the Second Temple Period, shaped rabbinic interactions with the pig and The Pig. In our examination of this development, three themes emerged.

First, the metaphorical weight of the pig leads to linguistic avoidance. As the pig is laden with more meaning, it becomes harder to utter the word itself. This has a snowball effect, as the harder it becomes to utter the word, the less it is said, which in turn makes it even more significant and, concomitantly, even harder to speak aloud. As we continue our story about Jews and the pig, we will see how other linguistic developments add further significance to the pig. This is but the beginning of that tale.

Second, Rome becomes The Pig. In this act of embodiment, each takes on qualities of the other: Rome is understood to be pig-like in actions and both physical and mental traits, and the pig is viewed as uniquely symbolic of colonial oppression, greed, and corruption. This association only grows and deepens over time, especially as Christianity and Rome become bound together in fact and in rabbinic imagination. Rome as The Pig, and The Pig as the ultimate

Other, is an important theme throughout our narrative, with who and what constitutes "Rome" changing over time.

Third, while all of this is happening, another important development occurs: the Rabbis allow a Jew to consume the pig rather than die. Theoretically, then, discussions of pig-related Jewish martyrdom should disappear. But, as we shall see as our story continues to unfold, this is not necessarily the case. The symbolic meaning of the pig—both internally and externally—leads to its appearance in a variety of rhetorical and actual instances of life and death, wherein the pig is used to index submission or rebellion. The story does not end; it only changes.

In all of these themes, we see that the pig has developed deep signification. In doing so, it sets the stage for its appearance in multiple important and fraught interactions for the millennium and a half to follow. Some of these events are traumatic, others are humorous, and still others are both. We are now ready to turn the page and see where the pig takes us next.

3

"THE PIGGISH TALMUD"

From Metaphor to Mockery in the Medieval Period

The Medieval Period often suffers from bad press. This begins with the various names by which the period is labeled. For example, Enlightenment thinkers—to play up their presumption to have shed the "light" of learning on the perceived "darkness" of previous superstition and unscientific reasoning—referred to this era as "The Dark Ages." Even the somewhat innocuous sounding "Middle Ages" positions the era as a way station (or, anachronistically, as akin to a historical "flyover" state) on the road from antiquity to modernity.[1] Both names do a disservice to the Medieval Period.

The complexity of the Medieval Period is readily apparent when one tries to label its beginning and end point. It depends on where geographically and/or on what data one focuses. Further, all discussions must begin prior (to set up the beginning of the narrative) and after (to follow through on reverberations and (re)interpretations of events/ideas). Thus, our conversation will explore roughly one thousand years of history, mostly in Europe but also beyond. Keep in mind, however, the necessary caution that we should not consider this period as a unified whole. It contains multitudes and nuances that I offer no pretense to cover fully.[2]

During this period, we watch as the reverberations of the past collide—sometimes violently—with the historical challenges of the present. In so doing, we encounter some of our most challenging sources, as the pig is put to work in service of goals ranging from basic theology to rabid antisemitism. From mammal to metaphor to mockery, the pig undergoes quite the transformation in the Medieval Period. Along the way, we observe the physical consequences of the embodiment of this metaphor on both textual and physical Jewish bodies; the pig leaves its mark, which too often appears in the form of a bruise. In order to understand how this comes to be, we need to back up a little and explain how it comes to be that to tell the story of Jews and the pig in the Medieval Period, we need to tell the story of Christianity and the pig.

"MY NAME IS LEGION": JESUS, DEMONS, AND PIGS IN THE NEW TESTAMENT

Christianity—in various forms, perspectives, and locations—becomes a central character in the story of Jews and the pig in the Medieval Period. I speak of "Christianity" as a character in this story—and not necessarily (but also not *not* necessarily) Christians—because, much like "Judaism," "Christianity" often serves as a symbolic identity defined in direct relation to the pig. Porcine texts commonly deal in abstractions, albeit embodied abstractions, and hence we often have to speak of Christianity, not Christians, much as elsewhere we have spoken or will speak of Judaism, not Jews.

It might seem surprising that, in a book devoted to Jews and the pig, Christianity plays such a large role—until you think about Jewish history. With the rise of Christianity, Jews had to interact with Christianity in the abstract—theologically, economically, politically—and Christians in lived reality: in various manners that ranged from collegial to violent and all points in between.[3] And in many of these interactions, both Jews and Christians imagine these relationships through a porcine lens.

This story begins in documents that, while they come to be viewed as (indeed, *the*) Christian texts, have their origins in Judaism: the Gospels of the New Testament. Jesus and his earliest disciples are Second Temple Period Jews. Jesus criticizes the Temple priests and various Jewish authorities, but his quibbles are an internal critique. Only with Paul does the conversation grow beyond the Jewish community, to include Gentiles. To offer one relevant example, Jesus is never described in any New Testament Gospel as either eating non-biblically-kosher food or as eating at a table with non-Jews.[4] Therefore, there is no reason to presume that Jesus ever ate pig. Indeed, the evidence more strongly suggests that he did not.

But that does not mean that Jesus never interacted with pigs. While Jesus's most famous pig-related statement—uttered during the Sermon on the Mount—is "do not throw your pearls before swine" and his most famous pig-related parable is the Parable of the Prodigal Son (in which a son blows his inheritance, is forced by his poverty to become a swineherd, and then repents), it is his most well-known interaction with pigs that merits our attention.[5] Arriving in Gerasa (in modern northern Jordan), Jesus immediately encounters a man in dire need of an exorcism.[6] Jesus talks with the demonic spirit tormenting the Gerasene man and asks it its name.[7] The demon replies, "My name is Legion; for we are many."[8] Conveniently, "there on the hillside a great herd of swine was feeding."[9] Legion begs Jesus, "Send us into the swine."[10] Jesus grants Legion permission to go into them. "And the unclean spirit came out and entered the swine; and the herd, numbering about two thousand, rushed down the steep bank into the sea, and were drowned in the sea."[11] The swineherds, who have just lost two thousand pigs, are understandably upset and run off to get reinforcements. Jesus is asked to leave, and he does so.[12]

The connection between an unclean spirit entering unclean beasts is clear. While that is worthy of note for our present purposes, one word in this text offers tantalizing possibilities. The demon's name is "Legion." Though the New Testament text is written in Greek, *legion* is a loan word from Latin. In Latin, *legion* is a military term, referring to an army unit of about five thousand soldiers.[13] Is this an allusion to Rome as The Pig? If so, it would fit with Second Temple (and beyond) Jewish sources connecting Rome with the pig / The Pig.

Further, as the scholar of biblical studies Lawrence M. Wills notes, "Many Jewish and Christian texts, especially apocalyptic texts, express a belief that God would destroy the Romans and establish a kingdom of God—albeit conceived in different ways. This story remains evocative of several far-flung possibilities without clarifying them: Do the swine represent the expulsion ("gerash") of unclean animals or the Roman armies? Are the Gerasenes angry over a symbolic battle or the loss of their herds?"[14]

Imagining Legion's pigs as symbolic of Rome seems reasonable also for the rationale that the historian Jamie Kreiner suggests: "a herd of pigs is the perfect host—unclean and rapacious—for an aggressively parasitic empire that many of its Jewish subjects resented."[15] For all of these reasons, the pig seemed like a perfect metaphor for the perceived colonial oppressor polluting the Holy Land.

While I think it likely that "Legion" is a gesture toward porcine Rome and it certainly fits with all of the evidence provided in the previous conversations about pigs in both the Second Temple and Rabbinic Periods, sometimes a pig is just a pig and not a metonym. Therefore I remain uncertain whether there is enough evidence to conclusively assert that this is another connection between Rome and The Pig. Likely? Yes. Definitely? Maybe.

"THE SORT OF PEOPLE WHO ARE LIKE PIGS": FROM MAMMAL TO METAPHOR IN EARLY CHRISTIAN TEXTS

From the first century CE onward, early Christian authors quickly begin to read Old Testament laws as allegories to learn from and not necessarily as literal laws to follow. Thus, the pigs into which Jesus casts Legion come to be viewed as metaphors for sloth and depravity rather than as tabooed sources of protein. In sum, Christians could eat the pig; they just could not act like the pig.[16]

This allegorical move plays a key role in our story. As pigs transform from literal beasts into embodied allegories for vice, impurity, and, importantly, heresy, the categories of pigs, Jews, and bad

Christians are conflated. This is further cemented by the common label of "Judaizers" for "bad" Christians, in that they act like "Jews." Eventually, this results in pigs serving as allegories for bad Christians as part of a broader trend of what the historian David Nirenberg refers to as anti-Judaism.[17] Christians talk about Jews and Judaism as a means to talk about Christianity. Therefore, pigs and Jews are hermeneutical pigs, and Jews embodied metaphors for Christians whom the authors of the texts consider to be wayward. This observation raises two important points: (1) the pigs/Jews should be read as metaphors, not mammals; and (2) this metaphorical move establishes pigs/Jews as a means by which to discuss "good" and "bad" Christians or manifestations of Christianity. Both of these developments will be important not only for our present discussion but also for the full narrative arc of the history of Jews and the pig.

The move from mammal to metaphor happens early in the history of Christian biblical interpretation. In the second century CE, for example, we find the Epistle of Barnabas declaring,

> And when Moses said, "do not eat the pig, . . ." So, then, the commandment of God is not a matter of avoiding food; but Moses spoke in the Spirit. This is why he spoke about the pig: "Do not cling," he says, "to such people, who are like pigs." That is to say, when they live in luxury, they forget the Lord, but when they are in need, they remember the Lord. This is just like the pig: when it is eating, it does not know its master, but when hungry, it cries out—until it gets its food, and then is silent again.[18]

Pigs are pigs. They take and take and take without gratitude and only pay respect to the Lord—whom they forgot during the good times—when they need something. Once a Christian learns this lesson, they are free to partake of the literal swine so long as they avoid the metaphoric sin it embodies. A good Christian must shun piggish ways in their decorum but need not (and, in fact, as we shall see both later in this chapter and in later eras, must not) shun pig in their diet.

This lesson is repeated several times in early Christian texts, in which the pig represents various sins and vices.[19] In this line of exegetical thinking, the Old Testament taboos the pig in order to call attention to the need to taboo these sins and vices. But that does not mean that one should avoid the pig. Again, good Christians know both how to distance themselves from moral and spiritual harm and that, in order to so, they need not distance themselves from ham.[20]

Not every early Christian seems to have gotten the memo. For several centuries, we learn of Christian communities that continue to follow Old Testament food laws literally, including—especially troubling—the pig prohibition. For example, Augustine of Hippo (a.k.a. Saint Augustine) notes with annoyance the fact that there are groups of Christians in the late fourth–early fifth century CE who still abstain from ingesting the pig.[21] The importance of food laws in general and the signification of the pig in particular clearly continue to influence the food practices of a variety of Christian communities. The power of The Signifying Swine endures.

A fascinating report of one such community is preserved in its own voice. In 654 CE, the Visigothic king of Hispania, King Recceswinth, received a letter from a group of his subjects living in Toledo. Decades before, this particular community had converted from Judaism to Catholicism. The letter reports how the community has embraced Christian practices (such as only socializing with baptized Christians) and abandoned Jewish practices (such as circumcision and celebrating Passover). But one Jewish practice proved especially vexing to abandon: the community still found it difficult to eat pig. Try as they might, the historical weight of the pig loomed large. Summarizing their arguments, the historian Jamie Kreiner notes,

> They knew that tasting pork was socially and historically conditioned, because they were trying, with great difficulty, to counteract the "nausea and horror" (*fastidio et orrore*) they had once felt at the thought of eating a forbidden meat. Their visceral reactions were rooted in the antiquity (*vetustas*) of their traditions. And in saying these things to

> the king, they were pointing out that changing one's tastes required a conversion of the innermost kind, not of the mind on its own, but more profoundly the turning of a body away from itself and from the foodways that had sculpted it.[22]

While "good" Christians in all other ways, even after decades had passed, these former Jews could not bring themselves to eat pig. Pig thus functions as an embodied remnant of their past. Their conversion would not be complete until they changed their tastes and ate the pig. In a theme that we shall return to later, one has not fully accepted Christ in their life until they have fully assimilated the pig into their diet.

Just as Jewish sources lade pig with more layers of meaning, so too do Christian texts. In doing so, both Jewish and Christian sources create "a feedback loop, with each party responding to developments in the other by ramping up their own attitudes towards swine."[23] In short, the more that the pig comes to signify Jewish identity, the more it comes to signify Christian identity, and vice versa. This highlights an irony we encounter throughout this period and beyond: the more that Christians use the pig to talk about Jewish identity, the more that the pig ends up defining and shaping Christian identity.

"AND LET THEM BE SWINE EVER MORE": MEDIEVAL MOCKERY AND DEHUMANIZATION OF JEWS

As pigs transform from literal beasts into embodied allegories for vice, impurity, and heresy, their association with Jews continues. While this directly leads to the connection between bad Christians and "Jews," discussed earlier, the association between Jews and pigs—both embodied and metaphorical—persists. And this connection proves useful for both laughter and derision. Here, we discuss two examples in which the association between Jews and the pig is used to both mock and dehumanize Jews.

The first example comes from the popular practice of writing about the infancy of Jesus. This practice develops in both antiquity and the Medieval Period because, while New Testament texts have much to say about Jesus's birth and adulthood, they are silent about his infancy and preteen years. Ancient and medieval Christians fill in the holes in Jesus's biography, writing fascinating (and occasionally humorous) gospels and poems.[24] In a handful of these texts, a story is told in which some Jewish children hide from Jesus in an oven while their parents lie to Jesus about their whereabouts. But Jesus being, well, Jesus, easily sees through this charade. In a version written in Middle English and dating to around 1280–1300 England, the following events unfold:

> He asked the Jews at once what had been put in that oven. The Jews began to vow and say that it was all swine. Jesus then said to them: "And let them be swine ever more." And each of them likewise became swine at that same time, and as swine they ate food. Thus was Jesus avenged on them. When Jesus Christ was gone, the oven was quickly opened, and those that had been put in there came out truly swine. Everyone considered them all dead and killed for their deserts. And ever after because of this, I believe, the Jews consider every pig a brother, according to their custom. This was an excellent miracle. Nor ever after, from that [time] to this, do Jews eat of swines' flesh, nor will they ever, raw or cooked, for their law has forbidden it.[25]

While Jesus is more famous for his miraculous ability to turn water into wine, in this tale he turns children into swine (see figure 3.1). Seen as just deserts for their behavior, this transformation clearly dehumanizes Jews, connecting the animality of Jews with that of pigs.[26] Further, Jews are explicitly blamed for this development. As the ethnographer Claudine Fabre-Vassas astutely observes, "It was the Jews who originally confused their children with pigs, who committed this most serious error in classification, and that is why they are forever separated from the animal. Thus, contrary to the

FIGURE 3.1. Illuminated manuscript of Apocryphal Childhood of Christ, written in French. People are astonished when pigs come out of the oven. Oxford, Bodleian Library MS. Selden Supra 38, pt. 1, circa 1315–1325 CE. © Bodleian Libraries, University of Oxford, used with permission, https://digital.bodleian.ox.ac.uk.

universal rule that associates the other, the foreigner, with what he eats, Jews are associated with the flesh they are forbidden. Sameness and prohibition are reconciled with one stroke."[27]

When Jesus transforms those Jewish children (hiding in an oven, into which food is usually placed), he is merely making true the false oath of the parents. Now, indeed, there are pigs in the oven. Jesus is being cheeky, but the parents are the ones at fault here. After all, Jesus just turned their words into (pig) flesh.[28] This story doubles as another origin story for why Jews do not eat the pig: if every pig could be a brother, then one best avoid the flesh of their brethren.[29] This ignores the fact that the Old Testament had already tabooed the pig in Leviticus 11:7 and Deuteronomy 14:8. Of course, one could invoke Jesus's own words, as he famously declared, "before Abraham was, I am."[30] But I do not think this is necessary, as the punch line is more about imparting a humorous joke rather than a historical lesson. The reader can both know the Old Testament law and laugh at this "origin" story.

Before turning to the next example, a recent study is worth our attention. In 2021, an interdisciplinary group of scholars analyzed organic residue, faunal records, and historical documents related to the Jewish Quarter in Oxford, England, in the eleventh to twelfth centuries. They found not only a strong prevalence of kosher fowl but also a complete absence of pig remains.[31] Therefore, when medieval English Christian authors retell this infancy story, they are not only regurgitating past texts but perhaps also presuming its veracity on the basis of observable practice in their contemporary world.[32]

A key detail in the preceding story serves as the perfect segue to our second example. When confronted by Jesus, the Jewish parents vow that the oven is filled with swine, not children. And pigs come to play an important role in a particular type of vow taken by medieval Jews.

In medieval Europe, there was a common legal practice known as the Jewish Oath (*Iuramentum Iudaeorum*), which refers to "the oath that Jews had to take to establish proof in lawsuits with Christians."[33] The Jewish Oath, and the ceremony involved in its recitation, combines "elements of Jewish and Germanic law."[34] One particular part of the Jewish Oath merits our attention. In a text that dates to around 1275, the following description of the Jewish Oath ceremony appears: "This is the Jews' oath, as they shall swear it, and everything that belongs to their oath. He shall stand on a sow's skin, and his right hand shall lie in a book up to the wrist; and that shall be the five books of Moses."[35]

Parts of this ritual conform with rabbinic law. The Babylonian Talmud, for example, prescribes standing and grasping a Torah scroll while taking an oath.[36] But the eagle-eyed reader will spot the part that does not conform with rabbinic law: standing on a sow's skin. (For a visual representation, see figure 3.2, which is a depiction of this ritual in a ca. 1425 manuscript of the just-cited text.) The tradition of a Jew standing on a sow appears in several medieval versions

FIGURE 3.2. Jew swearing an oath according to the Jewish Oath prescriptions, early fifteenth century CE, by Diebolt Lauber. *Schwabenspiegel*, MS Bruxellensis 14689–14691, fol. 204v. Used via Wikimedia Commons License, https://de.wikipedia.org.

of the Jewish Oath. For example, in a text from 1516, just in case the physical and rhetorical function of the pig is missed, it is made much more apparent: "[The Jew] shall stand on a skin of a sow that had born young within fourteen nights. The skin shall be split up along the back and be spread on [displaying] the teats; on it the Jew shall stand barefooted and wearing nothing but nether garment and a haircloth about his body."[37]

The role of the pig in this oath ritual seems obvious: it is meant to degrade Jews. While the ceremony accords with Jewish religious oath regulations by occurring while standing and holding a Torah scroll, it simultaneously mocks Jews by forcing them to stand on the pig—an animal explicitly prohibited by the document they hold in their very hands.[38] Further, evidence shows that the original form of the Jewish Oath ceremony required the Jew to stand on a goat. The pig was added in the thirteenth century.[39] Why would a goat—a biblically kosher animal—be replaced with the pig if not to debase the Jewish oath taker?

Moving forward, we will discover that the motif of using the pig to mock Jews becomes a central theme of our story. This is but the first step down that slippery slope. In the next step down that slope, the trends of the pig becoming an allegory for vice and using the pig to mock and dehumanize Jews intersect as we discuss the complex history of perhaps the most famous—and troubling—medieval image of Jews and the pig: the *Judensau*.

"THE RECTUM OF THE SOW IS THE TALMUD": THE *JUDENSAU* IN MEDIEVAL GERMANY

From the thirteenth through the sixteenth century, various forms of the *Judensau* image appear in Germany.[40] In its most basic form, the *Judensau* (literally: "Jews' sow") depicts Jews sucking on the teats of a sow.[41] Sculptures and images of the *Judensau* range from the relatively tame to the graphic—with the latter including depictions of Jews eating pig excrement. The historian Caroline Walker Bynum offers a concise summary of the development of this visual motif in medieval Germany: "At first one animal image among many in the cycle of virtues and vices and carrying as its primary meaning the accusation that all sinners are Jews in their greed and lasciviousness,[42] it became dissociated from such cycles and by the fifteenth and sixteenth centuries served as what German historians call a 'Schandbild,' an image intended to satirize, humiliate, and accuse. The association of Jews with an animal they considered unclean and with the filth (dung) of economic profit was drawn out explicitly."[43]

While the *Judensau* starts off as but one animal image in a series of animal images about virtues and vices, in Germany it very quickly becomes associated with Jews and "Jewish" vices. The historian Isaiah Shachar notes in his classical study of the *Judensau* that, though medieval English churches and cathedrals frequently used the motif of sow and piglets more generically, "allegorical representations of sows without Jews are quite uncommon in German religious sculpture."[44] Further, in Germany, this image proved popular, enduring for several centuries.[45]

Equally enduring was the obscene depiction of Jews. First of all, Jews are immediately recognizable in the majority of these images by their hats: "Jews can be recognized in high medieval art by various versions of the pointed or peaked headgear known sometimes as the *pileum cornutum* (horned cap) or simply as the 'Jewish hat.'"[46] This is important to note because the obscenity of the images hinges on the clear legibility of the humans as Jews. Second, as Shachar bluntly states,

> It is noticeable that, in spite of local and period variations, all examples of the motif share clear common features of rudimentary obscenity. The sucking of the sow's teats is shown in all but two, which show the sow embraced and kissed. Additional occupation with the animal's hind quarters, and the eating and drinking of its excrement, are shown in most. While the meanings attached to the *Judensau* changed considerably over the years, these obvious elements of oral and anal obscenity were always retained and, indeed, elaborated. This seems to suggest strongly that it was the extreme obscenity of the representation itself that made it so popular for some six hundred years.[47]

Obscene to begin with, *Judensau* images become even more obscene as they move from satirizing the vice of greed in general to satirizing the Jew as the embodied pig of greed in particular.[48]

Since a picture is worth a thousand words, let us look at a particularly graphic *Judensau*. Figure 3.3 shows a fifteenth-century German woodcut.[49] In the center of the woodcut is a large sow. Surrounding the sow are seven young boys and two adults—clearly identified as

Jews through various symbols, such as the Jewish hat worn by most of them. Four young Jewish boys are beneath the sow, vigorously sucking on her teats. Another young Jew (marked as Jewish both by his hat and by the mock Hebrew letters on his clothes) sits atop the sow and, facing backward, lifts its tail and sucks the tail's tip. Beneath the lifted tail, a young Jewish boy points at the sow's rectum and sticks out his tongue—seemingly preparing to dine on the sow's feces.[50] Another young Jewish boy snuggles the sow's snout, which belies how Jews are supposed to feel about the pig. Two bearded adult Jews look on and hold scrolls whose words reinforce the obscenity of the image. Shachar summarizes the visceral profanity of this image:

> As it stands, the woodcut is a single big anti-Jewish joke centred on associating the Jews, in an intimate and obscene manner, with the animal they most abhor. The inscriptions make the joke quite explicit. The caption reads: "This is why we do not eat roast pork. And thus we are lustful and our breath stinks."[51] While one Jew, probably the religious teacher, pronounces the exhortation "This we should not forget—swine's flesh we must not eat," the other elderly man invites "all the Jews" to "behold what came to pass between us and the sow." While most of the youngsters take the part of sucking piglets, one calls the sow "our mother" and another encourages his brother to suck the tail so as to uncover the rectum.[52]

This picture is indeed worth a thousand words, and every word is obscene.

In 1543, Martin Luther turned his attention to the *Judensau* (to be more specific, to the *Judensau* in Wittenberg).[53] Luther's poison pen spewed much venom on this subject, with complex and catastrophic effects for centuries to come.[54] To be fair, Luther found the *Judensau* useful not just for mocking Jews but also for mocking the pope. For example, in 1545, Luther commissioned a print in which "a bearded and hooked-nose Pope Paul III rides a sow

FIGURE 3.3. Fifteenth-century German woodcut depicting a *Judensau*. Used via Wikimedia Commons License, https://commons.wikimedia.org.

while holding a handful of steaming feces.... This 'Papensau' was doubtless inspired by and meant to evoke the Jews on their 'Judensau.'"[55] Luther's followers took his vitriol and built on it. Notably, in 1596, Laurentius Fabricius, as part of his profession as professor of Hebrew at the University of Wittenberg, published a volume that contained a lengthy discussion of the *Judensau*.[56] Extending the metaphor to absurd levels of both obscenity and debasement, Fabricius makes a new association: if the Jews are the pig, and the Talmud—not the Bible—is their central document, then the Talmud is the pig, and both embody the Jew. Thus, when a *Judensau* depicts a Jew gazing at a sow's rectum, Fabricius interprets it this way: "[The Jew's] facilities concentrated in earnest meditation, to be laying open I do not know what mysteries in the Talmud of the sow."[57] Fabricius develops this animus argument further: "Consider their own learning: they have a sow as mistress, a swinish pedagogue, and in brief, their whole discipline is swine breeding, and all their teachers swine-breeders. For once upon a time the pious Jews did not approve of the sow for eating and sacrifice; today the Jews ignore this and make her their mistress. Having neglected the Sacred Book, they occupy themselves with the rectum of the sow. . . . They take all their mysteries from the piggish Talmud, they suck all the impurity from the teats of swine."[58]

Fabricius accuses Jews not just of ignoring the Bible but of committing heresy: they are supposed to taboo the pig, and instead, he claims, they embrace the pig carnally. Concomitantly, they reject the Bible (= Christ and Christianity) and embrace the Talmud (= the pig and piggish Judaism). Fabricius believes that instead of gazing into the biblical truth of Christianity and drinking from the pure waters of Christ, Jews stare into the rectum of the pig (that is, the Talmud) and drink impure milk/texts of the sow/Talmud. In sum, the pig is the Talmud; and the Jews are the people of that book; ergo, the Jews are the pig.

This "piggish Talmud" association perhaps appears in other *Judensau*-adjacent imagery. Take for example German playing cards. Like modern playing cards, they feature not only numbers and suits but also images. "The smallest value in cards, the Two (= *Zwei*, *Daus*), was called all over Southern Germany, for etymological and folkloristic reasons, *Sau* [= Sow]."[59] Thus, sows are obvious images for Two cards in all suits. Shachar notes one fifteenth-century example that features a Jew, hugging a sow and holding a money bag.[60] Greed, Jews, and love of pigs are clearly indexed in this image, pointing the viewer directly toward the *Judensau*. In another version of the *Sau* playing card from the seventeenth or early eighteenth century, a Jew is depicted riding the sow and reading a book.[61] Though it is not clear, I think the implication is that the book in his hands is the Talmud. That being said, this later *Sau* card also represents part of the decline of the *Judensau* image: it is now less about outright abusive mockery and more of a clichéd joke of the Jew joyfully interacting with the supposedly abhorred pig.[62]

As obscenity piles on top of obscenity, the *Judensau* devolves over time into what it was at its very core: a vulgar joke. Eventually, this joke is deemed too childish and immature for polite company, and it comes to be viewed as too scatological and lowbrow for church sculpture.[63] But not before the damage, both physical and metaphorical, was already done.

"NEVER COULD I SLAY THAT TRACE OF CONVERSO": MARRANOS, PIGS, AND THE INQUISITION

Like many Americans, in elementary school I was taught a historical lesson in rhymed form: "In 1492, Columbus sailed the ocean blue." While most readers know that this refers to Christopher Columbus setting sail from Spain across the Atlantic Ocean, less well known is that another significant historical event occurred earlier that same year: Spain expelled the Jews.[64] Both of these events in 1492 had significant and long-lasting impacts across the globe—from Spain to the Americas and beyond.[65] And, though we will only focus on the Spanish expulsion of the Jews, both of these events feature enduring stories related to the pig.[66]

Before we get to this story, it is worth noting that when the Iberian Peninsula was under Muslim rule (and known as al-Andalus), the pig was a defining feature not for its presence but for its absence.[67] Given the fact that Islam taboos the pig, this should be expected. Building on prior assumptions, the pig was seen as dirty—and hence regions that consumed the pig were seen as dirtier than pig-free zones. This claim is made by the renowned twelfth-century Jewish philosopher Maimonides.[68] Writing in Judeo-Arabic in his famous *The Guide for the Perplexed*, he sullies the pig for its sullied reputation. Maimonides then asserts, "Now if swine were used for food [in al-Andalus], market places and even houses would have been dirtier than *latrines*, as may be seen at present in the country of the Franks."[69] In Arabic, "Franks" was a common way of referring to Europe.[70] Hence, Maimonides here uses the pig to divide pristine al-Andalus from the both literal and figurative pigsty that (in his opinion) is Europe. But when the Iberian Peninsula comes under Christian rule, the plot of the pig's story takes an interesting twist.

For many years prior to issuing the decree expelling Jews, Spain and the Catholic Church pressured Jews to convert. Apparently, in addition to laypeople, priests, and nuns, even the Virgin Mary reportedly exerted pressure to convert. In the thirteenth-century collection of poems known as the *Cantiagas de Santa Maria*, for example, the Virgin Mary appears in a dream to a Jew imprisoned by Christian thieves. The Virgin Mary promises the Jew that he will be with Christ in heaven if the Jew would "believe in Him and eat suckling pig and stop cutting the throats of goats."[71] While we learn that subsequently he was baptized, we never learn explicitly whether he adds suckling pig to his diet (nor whether he stops cutting goat throats). Jews became Conversos (Spanish for "converts," especially referring to Jews who converted to Christianity) for a variety reasons, ranging from genuinely held belief to genuine fear for life. Regardless of their reason for converting, Conversos were often treated with suspicion—both of the "Jewish stench" that was still considered inherent to them as former Jews and out of fear that Conversos continued to practice Judaism in secret (which some, but by no means all, did). Writing in the 1470s, Antón de Montoro—a poet, tailor, and Converso—laments in porcine terms that he is never viewed by his fellow Spanish Catholics as truly Christian:

> **I followed the credo and worshipped**
> **Pots of fatty pork**
> **half cooked bacon**
> **listened to mass and prayed**
> **crossed and crossed myself**
> **And never could I slay**
> **that trace of Converso.**[72]

No matter how much pig he eats, Montoro is always viewed as a Converso—with one foot still planted in the Jewish world—rather than as fully Catholic.[73]

This suspicion of the Converso is only exacerbated by the impact of the event that, according to Monty Python, nobody expected: the Spanish Inquisition. The Inquisition inquired into the sincerity of the Conversos. Their methods ranged from the bureaucratic to the brutal. Eventually, Inquisitors succeeded in convincing the Spanish monarchy to expel all Jews who would not convert to Catholicism. And it is here where the pig enters our story. Thus far I have referred to these Jewish converts to Christianity by the relatively neutral term "Converso."[74] However, a popular term used to refer to a Jewish convert was "Marrano." Cecil Roth summarizes the history of this term: "The word Marrano is an old Spanish term dating back to the early Middle Ages and meaning swine. Applied to the recent converts in the first place perhaps ironically, with reference to their aversion from the flesh of the animal in question, it ultimately became a general term of execration which spread during the sixteenth century to most of the languages of Western Europe. The word expresses succinctly and unmistakably all the depth of hatred and contempt which the ordinary Spaniard felt for the insincere neophytes by whom he was now surrounded."[75]

As Roth notes, there is a perverse logic to this association: Jews abhor the pig, and "true" Christians should abhor duplicitous converts. Further, a similar logic to *Genesis Rabbah* 65:1, a text discussed earlier, applies here: the pig looks kosher on the outside, which belies its nonkosher core; and so too, Marranos look like Christians when one sees them on the street or in church, but inside (their heart and their home, where they continue to practice Judaism) they are secretly corrupt.[76]

From the benign to the brutal, the association between Jews and the pig plays into conversations about Conversos for almost a millennium. We see it, for example, when Elvira del Campo is tried by the Inquisition of Toledo in 1567–1569 on charges including not eating pig. She confessed to this crime and was sentenced to torture.[77] Sadly, Elvira del Campo was not alone in suffering, as many Conversos were hauled before the Inquisition and condemned over claims that, among other things, they avoided eating pig.[78] Inquisitors found Converso avoidance of the pig—whether actual or perceived—as damning proof of their secretly practicing Judaism and meted out vicious punishments as condemnation of these "Pigs."[79] The pig also appears in pernicious stories accusing Jews of the blood libel.[80] The legacy has even influenced food history: in Portugal, a "blood sausage" that contains neither blood nor pork is called a *chorizo de Mariano*—a Marrano's sausage or, to make explicit that which is implicit, a Jew's sausage.[81] The pig plays an enormous role in the story of Conversos, as both Inquisitors and Conversos tell tales of how the legacy of Judaism (both knowingly and unknowingly) reverberated through generations—sometimes long after the connection between the Conversos and their Jewish past was forgotten.[82] Though the elephant may never forget, it would seem that the pig never lets anyone else forget.

"MILK FROM A CHRISTIAN WET NURSE": BREAST MILK, PIGS, AND JEWISH/CHRISTIAN INTERACTION

While the rhetoric and politics surrounding modern breastfeeding is quite polarizing, it might surprise readers to learn that there is a long history behind the various critiques of and apologies for breastfeeding practices.[83] And, in the Medieval Period, pigs enter into the discussion—by both Jews and Christians. For our present purposes of comparison, it is especially interesting that both sources that we will discuss relate to the same topic: non-Jews serving as wet nurses for Jews.

Our first source is by Rabbi Isaac ben Moses, a widely respected medieval authority who lived in thirteenth-century Vienna. As part of a consideration of whether young children are allowed to eat non-kosher food (in general, they are), he offers the following caveat:[84]

> Despite this, one should warn the [non-Jewish] wet nurse not to eat impure meat or pork and certainly not to feed them [the infants] impure substances, as it is written: "What caused [Aḥer to apostatize]..." And some commentaries on the passage explain, that some say that when she [his mother] was pregnant with him, she would pass in front of idolatry, and she smelled something of that *min* and they gave it to her and she ate and that *min* bubbled in her body.[85] ... For everything that a woman eats, the infant eats. And this caused him to turn to evil ways in his old age.[86]

It is important to note what might seem surprising: since the Classical Rabbinic Period, there are clear allowances for non-Jews (under certain, controlled circumstances) to serve as wet nurses for Jewish children.[87] But this creates a dilemma: What if the non-Jewish wet nurse eats forbidden food and/or feeds that food to the Jewish infant? While the infant is technically allowed to eat nonkosher food, it clearly is still a concern. Isaac ben Moses therefore suggests cautioning non-Jewish wet nurses against this eating/feeding practice. Why? Because eating the pig could lead to apostasy.

An example is offered with regard to Aḥer. "Aḥer" means "Other" in Hebrew and refers to the rabbinic figure Elisha ben Abuyah. Aḥer was famous—or, depending on your perspective, infamous— for first becoming a renowned master of rabbinic knowledge and practice and then a renowned apostate. It has long been the subject of speculation about why the pious Elisha ben Abuyah became the heretical Aḥer.[88] One explanation, offered here (not for the first time) is that, when pregnant with him, his mother smelled pig, and that kind of meat (*min*) led the child in her womb eventually to that kind of heresy (*min*).[89] The implications are clear: even if technically allowable, the non-Jewish wet nurse should neither eat pig prior to breastfeeding nor feed pig directly to the Jewish infant. Pig is embodied heresy (and, in particular, Christianity), so it cannot be fed to a Jewish child, lest it affect its spiritual development.

In our second source, the suspicion works the other way, as it is a text written from a Christian perspective. Reputedly reporting an incident that occurred in 1535 in Jägersdorf, Silesia, the following narrative is told:

> **A Jew offered to buy milk from a Christian wet nurse who instead sold him the milk of a sow. He then got a poor peasant who owed him money to execute his orders on the promise that his debt would be erased. He brought him to the foot of a gallows, made him cut off the head of the hanged man's corpse, and had him place it to soak in a receptacle filled with the milk. Afterward the Jew ordered the peasant to put his ear to the head and asked him, "What do you hear?" The peasant responded, "The grunting of a herd of pigs!" "Woe is me!" the Jew then cried, "the woman tricked me!" The next day all the pigs within a radius of eight kilometers gathered at this spot and killed one another.**[90]

While the Jew still buys "breast milk" from the Christian wet nurse, the concern here is for the Christian. The Jew is depicted as a deceptive sorcerer. Clearly, the role of sow's milk and pig squeals are meant to invoke the associations between the Jew, greed, filth, and heresy. The fact that the Jew is a usurer—after all, he turns to a poor Christian debtor for help—furthers this connection, as it marks the Jew as greedy and adds an ironic flavor to the story: the greedy pig is offered pig milk and does not realize that it is not human milk.

This association reaches its climax in a rhetorical question that concludes the narrative: "What would have happened if the good Christian had obtained human milk for the Jew?"[91] Unlike the wise Jesus in the infancy narratives discussed earlier, this narrative is of the conniving Jew who tries to buy Christian breast milk in order to perform black magic and kill Christians. Thankfully (from the perspective of the narrative), he is thwarted by the quick thinking of a Christian woman who tricks the trickster by substituting human milk for sow's milk. Gender plays a key role here, as the Christian woman emasculates the Jewish man by not only preventing his nefarious plot but also embarrassing him via the pig. Had she not done so, all of the Christians in an eight-kilometer radius might have died. Instead, only the neighborhood pigs (= Jews?) died. Categorical confusion also plays a key role here, as the substitution of one mammal's milk for the milk of another troubles the human/nonhuman binary by (perhaps not so subtly) placing two of the three mammals on one side of the equation and one on the other: Jews and the pig on the nonhuman side and Christians on the human side.

In our first example, Jews are worried because Christian pigs might harm Jewish babies. In our second example, Christians are worried that Jewish pigs might harm Christian babies. In both cases, breast milk and porcine identities combine to embody metaphors of fear of the Other. And once again, pigs are the metaphorical and physical beasts of burden for conveying these dire concerns. From the cradle to the grave, the pig has the potential to cause trouble.

"PORK TERRORISM": CONCLUSIONS

Of this entire book, writing this chapter was the most emotionally difficult experience for me personally. Engaging in a sustained manner with the antisemitic words and images that we have seen was quite taxing.[92] It is hard to read how the pig was weaponized against Jews in a manner akin to, in the words of the archaeologist Max Price, "pork terrorism" and not be affected.[93] And—as we should not forget—that was the explicit goal of many of these texts and images: to make Jews uncomfortable and feel threatened. But that is only part of the story.

Throughout our exploration of the Medieval Period, we have seen how medieval Christians use the pig to discuss Jews, Judaism, and bad (= Judaizing) Christians. The pig moves from mammal to metaphor to mockery and all points in between. Yet, as Jamie Kreiner rightly cautions us, we should resist the urge to view this as a fait accompli: "The pig's Christianization might seem inevitable to us.

Because Christians eat pork, and Muslims and Jews do not, we might assume that the pig had been a symbol of religious identity since those religions came into being.... The reason the pig seems to us to be an obviously meaningful boundary between the monotheistic traditions is because it *did* eventually become one—but only over the course of the early Middle Ages."[94]

It only seems inevitable because that is how things turned out. But it also seems inevitable because there was a vested interest by both Jews and Christians in presenting it as such. For Jews, Christians inherit the mantle of Rome—The Pig—and thus all of the historical baggage associated with Rome maps neatly onto their porcine bodies. For Christians, allegories of greed map neatly onto the people presumed to be greedy; and the pig's body—both literally and figuratively—seems a perfect vehicle through which to deliver this message. Thus, Christian identity ironically is also mapped onto, and thrown into relief by, the pig.

As we continue to follow the pig on its journey across the temporal and geographic landscape, the motif of using the pig to mock Jews becomes a central theme of our story. Over time, this devolves from mockery to murder. To understand why, we first needed to tell the pig's medieval story. Having heard that tale, now we turn the page to begin our exploration of the pig and Jewish persecution in the Early Modern Period.

4

"SAV'D HIS BACON"

Pig and Persecution in the Early Modern Period

LIKE the Medieval Period, the Early Modern Period is defined differently depending on one's historical and geographical perspective. In general, it encompasses roughly 1500–1800 CE, with some scholars tweaking the beginning and/or ending dates. These years saw much change across the globe. For example, in Europe—which is the main focus of this chapter—this era witnessed the Renaissance; the so-called Age of Discovery, in which Europeans "discovered" and then colonized great swaths of territory both near and far; and the French Revolution, among numerous other world-shaping events.

Throughout these major events, the pig continues to rear its head (sometimes, as we shall see, quite literally!). We find the pig in Shakespearean plays, at an Italian rabbi's funeral, and in the midst of debates ranging from whether to offer Jews citizenship in European countries to whether vaccines are a Jewish conspiracy. Unfortunately, the themes of antisemitism and violence encountered in the Medieval Period persevere into the Early Modern Period. The pig is used both to mock and to do harm to Jews, embodying both Jewish identity and implying/effecting physical violence against Jewish bodies (and, in theological terms, Jewish souls, as well).

Further, we discuss a development that will have additional significance moving forward: Jews using the pig to engage in acts of transgressive eating. In these instances, Jews intentionally ingest the pig as a symbolic act to violate Jewish legal norms and, in so doing, stake a claim to new and contested Jewish identities. While these

Jews were certainly not the first Jews in history to engage in acts of transgressive eating, the role that the pig plays in these early modern meal practices serves to highlight the accumulated historical weight of the pig. At this point in history, the pig had been endowed with the symbolic girth needed to signify *the* ultimate transgressive line. Therefore, when a Jew ingests the pig to make a statement about Jewish identity, that statement is written in bold, underlined, and capital letters. Indeed, with regard to symbolic practices to signify Jews transgressing against Judaism, the pig stands alone.

"I WILL NOT EAT WITH YOU": THE PIG PROBLEM IN SHAKESPEARE'S *MERCHANT OF VENICE*

In the waning years of the sixteenth century, William Shakespeare wrote *The Merchant of Venice*, a comedy that both provided memorable lines and inspired heated debate about whether the play is antisemitic.[1] In one scene, we find both a memorable line and—at the very least—a quite unfavorable depiction of Jews. And, as a reader of this book might have predicted, this scene features the pig:

> BASSANIO: If it please you to dine with us—
> SHYLOCK: Yes, to smell pork, to eat of the habitation which your prophet the Nazarite conjured the devil into. I will buy with you, sell with you, talk with you, walk with you, and so following; but I will not eat with you, drink with you, nor pray with you.[2]

In this well-known scene, the non-Jewish Bassanio invites the very Jewish (and very usurious) Shylock to dinner with his family.[3] Shylock declines this commensal invitation. His roundabout manner and reason for doing so are worth our attention.

First, Shylock focuses in on the pig—which he presumes will be served. Note that Bassanio has not provided the menu. But Shylock assumes—and we the audience are expected to agree—that pig will be on Bassanio's table. After all, what else do Christians eat or serve to

Jews?[4] This culinary quip injects a touch of humor, right as things turn heretical. And that brings us to the second point: what the literary scholar David B. Goldstein aptly refers to as "the problem of pork in the play."[5] If Shylock—a Jew—were to decline to eat pig, he should do so by citing *his* Bible: the Old Testament. "Instead, Shylock quotes the *New* Testament, and in so doing wields the Christian Bible against the Christians."[6] The New Testament story to which Shylock refers is one with which we are familiar: when Jesus (a.k.a. "the Nazarite") casts Legion into a herd of swine.[7] Shylock's blunt wording was deemed sacrilegious to some of Shakespeare's readers.[8] But the heretical subtext of Shylock's comment is quite important for understanding how Shakespeare depicts the usurer here—and throughout the play. Commenting on how the Bard's syntax and intertext combine to articulate a complex porcine concept in this passage, Goldstein observes,

> With its indecently dangling preposition, Shylock's rhetorical construction—"to eat of the habitation which your prophet the Nazarite conjured the devil into"—emphasizes the action of putting the devil into hogs, but says nothing about removing it. The implication is not only that pigs are disgusting creatures, fit only for devils, but that in eating pork, one eats a devil embedded within. . . . Thus, Shylock's insult operates metonymically: pork, the habitation of the devil, transfers its devilry to those who eat it. Those who allow pork into their bodies allow the devil in as well; to eat pig is to eat the devil himself.[9]

As pig-eaters, Christians are ingesting the devil—as they should very well know because it says so in the New Testament! Shylock here inverts a long-held antisemitic trope: "To put the devil in pigs is to put the devil in Christians, thus resisting, reversing, or deflating the same accusation that had for centuries been leveled against the Jews."[10] This tension is somewhat resolved a few lines later, when Antonio famously asserts, "The devil can cite Scripture for his purpose."[11] The Jewish devil devilishly uses Christian Scripture to make Christians feel wrong when they are, in fact, right.[12]

The pig is doing a lot of heavy lifting in Shylock's two sentences. Its split hoof draws a line in the sand down the center of the table, as Shylock uses the pig as a reason for declining to engage in commensality with non-Jews. And rather than bluntly state that, Shylock's cheeky remark serves both to invert the Jew-devil relationship *and* to devilishly cite Scripture for his own purpose. Commenting on these complex interplays, Goldstein offers an apt metaphor: "Pork in *The Merchant* acts almost as iodine does in a CAT scan, throwing the interconnections and blockages of the play's body into relief."[13] Once again, the pig serves to map the contours of Jewish and non-Jewish identities and relationships; and like many maps, the borders it draws are highly contested.

"THE SOUL OF THE RABBI INSIDE A PIG!": THE PIG ATTENDS AN ITALIAN RABBI'S FUNERAL

In the late 1640s, the esteemed Rabbi Tranquillo Corcos the Elder died.[14] Like other respected Roman Jews, his funeral procession began in the Roman Ghetto and proceeded east toward the Jewish cemetery on the Aventine.[15] But two features of Rabbi Corcos's funeral distinguish it from other early modern Roman Jewish funerals: (1) it was the subject of the first *giudiata*; and (2) the funeral procession included a pig.

Giudiate (the Italian plural of *giudiata*) were popular farces performed during Carnival, prior to Lent. Consisting of verses composed in mixed languages, they were sung by silly, comedic characters.[16] As the term *giudiate* implies, these farces targeted one particular group: "They owed their name to their mocking imitation of the Jews, who were represented in odd and discourteous ways."[17] The *giudiata* is but one of the many forms of anti-Jewish Carnival practices in medieval and early modern Italy.[18] Some of these practices incite violence against Jews; others are downright violent against Jews. To offer two notable examples: in the so-called Jews' Race, Roman Jews were forced to run naked down the Via del

Corso to Testaccio (yearly until 1668).[19] And there was a medieval Carnival tradition (yearly until 1312) of forcing the oldest Jew in the Roman community into a barrel filled with nails and then pushing the deadly barrel down Mount Testaccio.[20] This latter cruel Carnival practice has its own porcine history, as eventually Jews were able to pay the church a yearly fee of ten florins to replace the old Jew in the barrel . . . with two pigs![21] In this ritual, which Claudine Fabre-Vassas aptly refers to as "the spectacle of the pigs," the pigs were led in a procession to Mount Testaccio.[22] To the glee of the gathered crowd, the pigs were then violently thrown off the mountaintop. Instead of Jews, they murdered pigs—and used a fee imposed on the Jewish community to pay for the "murderous ceremony."[23]

The claim that Rabbi Corcos's funeral procession is the subject of the first *giudiata* is made explicitly in the manuscript that preserves the *giudiata*.[24] Although we cannot state this with 100 percent certainty (even the text itself notes that "it is believed to be the first *giudiata* in Rome"), the timing would fit with extant evidence, and there is nothing that contradicts this claim.[25] At the very least, we can certainly assert this to be among the first, if not *the* first, *giudiata*. And then, there is the matter of the pig.

The surviving manuscript of this *giudiata* opens with a brief description of its history and context. This description was written by Giovanni Pastrizio (ca. 1636–1708), who, among other professorial roles, was the *scriptor hebraicus* at the Vatican Library.[26] It is worth quoting in full Pastrizio's description of this *giudiata*'s history:

> Melchior Pallontrotti [sic] of Rome was very expert in the Hebrew language and severe against the Jews.[27] He printed [works] against their stupidities, went to synagogues and hurled abuse at them, and was often found at their sermons and interrupted them, noting their errors to the Rabbi. In his time lived the principal rabbi and teacher, highly esteemed by all the Ghetto, Rabbi Manoaḥ.[28] And when he died, Pallontrotti made a masquerade of the Jews who were on their way to bury Rabbi Manoaḥ, carrying him in a coffin. But in his own [casket]

> he had put a live pig, with a device so that he opened the box a little bit whenever he wanted to, and the pig, called a *chazir* by the Jews, would stick its head out.²⁹ The song that Pallontrotti wrote, he taught to the youths who made up his masquerade, and it is believed to be the first *giudiata* in Rome.... It pretends to praise him, but it mocks him.³⁰

As Pastrizio notes, Palontrotti is not subtle: he makes the vaguest pretense of pretending to praise Rabbi Corcos, which only further highlights his porcine mockery of the (dis)honored deceased.

This lack of subtlety leads to almost slapstick humor in the conclusion of the *giudiata*. When the pig arrives on the scene, it is greeted with the opposite of "mazal tov!": "*Mazal ra'!* The soul of the Rabbi inside a pig!"³¹ *Tov* means "good" in Hebrew, and *ra'* means "bad/evil"; so instead of signaling good luck, this signals that fate has turned against the Rabbi (and, by extension, the Jews).³² And in case it was not obvious what he was trying to allude to with the pig-in-a-coffin trick, he puts the words in an observer's mouth: the pig represents the Rabbi's soul.

Not just that, but the pig is now mockingly embraced in a messianic fervor and declared kosher:

> Have you read in the [Talmudic] tractate 'Avodah Zarah
> That pig is eaten in The World to Come?³³
> Behold our Teacher
> Who, to reassure men and children,
> Shows himself in the shape of a pig to everyone
> Happiness to the wise! Joy to the elders!
> Make a celebration, O Jews!
> Sound the *shofar* for all the Ghetto
> Eat pig without any respect.³⁴

This biting farce blends Hebrew with Italian to great (and acerbic) comedic effect. In the messianic age, pig will be kosher.³⁵ And the Rabbi's porcine soul appears as a pig to inform Roman Jews to rejoice and embrace that fact. Get the party started. Take out the *shofar* and eat pig without concern for biblical and rabbinic legal prohibitions.[36]

This invitation to party like it is messianic times points to the overall goal of this *giudiata*. As the historian Martina Mampieri persuasively argues, "While the employment of Jewish themes and the imitation of the Italian Jews' manner of speaking were intended for comic effect, Palontrotti exploited them as support for his narrative and specifically for its polemical purpose. The final exhortation to eat pork, though undoubtedly flippant, may reveal a not-so-subtle prompt to conversion."[37]

Once again, the pig is used to mock Jews who stubbornly refuse to accept the "truth" of Christianity. Further, the pig points toward real and potential violence against Jews. As the historian Emily Michelson notes, "The pig in its box was carried directly along the thin line between speech and violence, and that line remains blurred or half erased, and sometimes eliminated entirely."[38] Like the pig in its box, at any moment violence could rear its ugly head. Unfortunately, far too often that proved to be the case.

"THE SANCTIFIED MORSEL": FORCE-FEEDING PIG AND FORCED CONVERSION

Palontrotti's exhortation for the entire Ghetto to "Eat pig without any respect" points to a common motif in early modern Europe (and, both temporarily and geographically, beyond) that force-feeding Jews pig "could be used as a crudely effective means of expediting their conversion to Christianity."[39] The motif of force-feeding Jews pig as a means of forcing them to convert obviously harks back to past events, most especially to the Inquisition. In some accounts, the Inquisition is explicitly mentioned. Famously, for example, Voltaire refers in his 1759 classic novel *Candide* to two Portuguese Conversos who were burned to death because they were convicted of having secretly thrown away the bacon that accompanied their chicken dish.[40] While we have seen, and will continue to see, several examples of this widespread, violent presumption, we take a moment now to reflect on one particular blunt and satirical illustration of this phenomenon.

Thomas Bonner's 1764 print *The Conversion of Nathan* (see figure 4.1) features an illustration, which we shall discuss shortly, and the following rhymed verse:

> A wandering Levite who visited Fairs
> A dealer in Penknives and such Sorts of Wares
> At a little Hedge Ale House fell deep in dispute
> With a Butcher of Swine a Man of Repute
> After Canvassing o'er the Mosaical Laws
> Old Customs and soforth they came to the Cause
> Why Hoggs Flesh to Jews was so horrid a treat
> When Christians esteem'd it most Excellent Meat[41]
> But Nathan whose System put a side all his Art
> On Bacon and Pork was now somewhat too tart
> Swore Christians were fools & D—m the whole Nation
> Which (soon fill'd) the Butcher with terrible Passion
> He brandish'd his Cudgell—the Jew on his Knees
> Frighted out of his Senses would his wrath fain appease
> But on this Condition the Butcher relents
> To instant turn Christian, poor Nathan Consents
> But what could be done n'er a Priest to be got
> When the Butcher conceiv'd a most excellent thought
> A Yard of Pork Sausage to carry the farce on
> Shou'd make him a Christian as well as a Parson
> That this was not legal the Jew would have pleaded
> But he saw the strong Cudgell—so Silent proceeded
> All the folks were call'd in to behold the droll sight
> Sure there ne'er was a Scene of such mirth & delight
> The sanctified Morsel at length having eaten
> He became a Stanch Christian & so sav'd his Bacon.[42]

FIGURE 4.1. Thomas Bonner, *The Conversion of Nathan*, etching, London, April 23, 1764, published by Henry Roberts, engraver, near Hand Alley facing Great Turnstile in Holborn. The Jewish Theological Seminary Library, Call Number: PNT E12.23.1. Courtesy of the Jewish Theological Seminary, used with permission.

Of all the ale houses in all the towns in all the world, Nathan had to walk into this one. Nathan proceeds to get into a theological debate with a butcher of swine—whose particular profession is hardly coincidental. Foolishly, Nathan swears that all Christians are fools and damns them all. Incensed, the butcher of swine brandishes his cudgel, threatening Nathan, who falls to his knees. Nathan is then faced with a choice that Jews had been forced into for nearly two millennia: eat the pig and convert to another belief, or refuse the pig and violently die as a Jew.

Here, the verse takes a turn for the comical (or tragic, depending on your perspective). With no priest to be found, an official conversion is not possible at that moment. The butcher of swine proves to be both cunning and cruel by conceiving of a practical solution: Nathan shall be baptized a Christian by means of forcibly eating pig. Even Nathan the Jew knows that this is not legal, but that does not matter—what matters is the farce of making a Jew Christian by means of the pig. This is what we see in Bonner's illustration that accompanies the verse. The butcher of swine is on the left, brandishing his cudgel. Nathan is down on one knee, his wares off to the side. Depicted in stereotypical manner as the grotesque, bearded Jew, Nathan stuffs pork sausage into his mouth. To the right (from our perspective) of Nathan stands a young Christian boy, who jeers at Nathan while he holds onto the end of the long string of sausage links that Nathan is being forced to consume. The crowd drinks and laughs, whooping it up at this "Scene of such mirth & delight."

The conclusion is jam-packed with content. Nathan's conversion is effected by means of "The sanctified Morsel"—which is not the Eucharist but the pig. The reader is meant to laugh at this joke, rather than ponder the possibilities of equating the pig with the body of Christ.[43] By ingesting this porcine morsel, Nathan becomes Christian, a member of the foolish nation that he has just damned. The pig simultaneously indexes both his former Jewish identity and his new identity as a Jewish convert to Christianity. And finally, the zinger to end all zingers: by eating the pig, he saves his bacon. This pun still works over 250 years later.[44]

The violence imagined in this text is realized over the coming decades in particular in England, where we encounter several instances in which the pig is used in physical assaults against Jews. For example, in 1769, a Jewish peddler in Monmouth Assizes had his hands tied behind his back and hot bacon stuffed down his throat.[45] More commonly, there was the (sometimes realized) threat of greasing a Jew's beard with pork fat. The menace of such porcine assault appears in numerous literary accounts and is even recorded in a 1776 case in which "a woman who kept a public house was found guilty at Westminster Quarter Sessions for assaulting a Jew and greasing his chin with pork."[46] Summarizing the extant evidence, the English scholar Frank Felsenstein notes, "The anointment of the Jew's beard with swine's grease, while having the primary purpose to humiliate or degrade him, may also be perceived . . . as a facetiously unholy replication of the sacred act of Christian baptism."[47] Once again, the Jew is both mocked and—ironically, as via a "sanctified Morsel" and/or baptismal grease—saved by bacon.[48]

"THOSE FOES TO THE PORK OF OLD ENGLAND": PIGS AND JEWISH EMANCIPATION

The Enlightenment reimagined myriad theological, political, and philosophical models. Part of that conversation involved questioning who could or could not and should or should not be citizens of various (often newly emerging) nation-states. As these debates occurred across Europe, a question was asked time and again: Can or should Jews be granted citizenship? Consideration of Jewish emancipation—that is, whether to offer Jews full civil and political rights—took many forms over five centuries.[49] And some of those forms involve making jokes about Jews and the pig.[50]

To set the stage for this porcine encounter, we once again return to Shakespeare's England (though now 137 years have passed since the Bard's death). In May 1753, the British Parliament enacted a controversial act.[51] Commonly referred to as "The Jew's Bill," the act—whose official title was "The Jewish Naturalization Act"—declared "That Persons professing the Jewish Religion may, under Application for that Purpose, be naturalized by Parliament, without receiving the Sacrament of the Lord's Supper."[52] This victory, however, was short-lived. Opposition to The Jew's Bill was sufficient to lead to the act's repeal less than a year later, in 1754. Once again Jews—even if, as the Jewish Naturalization Act conceded, were one of the "many Persons of considerable Substance professing the Jewish Religion"—could not become naturalized as British citizens; only Christians, born or converted, could be granted British citizenship.[53] Unfortunately, the antisemitic forces of the day prevailed. In retracting this briefly granted right, England once again endorsed the racist logic of exclusion. Clearly articulating this logic, Jonas Hanway—a contemporary outspoken critic of The Jew's Bill—bluntly asserted, "The Jews, I conceive, are not entitled to naturalization for two plain reasons; the first is, because they are Jews; the next is, because they are not Christians."[54]

Those who were against naturalizing Jews as British citizens turned to mockery to ridicule Jews. As the historian Isaiah Shachar observes, "The prohibition of swine's flesh and the commandment of circumcision were the best known facts about Jewish existence, and these emerged as a popular subject for satire when the naturalization of Jews became a public issue."[55] Both of these themes combine, alongside another long-enduring antisemitic cliché—that of Jews as manipulators of world financial markets for their own gains, explicitly at the (literal and figurative) expense of Christians—in a popular contemporary doggerel:[56]

> In brave Edward's days they were caught in a gin,
> For clipping our coin, now to add sin to sin,
> As they've got all our pelf, they'd be clipping our skin.
> Those foes to the pork of old England,
> Oh! the old English roast pork.
>
> When good Queen Elizabeth sat on the throne,
> When Jonathan's jobbers and Jews were unknown,
> Each Briton might then call his birthright his own,
> And feed on the pork of Old England,
> Oh! the old English pork.[57]

Not content with having taken all of England's riches ("pelf"), the poem claims that Jews are now coming for their foreskins.[58] It then imagines the pig as representing British identity. Jews are "foes to

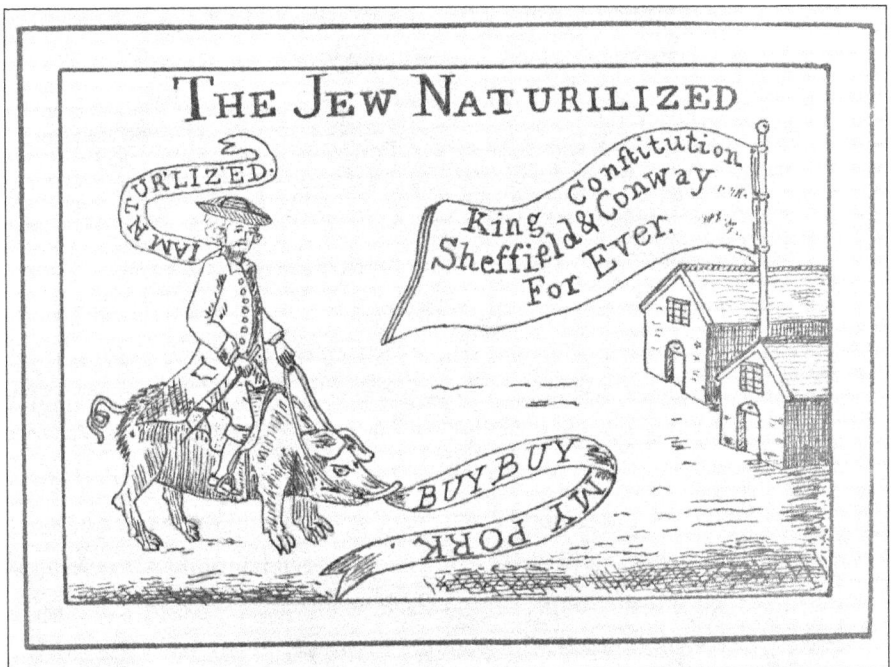

FIGURE 4.2. "The Jew Naturalized," English etching, 1753–1754. Courtesy of the Jewish Museum London, used with permission.

the pork of old England." Jews hate the pig—both the animal and the empire it represents.⁵⁹ The poem then reminisces about the good old days—defining "the greatness of the Elizabethan era in terms of it having been an England free of Jews."⁶⁰ Without Jews, Britons could "feed on the pork of Old England."⁶¹ Here, "pork" has yet another meaning: the resources and riches of the country that, prior to the arrival of "Those foes to the pork of old England," used to benefit only the British. But now those pork-haters have devoured all of the English pork, leaving the British hungry.⁶²

Though The Jew's Bill was law for less than one year, the controversy "inspired more pamphlets and cartoons than any other political issue in eighteenth-century England."⁶³ In some of the associated cartoons, Jews appear riding pigs. Importantly, as Isaiah Shachar points out, these images should not be read as directly connecting to the medieval *Judensau*, as that image "had not struck root" in

England.⁶⁴ Instead, they draw on the pig to mock Jews; since Jews were so famous for abhorring the pig, it was seen as funny to depict Jews riding the animal that they so abhorred. One oft-cited image is an English etching from 1753–1754 (see figure 4.2). In this image, a fashionably dressed Jew rides a pig and declares, "I Am Natur'liz'ed." The pig then says, "Buy Buy my Pork."⁶⁵ The image juxtaposes the Jew, pretending to act like a wealthy British citizen, and the tabooed pig, which represents Christian British identity. If you are so British, the pig that the Jew rides suggests, then you should eat pig. To be British is to act British; and to act British is to ingest the pig. The reader presumes that the Jew will not, belying his claim to truly be British. Another layer of humor is added when one realizes that, in the end, the pig comes across as more British than the Jew does.

This Jew might be a generic stereotype of a Jew or may be intended to depict the famous Sephardic Jewish banker Sampson Gideon. Among other financial dealings, Gideon was involved in the 1753 lottery, in which he made (and, more importantly, was perceived to have made) a hefty profit. This fed into the usual antisemitic stereotypes, especially given the timing and his public support of The Jew's Bill. While it is not certain that the pig-riding Jew is Gideon, another image from 1754 of a pig-riding Jew is clearly identified as Gideon.⁶⁶ This image is rather blunt, referencing Shylock, mocking Gideon's English, and depicting Gideon carrying lottery tickets and a sack of loot, among other well-worn antisemitic tropes.⁶⁷ For our purposes, what matters most is that, once again, a Jew rides a pig, a means of travel meant to mock the Jew.

Gideon appears in another print that references—but does not depict—the pig. In a 1753 engraving titled *Vox Populi, Vox Dei, or the Jew Act Repealed*, Gideon leads a mob toward the promised land. Amid various other religious and political images, we also find Sir William Calvert, who in his capacity as the City of London's member of Parliament had voted in favor of The Jew's Bill. And what does Sir Calvert allegedly utter? "The Devil's in the Swine and the Swine in me."⁶⁸ Once again, we return to the habitation into which Jesus conjured the devil, with the devilish swine infecting the mighty member of British Parliament. Further, the engraving strongly implies that the swine here are to be equated with those who are supposed to abhor the swine: that is, the Jews.[69]

Long after the repeal of The Jew's Bill, English cartoonists continued to draw (and draw on) images that juxtapose Jews and the pig. In these images, Jews (often depicted as the common stereotype as peddlers) interact with pigs in various ways, all with the intention of using the pig to mock the Jew.[70] The joke never seems to get old. Time and time again, pigs mark Jews as "foes to the pork of old England."

"THE MORE WE ENJOY THE PIGLET / THE BETTER CATHOLICS WE BECOME": JEWS, PIGS, AND EASTER

In eighteenth-century Burgundy, we encounter the following line in songs to be sung at meals on Christian holidays:

> While the Jewish law
> Prohibits lard as heretical
> The same is not so in Christian lands.
> Let us eat fresh pork, Let us eat!
> The more we enjoy the piglet
> The better Catholics we become.[71]

In isolation, this French song might not make sense. But once we place it into the full trajectory mapped out here, it clearly fits into the larger story. For example, it underlies the spectacle of porcine violence of the *giudiate*, which were regularly performed as part of Carnival celebrations. And it connects with the Christian holiday celebrated at the other end of Lent: Easter.

We have seen how the pig was used in numerous times and places to mock Jews. This is certainly true at Easter—a Christian holiday that celebrates the resurrection of Jesus Christ. Since Jews are often depicted as complicit in—indeed even directly responsible for—Jesus's crucifixion, this is deemed by some Christians as an appropriate time to ridicule Jews. And one way to do so is to include pig in Easter celebrations.[72]

Further, pig was also used to distance the Christian Easter from the Jewish Passover. Given the (not historically accurate) traditional belief that Jesus was crucified on Passover—and that his Last Supper was a Passover Seder (also not historically accurate)—the two holidays had been coupled until the Council of Nicaea in 325 CE separated them. Over a thousand years later, however, the connection between Easter and Passover was still too close for some Christians. This is where the pig proves useful. For example, in a Provençal dialogue from 1683, the Christian custom of consuming pig on Easter is explained thusly:

> What we do with the pig is only to distinguish ourselves from the Jews and show by the consumption of this meat, prohibited to all those of their Nation, that no longer being under the yoke of their law, we also no longer wish to take any part of their Easter. It seems most likely that this custom was introduced among us during a sojourn of the Jews long ago in Marseilles, during which time our citizens, so as not to meld their Easter with that of this people, knowing that piglet flesh was prohibited to them and that abstinence from this meat was something of the characteristic of Judaism, chose to eat some on this day, the better to demonstrate the Easter they were celebrating had nothing in common with theirs.[73]

What better way to prevent melding "their Easter" from our Easter than to serve pig? This further explains why "The more we enjoy the piglet / The better Catholics we become." Jews—and, importantly, Judaizers—do not eat the pig. Once again, in representing the opposite of a Jewish identity, the pig ironically comes to index Christian identity, as well. Good Catholics eat the pig and in so doing ingest their true Christian identity. If this is true every day, it is all the more so true on Easter, when ingesting the pig proves that the holiday that good Catholics are celebrating has "nothing in common" with the pig-free Jewish holiday of Passover.

"A PIECE OF PORK . . . IN [THEIR] SHABBAT MEAL": EATING PIG WITH FALSE MESSIAHS

In the seventeenth and eighteenth centuries, a messianic fervor swept across Jewish communities spanning the globe. Two main figures emerged as charismatic—indeed, messianic—leaders, propelling this fervor to even greater heights: Shabbatai Tzvi and Jacob Frank. Tzvi was a seventeenth-century Turkish Jew who rose from obscurity to lead a worldwide messianic movement. Frank was an eighteenth-century Polish Jew who proclaimed himself to be the reincarnation of Tzvi. We cannot do justice here to the fascinating and complex histories of either of these two men who claimed to be the messiah or of their movements. To give you an idea of the massive scope of their stories, the classic study of Tzvi's life by the influential scholar Gershom Scholem numbers nearly one thousand pages, as does the Nobel Prize–winning literary novel written about Jacob Frank by Olga Tokarczuk.[74] These were enormous figures, with massive followings (and egos), which require voluminous words to survey comprehensively.

Without getting too into the weeds with these messianic figures, it is important to note that they both ended up advancing versions of a controversial theology, in which subversion of normative Jewish law and practice was seen as now allowable and, in some cases, even necessary. Adapting elements of medieval Jewish mysticism as a means of justification, both figures ended up converting to other religions, deeming these conversions a necessary component of their messianic mission.[75] Further, since certain actions—such as the ingestion of pig—would be allowable in the messianic age, would not ingesting pig be allowable now that the messiah (Tzvi or Tzvi's reincarnation, Frank) is on the scene? As should be obvious, these arguments were not everyone's cup of tea; indeed, many Jews and Jewish communities deemed them heretical.

Ritual transgression and inversion played a part in various rites in these messianic communities.[76] And, if you are going for shock value, what is more scandalous and stupefying than a Jew eating pig as part of a Jewish ritual?! Evidence for the existence of this practice comes from a Polish rabbinic court's 1756 investigation of Sabbatians—that is, those who continued to follow the teachings of Shabbatai Tzvi, even after his death in 1676. Amid the twenty-seven short depositions (plus one long confession) of Sabbatians collected by the Satanów rabbinic court, one Sabbatian confessed to participating in pig-related rituals. The historian Paweł Maciejko summarizes the deposition: "Thus Joseph of Rohatyn, who did admit to having taken part in prohibited rites, described in detail how during Passover he had eaten a slice of bread with 'the other thing' (pork) and butter and had drunk nonkosher wine;[77] he also stated that it was customary among the Sabbatians to include a piece of pork and a piece of cheese in a Shabbat meal."[78]

Joseph of Rohatyn paid a steep price for his actions as a Sabbatian—including receiving thirty-nine lashes, literally being walked over by Jews entering and exiting the synagogue, being forced to divorce his wife and declare his children bastards, being banished from his community, and being forbidden from interacting with any Jew ever again.[79] These penalties were designed to serve as stark warning to anyone who dared transgress like the Sabbatians; for in doing so, you risk painful and humiliating punishment, followed by social isolation of yourself and your family.

Consuming pig is grouped with other ritual inversions to elevate the level of transgression. For example, eating leavened bread on Passover is punishable by excommunication in the Hebrew Bible.[80] That alone would be violating a major taboo. Eating a pig sandwich heightens the transgression.[81] But that was not enough. Joseph of Rohatyn also washed down that sandwich with nonkosher wine, a major rabbinic taboo.[82] Interestingly, Joseph of Rohatyn's claim to add butter to his pig sandwich does not worsen the transgression, as he seems to think it does. Already in the Mishnah, the Rabbis decreed that the prohibition against mixing milk and meat only applied to kosher meat; mixing milk and pig did not violate that prohibition (though it obviously violated the pig taboo).[83] Perhaps the Sabbatians were not aware of this ruling; or, perhaps they still viewed it as transgressing, violating a legal and/or cultural food norm. Either way, they made sure that their ritual inversions were not just a yearly practice but a weekly one as well. They marked the Sabbath (a very Jewish thing to do) by eating a pig-and-cheese meal (a decidedly *not* very Jewish thing to do—that is, perhaps, until now).

In using pig to mark ritual inversions, Joseph of Rohatyn and his Sabbatian community members turn to "the other thing" to signal a willing transgression against Judaism. It becomes an internal critique.[84] Ironically, they use pig to violate Jewish law and thus to establish a new—and highly contested—Jewish identity. This is a theme that we shall return to later in our story: namely, that eating pig can both transgress Jewish law and custom and still, at the same time, intentionally be used to establish a claim to Jewish identity. The signification of swine continues, developing in new and fascinating directions.

While Sabbatian communities used pig ingestion as a form of ritual inversion, this relationship was neither uncomplicated nor consistent. For example, although Frank and his followers ate pig, at one key—and quite public—moment, they sought a concession *not* to be compelled to eat pig.[85] In 1759, Frank and his followers agreed, under significant pressure, to convert to Catholicism. However, they were able to negotiate their terms of religious surrender. Among a list of conditions, which included retaining their Jewish names and being allowed to marry only within their own community, they secured agreement that they would not have to eat pig.[86] These sorts of stipulations were not unprecedented, as we have evidence from twenty years prior of another Jewish community in Poland negotiating conditions prior to converting to Catholicism that included a concession that they not to be required to consume pig.⁸⁷ It is unclear why Frank's followers sought this concession. Perhaps there is a difference between knowingly and intentionally transgressing and being externally compelled to do so. Perhaps this reflects the fact that the Frankists were not a homogeneous group—some were wildly antinomistic, while others were much more normative.⁸⁸ Regardless, the role of eating pig as a means of symbolic inversion reverberated long after Frank and his followers exited the scene.

"GIVE IT TO A JEW BOY": CONCLUSIONS

Throughout the Early Modern Period, the pig is used to poke fun at Jews. These jibes are both highbrow and lowbrow—ranging from the theological to the scatological (and sometimes both). And while we have spoken almost entirely about adults in this chapter, children partake in swine satire, as well. For example, a jingle popular among schoolchildren in 1790s London went,

> Get a bit of pork
> Stick it on a fork
> And give it to a Jew boy, a Jew⁸⁹

Both young and old taunted Jews with implied—and too often realized—malice and violence.

Some of these moments feel far away from the modern world. For example, readers familiar with Mount Testaccio today probably first think of it as an ancient garbage dump and tourist location in Rome rather than a hill on which yearly an old Jew was placed in a nail-filled barrel and rolled downhill to his death. Others, unfortunately, hit way too close to home. I personally felt this most acutely when finishing research on this early modern material while living in the post-2020 pandemic world. Flipping through Isaiah Shachar's classic book *The Judensau*, which has been cited numerous times throughout our story, I stopped dead in my tracks when I came to plate 57b, which features a Jew riding a pig as part of a 1799 satirical etching from Hamburg, "in which vaccination is represented as a Jewish-inspired invention."[90] I was not prepared for antisemitic and vaccine conspiracies to intersect with the pig. But I should have been. After all, as we have seen, and will continue to see, the pig is used to index Jewish identity—including the litany of antisemitic stereotypes of Jews as usurious, coin-clipping, Christ-killing, vaccination-supporting, and so on.

From the tip of Shakespeare's quill pen to the last crumb of the Sabbatians' pork-and-cheese Sabbath meal, the pig has much to tell us about Jewish identity in the Early Modern Period. Time and again, we find the pig and Jews being not only compared to but equated with each other. For example, well into the late eighteenth century in many German states, both Jews and pigs who traveled on highways were required to pay a special fee. Every time that travelers on these roads—whether Jewish or non-Jewish—saw a sign declaring, "Jews and pigs pay toll here," the comparison between Jews and pigs was unavoidable.[91] And whether financially, physically, or psychologically, Jews always paid the price.

Like fattening a pig for market, each generation adds layers of meaning to the pig, making it heavier with signification. As the pig adds weight, its marbling reflects the twists and turns that the pig has taken on its journey to explore Jewish and non-Jewish identity. The pig puts on many more pounds in the Modern Period, for which the evidence is voluminous enough to warrant two separate chapters.

5

"PIGS REPRESENT FOR US A NEW PROBLEM"

Pig Polemics across the Globe in the Modern Period

THE Modern Period covers over two hundred years, from roughly 1800 to the present. Despite the fact that this is the shortest length of time of any era discussed in this book, more so than any other previous era, the world has radically transformed since 1800—from locomotion (planes, trains, and automobiles) to communication (telegraph, telephone, smartphone) and beyond.

In this first of two chapters to delve into this rich era, we explore Jews and the pig across the globe, except for the United States, which has more than enough material to merit its own chapter. Further, to highlight the global reach of the pig in the Modern Period, I organize this chapter geographically, with individual countries and/or regions receiving their own sections. As always, my aim is not to be exhaustive; after all, both Jews and the pig have reached all four corners of the Earth. However, by crisscrossing the globe in a "world tour of the pig," we shall see how—at whatever latitude and longitude we explore—the pig is used time and again to negotiate and navigate Jewish and non-Jewish identities. To use yet another porcine pun, the pig continues to hog the spotlight.

"A PIG HAS GOT A LOOK / THAT FOR A JEW MAY BE MISTOOK": JEWS AND THE PIG IN MODERN ENGLAND

We return once again to England. Simultaneously, we return to Gerasa, where Jesus cast Legion into a herd of swine. Here, we find the poet William Blake joining in the British tradition of numerous authors, including Shakespeare, who have drawn on this scene in order to mock Jews.[1] In his poem "The Everlasting Gospel," written in about 1818, Blake scribes the following biting remark:

> He turn'd the devils into Swine
> That he might tempt the Jews to dine;
> Since which, a Pig has got a look
> That for a Jew may be mistook.[2]

In Blake's exegesis of the New Testament account of the demonic spirit tormenting the Gerasene man, he finds "the telling factor by which Christ has distinguished the Jew by endowing him with a porcine physiognomy or, more accurately, the pig with a Jewish visage."[3]

This association plays out in a fascinating manner in George Cruikshank's 1815 engraving titled *Suitors to the Pig Faced Lady* (figure 5.1).[4] At the center of this obviously gendered (and sexist) image is a wealthy Christian heiress, whose attractive bank account is deemed inversely proportional to her unattractive face. She is quite literally pig faced, as both the drawing of her and the title of the engraving make explicit. The wealthy, Pig Faced Lady is surrounded by potential suitors, who make a variety of porcine puns as they claim to find her (or at least her checkbook) attractive. The suitor who interests us is to her immediate left (the viewer's right). His facial features, beard, attire, and open sack clearly mark him as a Jew. In his pitch to win her hand, he asserts, "For all my dislikes to de Griskins—yet de Monish gives me a relish for de Pork Chops—so I have brought my *bags* to take you home in . . . my pretty little Miss Porker."[5] The Jew declares that while he dislikes pig, her money ("Monish") excites him sexually ("gives me relish") for the Christian heiress ("de Pork Chops").[6] He wants to (literally) bag her and bring her home. The Pig Faced Lady responds to her suitors thusly: "If you think to *gammon* me?[7] you'll find you've got the Wrong Sow by the Ear. . . . I'll not be *plagued* with any of you." While the lady is addressing all of her

FIGURE 5.1. *Suitors to the Pig Faced Lady*, by George Cruikshank, engraving, 1815. Courtesy of the Jewish Museum London, used with permission.

suitors, the proximity of the Jew to her and the fact that she seems to be physically fending him off, in particular, suggests a stronger connection between him and her words. While one could read a lot into the "plagued" comment, I wish to focus on her remark that the Jew has "got the Wrong Sow by the Ear."[8] There is much to unpack in the Pig Faced Lady's remark. First, it plays on the sexual tension rampant throughout the image. The animalistic Jew is carnally lusting after an animal; but, despite her face, she is a human woman and not a nonhuman pig. This also draws on the common nefarious claim that Jews have unquenchable and uncontrollable bestial desires for pigs.[9] Second, the Jew's stated coveting of wealth—in line with clichéd antisemitic stereotypes of Jewish greed—leads him to ignore the fact that she is the "Wrong Sow." Though the Jew might be willing to set aside dietary and cultural aversions to the pig, the Pig Faced Lady is a Christian woman. She is the "Wrong Sow" because she is Christian, not because she is a pig. The "Right Sow," according to the logic of the text, would be a Jewish woman. Third, and connected to the previous point, Jews may sexually desire pigs, but that is also because Jews are pigs. When the Jew looks at the wealthy, Pig Faced Lady, he sees a wealthy, *Jewish* woman. After all, as William Blake claimed, pigs have got that Jewish look. Therefore, the Pig Faced Lady reminds the Jew that she is not the sow that he is looking for. Her pig face might make her appear as a Jew, but she is in fact a Christian. The Jew should take his empty bag and go home.

Antisemitic stereotypes often like to have their cake and eat it too. Jews are presumed both to be pig-like and desirous of the pig *and* to be repulsed by all things pigs. In the ironic logic of these antisemitic stereotypes, such contradictions prove rather than undermine their point. The assumed belief that Jews are repulsed by the pig was the presumption in an antisemitic assault in London in 1824. On the first day of Passover, Leah Meldola was assaulted by a non-Jewish donkey driver named Joseph Jones. "Jones grabbed her by the arms and threatened to drag her into a nearby house and force her to eat pork and bread. She was rescued by a young Jewish man before Jones could carry through his threat."[10] As the chief rabbi of the Sephardic community in England, Leah's father, Haham Meldola, might have assumed that both the facts and his status would sway a British magistrate when he sought to press charges against the donkey driver. But the charges were dismissed in an opinion obviously colored by blatant antisemitic bias: "'You Jews,' he told them, are 'a quarreling people' who are 'continually bringing forward frivolous cases.'"[11]

Other times, the connection between pig and Jews is simply used as a stereotyped shorthand for Jews.[12] For example, an April 1823 boxing match at Harpenden Common in Hertfordshire featured a battle between pugilists Aby Belasco and Patrick Halton.[13] Playing on the fact that the former was Jewish and the latter was Irish, the match was hyped as "Pork and Potatoes, or Ireland versus Judea."[14] Anthropologists have long observed that groups often describe the Other through their foods. In this case, the Irish are represented as "Potatoes" and the Jews as "Pork." While the historical association between the Irish and potatoes has its own complex history, by now we are well acquainted with how Jews come to be identified with the pig.[15]

Jumping forward in time, we briefly visit with George Orwell. Though more famous for his novels *1984* and *Animal Farm*, he authored several other works, including *Down and Out in Paris and London*. Written in 1933, this novel famously focuses on the poor and poverty but is less well known for its antisemitism. Among the many less-than-flattering depictions of Jews throughout the novel (including a cocaine-dealing, double-crossing Jew), we find the following tidbit, which appears amid a description of a London coffeeshop: "In a corner by himself a Jew, muzzle down in the plate, was guiltily wolfing bacon."[16] One wonders how we know that the Jew is eating bacon "guiltily," given the fact that he does not speak and his face is obscured. Clearly, Orwell is drawing on the connection between Jews and the pig in order to portray this Jew as hypocritical (he knows he should not eat pig, but nevertheless he hides in a corner and does so, guilty conscience and all). Further, he uses animalistic rhetoric to dehumanize the Jew's actions—he has a muzzle, not a face, and he wolfs down bacon rather than eats it.[17]

We arrive next in 1992, when—in my opinion—the single best film whose plot centers on Jews and the pig was released. Of course, I am talking about *Leon the Pig Farmer*.[18] This slapstick comedy tells the story of Leon Geller, a young Jewish man from London who is trying to find his path in life. Early in the film, we learn that Leon is as equally clueless in love as he is scrupulous in his avoidance of pig. And this is when the fun really begins: Leon accidentally learns that his parents had sought the help of a fertility clinic in order to conceive him and, as a result of a clerical error, his father's sperm was mixed up with that of another man—which means that his biological father is not Sidney Geller, the Jewish man who raised him. Who, then, is his biological father? None other than Brian Chadwick, a Gentile pig farmer from Lower Middle Dinthorpe, Chadwick.[19] Leon travels to Chadwick to meet the Chadwicks. There, he must grapple with his identity.[20] That struggle becomes real when he tries to suppress his lifelong aversion to the pig in an attempt to fit in with his new Gentile family on their pig farm.[21] The metaphor of Jewish/non-Jewish identity and pig avoidance / pig farming is mined for every bit of slapstick humor imaginable. Leon eventually figures out a way to navigate this hybrid identity. While I will not spoil the ending, suffice it to say that the deus ex machina (or, in this case, the *porcus ex machina*) involves a pig, a mixed-up tube of sperm, and a rabbinic conclave.[22] And this is precisely why this film is the apotheosis of films on Jews and the pig: the entire movie centers around using pig to negotiate Jewish and non-Jewish identity. After all, how can Leon Geller be both a pig-avoiding Jew *and* a pig farmer?

Pig plays into other British texts that grapple with Jewish identity in England. For example, the pig rears its head in Natasha Solomons's novel *Mr. Rosenblum Dreams in English*.[23] Jack Rosenblum escapes World War II Germany and settles in England, where he seeks to assimilate as a proper English gentleman. The novel centers around his attempt to use golf to fit into British society. On a few occasions, the pig is used as a mechanism by which to probe Mr. Rosenblum's continued Jewish identity. When he is dining with his very assimilated daughter, Elizabeth Rose (who has changed her name), she orders a pork sausage.[24] Jack must decide if he, too, will eat the pig. As he ponders his decision, the narrator notes, "Pig was the one deep-rooted aversion he did not think to overcome. It was as unnatural as drinking seawater." Ultimately, Jack decides to join his daughter and "hesitated only for a moment before biting into the bread and blackened pork."[25] In another novel, *The Marrying of Chani Kaufman*, which was long-listed for the Man Booker Prize, the pig occasionally appears at moments when Orthodox Jewish characters are negotiating their Orthodox, Jewish, and British identities. As the eponymous Chani struggles to understand the secular world that surrounds her insular Orthodox community in the London suburb of Hendon, she wonders, "What did the non-kosher world taste like, for example? Every morning she walked past a cafe on her way to school. A salty, smoky tang wafted from its doorway. Shulamis had told her that the smell was that of bacon. How had she known? Shulamis had shrugged and said another girl had told her. What did bacon taste like? In America, you could buy bacon flavored kosher chips—a puzzling concept, as how did the kosher producers know what bacon tasted like? Was a goy [non-Jew] involved in the taste testing?"[26] Chani wonders about the pig as means of speculation on life beyond her Jewish world in Hendon. "What did bacon taste like?" stands in for the bigger question: What would it be like to experience the world as a nonobservant Jew or even as a non-Jew?

"ITZIG CAME RIDING ON A FAT SOW": JEWS AND THE PIG IN MODERN GERMANY

Long before Karl Marx was a household name whose words and ideas greatly impacted sociopolitical events and college syllabi across the globe, he was a young boy whose Jewish parents had converted to Christianity. Navigating an enduring Jewish past and a Lutheran present, Marx engaged in what might seem like a curious culinary practice:[27] "On the eve of Easter Karl would make his way to the ghetto of Trier. The Jewish Passover preceded the Christian Easter. The members of his Uncle Jacob's house would be busy baking *matzah* and preparing the stuffed fish for the *Seder*.... In Brueckengasse [outside the ghetto] they were coloring eggs and roasting a piglet. Karl used to bring some *matzah* home and eat it with thin slices of Paschal pork. 'We all have the same God,' his aunts would say indulgently. 'Sacrilege!' Henrietta [his mother] would storm indignantly, trembling in expectation of God's wrath."[28]

This *matzah*-and-pork sandwich—which I have taken to jokingly refer to as the "Karl Marx Special"—is less a heresy between two pieces of ritual carbs than a complex expression of Marx's identity.[29] Clearly, the pig represents his Lutheran present and the *matzah* his Jewish past.[30] Karl enjoyed them both combined together—literally ingesting his identity in the form of a sandwich. For Henrietta,

Marx's mother, however, this was sacrilege. She was a reluctant convert, which explains her stormy reaction to what she perceived as culinary heresy.[31] The pig represented not just Christian identity but also the ultimate Jewish taboo. Putting them together in one sandwich was a bridge too far for Henrietta. But for Karl, this sandwich was a bridge that brought together his past and present. It is unclear whether this was a bold statement foreshadowing his future revolutionary disposition or just a tasty combination of foods he enjoyed eating in spring. Religion may be the opiate of the masses, but this religion sandwich probably just satisfied Marx's hunger.

While the Karl Marx Special was a means of personal identity negotiation, other associations between Jews and pigs were more dehumanizing than humanizing. We should not be surprised to discover, for example, that the *Judensau* continued to have cultural cachet as a casual form of "humorous" antisemitism. According to the scholar of religion Jay Geller,

> As "the Jew"'s familiar or constant companion, the *Judensau* also appeared in various early broadsheets . . . , and it continued to be reproduced into the nineteenth century in prints and on playing cards as well as embossed on or sculpted into *tchotchkes*. . . . Traveling theaters exhibiting a pig marionette that would transform into a Jewish peddler were a regular fixture of country fairs into the early twentieth century. While Jewish peddlers were also frequently caricatured as pigs in so-called "humorous" postcards, their wealthier assimilated confrères were no less wallowing with swine in adjoining cards: They were emblematically displayed feasting on pork roast to exemplify the fruits of Emancipation.[32]

We have previously discussed *Judensau* images on playing cards and pig imagery associated with Jewish emancipation elsewhere in Europe, as well as porcine associations with Jewish peddlers. What Geller teaches us about here is the enduring popularity of these associations in modern Germany. For example, we learn that, starting in

1887, these postcards were mass-produced and thus widely available and disseminated.[33]

The popularity of the *Judensau* is also attested linguistically. According to Isaiah Shachar, the *Judensau* "persist[ed] as an expression of abuse in the German language until the present [twentieth] century. Folk-songs and children's rhymes still current at the beginning of the twentieth century describe how 'Itzig came riding on a fat sow,' 'Hob mounted on a wild boar,' or how the Jews lost a contest of cleanliness against the swine."[34] It was referenced in the common jeer *Saujud*, meaning "Jewish Swine." All too often, these remarks were ignored; occasionally, they were not. In 1884, for example, a non-Jewish surgeon at the Vienna General Hospital got into a heated argument with a Jewish doctor named Carl Koller. According to Koller's friend and colleague Sigmund Freud, the surgeon called Koller *Saujud*. To Freud's delight, Koller responded by punching the surgeon in the face.[35] Over and again, the *Judensau* was invoked in Germany to mock Jewish public figures, including Theodor Herzl and Walther Rathenau.[36] The latter, a Jew who served as Germany's foreign minister in 1922, was greeted across the country with the decidedly unfriendly chant, "Kill Walter Rathenau / The goddamn *Judensau*."[37]

I must confess to not having the stomach to wade through Nazi references to Jews and pigs, both in Germany and in surrounding regions leading up to and during World War II. Drawing on old stereotypes, ultimately they turned venomous words and images into massively deadly action (see, e.g., figure 5.2). To illustrate this phenomenon, I believe that only one—of the far too many—examples should suffice. In Heinrich Himmler's famous secret speech on the Jewish Question, delivered on October 8, 1943, he remarks, "The sentence, 'The Jews must be exterminated,' is a short one, gentlemen, and is easily said. For the person who has to execute what this sentence implies, however, it is the most difficult and hardest thing in the world. Look, of course they are Jews, it is quite clear, they are only Jews, but consider how many people—members of the Party

FIGURE 5.2. Poster from circa 1930. In Polish, it declares, "This Pig Buys from a Jew." United States Holocaust Museum Collection, Gift of the Katz Family, used with permission, https://collections.ushmm.org.

as well—have sent their famous petitions to me or to the authorities, declaring that all Jews, naturally, were pigs, but that so-and-so was a decent Jew and should not be touched."[38] Based on what became a shared assumption among the Nazis "that all Jews, naturally, were pigs," the solution to the Jewish Question was to force them to march like pigs to the slaughter, turning the metaphor into a violent, embodied reality.[39]

Amid genocide, famished Jews sometimes were forced to decide whether to eat pig when given the rare opportunity to actually consume meat (pig or otherwise) or to avoid it and perhaps die of starvation. From a rabbinic perspective, as we have learned, the answer is straightforward: preservation of life supersedes the pig prohibition. For some Jews, this answered the question, and they ate pig. For other Jews, they ate pig before the Holocaust, so they had no compunction eating it during this time of emergency.[40] And for others, even though ingesting pig is allowed under these circumstances, the symbolism of the pig carried too much weight to transgress even during this moment of crisis. In the words of one survivor, who was explaining to her grandson (the award-winning author Jonathan Safran Foer) why she refused to eat pig offered to her at the very end of the war, even when she was starving, "If nothing matters, there's nothing to save."[41] What the pig represents—Jewish tradition and identity—mattered more to her than her ravenous hunger. For her, Jewish survival requires both Jews and their (pig-free) identity to survive.

It is important to acknowledge that there is more to the history of Jews and Germany than the Holocaust and antisemitism. Therefore, I conclude this section by quoting from a 1918 memoir by the German-Jewish socialist Eduard Bernstein.[42] Raised by Reform Jews in a nonobservant household, Bernstein recounted his act of teenage rebellion.[43] At the age of eleven (in 1861 or 1862), Bernstein "decided to be a proper Jew." What did this entail? "Accordingly, in my opinion, I had to refrain first of all from eating pork. Whereupon I revealed to my parents one day that, in the name of Judaism, I would touch pork no more. Surprisingly, there was no opposition. 'If you don't want to, my son, don't eat pork,' replied my father. This absolute tolerance was poison to my intention. A bit of opposition would certainly have strengthened it, but now it lacked the attraction of a conquered right and consequently did not last very long."[44]

Bernstein's youthful rebellion was quieted by his parents in textbook fashion: they did not take the bait. Their tolerance took all the mischievous fun out of his act. (Perhaps the strong reaction by Karl Marx's mother, Henrietta, added to his enjoyment of his *matzah-and-pork sandwich*?) Further, as Bernstein goes on to note, he soon realized that just skipping pig was not the only Jewish dietary regulation. Realizing that his "decision was actually much more far-reaching than [he] had thought," his culinary rebellion lasted only a few weeks.[45] Important for our present purposes, however, is Bernstein's original plan: when he "decided to be a proper Jew," his immediate action was "to refrain first of all from eating pork." He did not start with prayer or text study or giving charity or any other of the myriad ritual practices mandated of the "proper Jew." He started with the pig.[46] In his mind, to be a "proper Jew" first and foremost required one not to eat pig.

"THE LEAST KOSHER MEAL IN THE UNIVERSE": JEWS AND THE PIG IN MODERN FRANCE

In 1896, Captain Alfred Dreyfus—an officer in the French artillery and a Jew—was wrongly convicted of treason. In the ensuing decade, what became known as the "Dreyfus Affair" unfolded. Behind these false accusations was thinly veiled—if veiled at all—antisemitism. For example, Dreyfus and his supporters were mocked in a series of forty-seven posters that appeared from 1899 to 1901. Titled "Museum of Horrors" (*Musée des Horreurs*), these posters depicted the heads of Dreyfus supporters (both Jewish and non-Jewish) on animal bodies. Two of these posters included pigs. In one, Henri Rothschild (from the Rothschild family, which was famous both for its wealth and for its Jewish identity) is depicted as a pig and expressing a lack of concern for running over someone in the car he is driving.[47] In this image, the long-held associations between greed, pigs, and Jews exist side by side with the novel: the recently invented automobile.

While the Dreyfus Affair captured headlines in France and across the globe, it was common in southwestern France, for example, for a Jew walking on the street to be greeted by the following scene: a passersby would "grasp the corner of their coats with one hand and twist it sharply with the other.... And, at the same time, they produced a kind of guttural, nasal grunting sound—a swinish grunt to be exact: 'Oink! Oink!'"[48] The twisted cloth was widely understood to represent a pig's ear; the "Oink!" obviously represented the pig's vocalizations; and the fact that these pig symbols were directed at a Jew was an overt porcine act of antisemitism. Referring to Jews as pigs, and particularly pigs' ears, is attested long before 1900. To cite but one example, over twenty years earlier in Provençal, a well-known antisemitic gibe was to twist the corner of one's clothes, mimicking the pig's ear, and to shout, "Black infidel, here's your father's ear!" Just in case the Jew–pig–pig's ear connection is not clear enough, this expression contains one more linguistic clue: the term for "infidel" in French was *bardaian*, which derives from *bard*, which refers to "the mud or silt where pigs like to wallow."[49] As we have seen before with the case of the term "Marrano," porcine jibes at Jews often proved popular, quickly spreading from their land of origin across Europe. Thus, we find references to these gestures and terms also in Alsatian, Italian, and Catalan witnesses.[50]

While a Jew walking down the streets of Paris today might not be met with gestures and shouts associated with pigs' ears, that does not mean that they would be free from pig-related molestation. In 2014, as part of anti-Muslim (with a healthy dose of antisemitism thrown in for good measure) sentiment, French far-right-wing party leaders sought to "save secularism" by removing nonpig alternatives from the menus of French public schools. Deploying rhetoric that made no attempt to mask their xenophobic intentions, these politicians, which included the former president of France Nicolas Sarkozy, argued that the only way to save secularism—and prevent sharia law (and Jewish religious law, too, though anti-Muslim sentiment is clearly at the forefront of their minds)—was to implement a "pork or nothing" school menu.[51] For these xenophobic politicians, when French Muslims and Jews refuse to eat pig, they are perceived as rebuffing a form of exclusionist culinary nationalism.[52] In a rhetorical move that by now we have seen time and again, to refuse to eat the pig is understood not as a sincere expression of one's religious beliefs but as an explicit rejection of integration into a dominant (in this case, French) society and culture.

Once again, I want to reflect on the fact that the pig symbolizes so much more than antisemitism. Further, Jewish identity is more variegated than just pig avoidance. Two notable examples of this complex porcine dynamic are found in recent works by French authors: Joann Sfar's graphic novel *The Rabbi's Cat* and Amanda Sthers's novel *Holy*

Lands.⁵³ In both of these works of fiction, "the pork-humor spectacle" plays out. This concept was developed by the scholar Nicole Beth Wallenbrock in order to discuss the pig, culinary nationalism, and Islamic identity in millennial French comedic films. According to Wallenbrock, the pork-humor spectacle refers to "the comedies that visually present pork in comic scenarios of cultural and religious differences, as well as the society (as the images reflect and encourage its pork symbolism)."⁵⁴ While previously we have discussed material that could be read through this scholarly framework, it is fitting to utilize Wallenbrock's concept here when analyzing the pig and Jewish identity in millennial French comedic novels.

Our first example of the pork-humor spectacle comes from a restaurant scene in the French graphic novel *The Rabbi's Cat*. In a book about religion in comics and graphic novels, the scholar of religion Ken Koltun-Fromm aptly summarizes this graphic novel thusly: "*The Rabbi's Cat* is a meandering tale of a once-speaking cat who tells all about his host family—the rabbi and his daughter Zlabya—offering delightful stories of Algerian Jews and their sometimes comic, sometimes traumatic encounters with a colonizing French elite."⁵⁵ In one pivotal scene, the pious rabbi (of titular cat-owning fame) travels to Paris, where he is disoriented by both its Jewish and non-Jewish life. He ends up wandering the streets of Paris on Friday night. As an observant Jew, there are various rules and regulations for the Sabbath, which means that he neither carries any money on his person nor can venture into certain places. But then he does what we least expect based on everything that we have learned about him thus far: he walks into a fancy, nonkosher French restaurant, sits down, and orders nonkosher food—and not just any nonkosher food. First, he asks the waiter, "Do you have any ham?" Next, he ventures out further, requesting, "And blood sausage? That thing made with pig's blood, you serve that to your customers?"⁵⁶ Then, he goes whole hog, ordering, "So give me some ham, some blood sausage, snails, seafood, and swordfish, which is a fish without scales, and oysters—and please check that they're really alive. And a glass of milk with the ham. And a really good wine named after a church or a Virgin Mary. . . . Hmm . . . and please make sure that the bottle isn't opened by a Jew and that no Jew says any prayer over this food."[57]

As the rabbi waits for the arrival of his feast, he turns to his cat (and a random dog they met in a Parisian church) and declares, "You're going to witness the least kosher meal in the universe."[58] Like the rabbi's cat and the Parisian dog, we collectively witness as this pork-humor spectacle unfolds. With "the least kosher meal in the universe" spread before him on his table, the rabbi speaks to God: "Lord, talk to me. Lord, you can see me, I'm about to break your commandments. Tell me not to do it. Tell me that I've deprived myself of these foods for sixty years and that it served some kind of purpose. Tell me you'll be sad if I break your Law."[59] When the rabbi does not hear from God, "looking forlorn and beaten," he resolves, "Just this once, I'll have eaten all this, Lord. Tomorrow I'll go back to fearing you."[60]

Part of the pork-humor spectacle plays out here, as the rabbi does not entirely tell the truth. Right before he puts the nonkosher food in his mouth, he recites a blessing: "Blessed are you, Lord our God, who allow us to transgress."[61] Remember that he instructed the waiter to make sure "that no Jew says any prayer over this food."[62] Analyzing the rabbi's claim to fear the Lord tomorrow but not today, Koltun-Fromm asserts, "This is not altogether true: the rabbi still fears his God (he even offers a blessing over his non-kosher meal), because even in his decisive moment of interchange he never crosses over. As a voyeur he peeks over the edge, but he remains tethered to the world he knows."[63] The rabbi transgresses but does so piously. In a porcine act intended to question everything about his Jewish life, he engages in practices that reinforce his Jewish identity.[64] Eating pig as part of "the least kosher meal in the universe" becomes an act of rejection transforming into reacceptance.[65]

In a completely different but yet analogous way, Amanda Sthers's novel *Holy Lands* grapples with pigs and rejection/acceptance of complex notions of Jewish identity. Though originally written in French by a French author and including one French main character (Monique Duchêne), plus her two half-French children (David and Annabelle Rosenmerck), the novel focuses on an American Jewish family. In particular, it explores the complicated—and often fraught—relationships that these, and other, characters have with a Jewish American father, ex-husband, and retired cardiologist named Harry Rosenmerck, who, after divorcing his wife, decides to move to Israel and buy a pig farm.[66] The novel consists of a series of letters and emails, written between the main characters, in which they discuss interpersonal dynamics, family history, and why the heck Harry Rosenmerck decided to buy a pig farm in Israel instead of retiring to play golf in Florida.

While the humor of being a Jewish pig farmer in Israel is consistently mined for laughs, the complexities of the pig and Jewish identity are explored in other contexts, as well.[67] For example, Monique writes a letter to Harry while visiting her parents in La Capelle-et-Masmolène (a commune in southern France), where she recalls the first time Harry met her non-Jewish parents: "Do you remember our first weekend here? Mother had, of course, prepared a pork roast for the first dinner with my Jewish boyfriend. She swore she didn't know that Jews didn't eat pork or that she'd forgotten. I laugh about it now, but it nearly broke us up."[68] Clearly, Monique's mother disapproved of her daughter dating a Jew (or perhaps that particular Jew?), and she expressed her displeasure by means of the pig. While we are not told how she reacted to Monique's eventual conversion to Judaism, we can infer from the pork roast that it was not greeted with unmitigated joy.

Throughout the novel, various characters' opinions on the pig— what at one point is referred to as "porkology"—are conveyed, usually as a means to understand why Harry has become a pig farmer and how this decision symbolizes his past, present, and future relationships with his family and friends.[69] Harry never offers a serious answer. His tongue is always placed firmly in his cheek. The closest he comes to solving this mystery for his friends and family (and for the readers) is when he remarks, "I bet on the golden calf. I'm like a dealer. Every society needs a transgression, and my pigs are a reasonable one!"[70] Pigs are Harry's reasonable transgression. But why he needs one, and why he cannot connect with his family, is a question to which he never provides a satisfying answer.

"LAZIO FANS DON'T EAT PORK": JEWS AND THE PIG IN MODERN ITALY

Italian cuisine seems to celebrate the pig in all its culinary glory. From prosciutto to pancetta to porchetta and beyond, the pig features prominently in myriad Italian recipes. Given the fact that Jews have lived continuously in Rome (the capital of the Roman Empire, which represented "The Pig" for the ancient Rabbis) since before the destruction of the Second Temple, Italian Jews have an over-two-thousand-year history of navigating the pig.

Many Italian Jews long engaged in a common culinary practice: substitution. From antiquity unto today, Jews often adopt local recipes and adapt them, switching out pig for other proteins, for example.[71] In Italy, there is a venerable tradition of substituting goose for pig. Ariel Toaff, a historian and son of a former chief rabbi of Rome, devoted an entire chapter of his book on the history of Italian Jewish food to "L'oca, il maiale deli ebrei"—that is, "Goose, the Pig of the Jews."[72] At the same time, there is a long history of Italians (both non-Jewish and Jewish) presuming that many regionally specific Italian dishes have a Jewish history. For vegetable dishes like the Roman *carciofi alla giudia* (Jewish artichoke), this historical connection is well documented.[73] For those that involve the pig, it is more folklore than established fact. Take for example the oral testimony of Renata, a Roman non-Jewish woman born in 1931 in San Lorenzo, an impoverished quarter of Rome. Discussing life in the Roman Jewish ghetto prior to its population's decimation due to mass deportations and executions during World War II, Renata repeats a claim that she grew up hearing: "Food is a mighty force in their culture, but also because they are Italians. The *cucina romana*, Roman cooking, *is* Jewish. Everybody in the world knows about *pasta alla carbonara*, in America and China and everywhere, and it comes from Italian-Jewish cooking. Have you ever had pig's liver *alla Romana*? Pig's liver is a dish that has been passed down to us from the time of the Roman Empire! And it is Jewish. What about the *pajata*? The intestines of lambs that have only ever had their mother's milk? Jewish, all of it."[74] In this quote, Roman Jews are seen as Romans—"they are Italians"—and, in succinct culinary terms, "Roman cooking, *is* Jewish." Leaving aside the dubious claims that Renata makes about the long history of certain Roman dishes, we still must grapple with the centrality of pig in two of these dishes (*pasta alla carbonara* includes pancetta, and pig's liver *alla Romana* obviously includes pig's liver).[75] In much of this folklore, the known antiquity of the Jews and their comparative isolation from the rest of Italians is used to cloak the unknown and desired-to-be-ancient history of Roman foods. The fact that these recipes involve pig is ignored in service of these pseudohistorical culinary claims.[76]

However, the modern history of Jews in Italy in general—and in Rome in particular—proves that neither is Jews' aversion to the pig always forgotten nor are Jews always considered truly "Italians." While Renata ignored the pig and accented the Romanness of Roman Jews, recent antisemitic acts take the opposite approach. For example, on January 25, 2014, three packages of pigs' heads were sent to the Great Synagogue of Rome, the Israeli embassy, and a museum featuring a Holocaust exhibit (the international commemoration day of the Holocaust was two days later, on January 27). Just in case the symbolism of the pig's head was not subtle enough, one package contained an antisemitic letter, and coordinated graffiti around the city claimed that the Holocaust was a lie.[77] Like the pig at Rabbi Corcos's funeral procession through Rome nearly four hundred years prior, the pig was used to denigrate Roman Jews and to contradict Renata's claim that "they are Italians."

In recent years, Jews and the pig have made several appearances in that most sacred of Italian institutions: the soccer pitch. In particular, the fans—which, lest we forget, is short for "fanatics"—of the bitter regional rivals of A.S. Roma and Lazio have both continuously drawn on the pig as part of antisemitic mockery of their counterparts. A.S. Roma fans unfurled a banner with the slogan "Lazio fans don't eat pork" (*Laziale non mangia maiale*). Lazio fans then produced stickers depicting Anne Frank wearing an A.S. Roma shirt. In the years that followed, the slogan "Lazio fans don't eat pork" has been regularly scrolled on Roman walls, usually accompanied by a swastika.[78] In each of these cases, the fans of one team wish to mock their opponent by comparing them to Jews by claiming that they "don't eat pork" or were murdered in the Holocaust. Whether shouted across the soccer pitch; printed on a sticker, shirt, or sign; or spray-painted on a wall, the pig embodies the very real threat of antisemitic rhetoric turning into physical violence. Sadly, in Rome, the more-than-two-thousand-year history of weaponizing the pig against Jews continues.

"AT THE REPASTS IN THE VALHALLA THEY ATE SO MUCH PORK": JEWS AND THE PIG IN MODERN SCANDINAVIA

Born in Copenhagen, Denmark, Isaac Euchel (1756–1804) in 1773 moved to Königsberg, where he made a name for himself as an important Jewish Enlightenment figure.[79] Like many of those who are associated with the Jewish Enlightenment, Euchel distanced himself from, and ultimately rejected, Jewish religious practice. As a cofounder and editor of the important Haskalah journal *ha-Meassef*, Euchel drew the ire of many anti-Enlightenment Jews.[80] One such critic was Rabbi Tsvi Hirsch Levin of Berlin, who used a porcine pun to mock his Danish opponent: "Indeed, truly a world turned upside down. Once pigs used to eat acorns (*Eichel*), and now Euchel eats pig."[81] The pig stands in both for Euchel's transgressions (in the form of the food he now eats) and for Euchel as transgressor (he is the pig).

The pig makes several appearances in Meïr Aron Goldschmidt's 1845 Danish novel *En Jøde* (literally, "A Jew," but sometimes titled in English, "The Jew of Denmark").[82] Once in the novel, Jews are ridiculed by means of the pig ("Jew—can you eat pork?"); but far more often, the pig is used to discuss Jewish identity and assimilation into Danish society.[83] This porcine theme begins when Jacob, the main character, is about to become Bar Mitzvah and then go to Copenhagen to continue his studies.[84] Wishing to assure that Jacob remains steadfast in his commitment to Jewish practice, Jacob's father takes him for a walk and asks his son a question: given (a) that "all mankind" eats lamb but many peoples (including, according to him, Jews, Muslims, Hindus, and all but the poorest of Christians) eschew eating pig and (b) that ewes birth one to two lambs at a time while sows birth six to nine piglets in a litter, why are there more sheep in the world than pigs? When Jacob cannot solve this puzzle, "his father enlightened him as follows:—'Seest thou, my son, it is a striking proof of the truth of the Jewish religion. The God we worship accords not his blessing to that, which, according to laws he bestowed upon the Jews, is *unclean*; so, notwithstanding all its fruitfulness, it cannot thrive.' And then he launched out into a history of the laws and promises of God, of the prophecies and their fulfillments, until their walk was finished and they had reached their home."[85]

If, as Jacob's father claims, the pig is "striking proof of the truth of the Jewish religion," then we should not be surprised that questioning whether to eat pig serves to question the entire enterprise. And Jacob begins to question. In the author's words, "religion which is either composed of ceremonies and superstitions, or else is purely spiritual, is not like a building out of which a single stone can be taken and another placed it its stead. The moment a doubt is admitted, the whole structure totters,—it falls at one crash, and the materials can never be used to raise a new one."[86]

What shakes Jacob's religious structure? The pig. After pondering ancient Greek and Norse gods and history, Jacob struggles to untangle his thoughts, which are twisted into a porcine pretzel:

> The only thing which he could not reconcile to himself in the acts of these old warriors was, that at the repasts in the Valhalla they ate so much pork.[87] But now he began to reflect upon the matter, and at length asked himself what offence the Deity could take at the quality of a man's food—whether the flesh of this animal or that entered within his lips.[88] "Is it conceivable," he said to himself, "that the sort of meat I put into my stomach can in any way be obnoxious to the moral law of God? Can it be possible that God sits up in the heavens and keeps watch to see that I let an hour elapse before I eat meat if I have been eating butter?" He remembered that, at the rector's bread and butter was eaten along with meat at breakfast, and no evil seemed to come out of it.[89]

And so it begins. Inevitably he must tell his father (and his uncle) that he neither believes in nor practices Judaism. With knees knocking together, he confesses to his father that he now eats pig. This is quite the metaphorical blow to his father (and literal blow to Jacob, as his uncle immediately boxes Jacob's ear after hearing this confession).[90]

Jumping ahead in time 260 years or so, we turn to a topic we have seen time and again: the use of the pig and antisemitic imagery to mock the Jews. But in this case, it might be a bit more complicated. In 2019, Norway's public broadcasting network (NRK) posted a cartoon video online (since removed from YouTube) that featured a stereotypical (and, at the very least, verging on antisemitic, if not outright antisemitic) image of an Orthodox Jewish man playing Scrabble. The viewer has the vantage point of the Jew's opponent. What Scrabble tiles does the opponent have to play in their hand? "JØDESVIN"—that is, "Jewish Swine." The player is deciding whether to play this word, which would be worth at least sixty-nine points, when the Jewish opponent taunts him, stating, "We are clearly on different cognitive levels."[91] The fact that this cartoon inspired controversy should not be surprising. After all, by now we are well acquainted with the antisemitic jeer "Jewish Swine." While there is plenty of evidence to suggest that the cartoon was a crass antisemitic joke, NRK entertainment editor Charlo Halversen rejects this allegation and offers his own interpretation: "The Scrabble player made an indecent and indefensible word that we can't and shouldn't use. But he's tempted to win."[92] Even if we accept this reading, the fact remains that the humor of this cartoon centers around the long-held association between Jews and the pig and how harmful it is to refer to a Jew as a "Jewish Swine."

Finally, similar to elsewhere in Europe, there is recent debate in Scandinavia about whether public schools and other public institutions should serve pig. While this debate has centered around halal food and Islam, kosher food and Jews are never far from the scene. As we have seen before, these debates tend to depict Muslims and Jews as nonnative outsiders and use their reluctance to eat pig as a reason to suspect them of radical and/or subversive tendencies. In coded language, pig stands in for "Danish food culture"—that is, for a white, Christian, and European notion of Danish culture. After all, if crispy pork with parsley sauce is the Danish national dish (proclaimed in 2014), then what does it mean if someone purports to be Danish and refuses to eat the pig?[93]

"HE MADE KOSHER PORK": JEWS AND THE PIG IN MODERN SOVIET RUSSIA

At the outset, it is worth remembering that when we consider Soviet Russia, we are discussing the region (the Pale of Settlement) where—at the time—the majority of the world's Jewish population resided.[94] Joining the many communities of the region was a language: Yiddish. While there are various dialects of Yiddish (and while most of these Jews spoke at least one or more additional languages), the language's dialects were mutually intelligible—even if there are major disagreements on how to pronounce such essential culinary words as "bagel" and "kugel." In a language famous for its humorous idioms, we should not be surprised to learn that "pig" appears in several, ranging from "A spoiled child makes itself comfortable like a pig in cabbage" to "A cantor in his old age barks like a dog and eats like a pig."[95] Also unsurprising is that Yiddish's technical vocabulary for the pig was lacking; basically, it imported two Hebrew words for the pig: "pig" (Yiddish: *khazer*; Hebrew: *ḥazir*) and "that thing" (Yiddish: *davar akher*; Hebrew: *davar aḥer*).[96]

Yiddish's porcine vocabulary expanded in the first half of the twentieth century as some Jews contributed to the Communist cause in Soviet Russia by participating in a particular agricultural collective act: namely, pig-breeding.[97] Jews are just part of this much-larger story, as pig-breeding became a major component of the Communist effort to produce protein for its massive population across the region.[98] While the inclusion of Jews in Communist pig-breeding might seem shocking, it also makes sense. After all, what better way is there for a Jew to express their devotion to Communism than by eschewing traditional religious aversion to the pig in order to raise pigs for the Communist cause?! But in order to do so, they needed a vocabulary to talk about what they were doing. Joking about this linguistic phenomenon, the satiric Yiddish poet Tsodek Dolgopolski (1879–1959) wrote,

> pigs represent for us a new problem,
> "pigs" (particularly of the Yorkshire breed)
> is a new word,
> introduced only last year.[99]

While Dolgopolski is correct that pigs represent a new linguistic problem, his tongue is firmly in his cheek when he claims that "pigs" is a year-old word. However, he is not far from the truth, as words such as "to farrow," "sow," and others needed to be created (or, more often, imported from other languages).[100]

Perhaps the most well-known representation of Jewish pig-breeding is from Leyb Kvitko's 1935 Yiddish children's poem "Anna Vanna," which was popular with children—both Jewish and (translated into Russian and Ukrainian) non-Jewish—for several generations. The poem begins,

> Anna Vanna, brigade leader,
> Open the sty door.
> Show the beautiful new
> Little piglets [Yiddish: *khazerlekh di kleyne*].[101]

Part of a genre of Yiddish songs about Jewish collective farms, "Anna Vanna" celebrates how cute and clean pigs are—in an attempt to rewrite thousands of years of Jews (and non-Jews) viewing pigs as repulsive and unclean.[102] For the many Jews who participated in this enterprise (see figure 5.3), breeding pigs was an effective means to communicate their complete participation in Communism.[103]

Of course, these Jewish Communist pig-breeders do not cover the vast range of practices among Jews in this region. Many Jews adhered to biblical and rabbinic laws prohibiting pig ingestion (and raising); some eschewed all Jewish practice and partook of the pig.[104] Others ate pig but observed other Jewish practice.[105] There was even a Jewish poet, Melech Ravitch (1893–1976), who wrote poems in Yiddish about animals and his vegetarianism; and yet, despite his commitment to secularism, he never could bring himself to write about the pig.[106] Incidentally, we know that Ravitch knew about pigs, if only because the earliest attestation that we have of the Nobel-laureate Yiddish author (and vegetarian) Isaac Bashevis Singer's common practice of signing his name by drawing a picture of a pig is from a postcard that he wrote to Ravitch, stating, "'*A sheynem dank. Ikh bin a—*' (Thank you very much. I am a—) followed by the drawing of a pig" (figure 5.4).[107] However, a significant segment of the Jewish population "increasingly became, in the words of Menshevik Grigori Aronson, a *khazeyrim-yid*, or 'pigs-Jew,' crossing the important line that divided cultivation of pigs from eating pork."[108]

And this brings us to a fascinating phenomenon, wherein several Jews from this region imagine the pig as being, under the right

FIGURE 5.3. Soviet Yiddish propaganda poster from 1931. The title declares in Yiddish, "The pig is our main machine for production of meat in the coming years!" Published by Tsenroizdat (Central Publishing House for the USSR Peoples, 1924–1934) in Moscow in 1931, designer unknown. Blavatnik Archive Foundation, used with permission, https://www.blavatnikarchive.org.

conditions, a Jewish—even a kosher!—food. Thus, we find a scene in "Family," a documentary story by Peretz Markish published on the Proletarian May Day of 1935, in which a Jewish family's dinner table "blossomed with the most exquisite choice of traditional Jewish dishes. [There was] excellently stuffed fish, chopped liver, amazingly prepared horseradish, and pork cutlets of an unparalleled fatness."[109] Sure, gefilte (stuffed) fish is a traditional Jewish food, but pork cutlets?![110] Perhaps this connects to an interesting case study by the scholar of Yiddish and Jewish-Slavic culture Anna Shternshis. Shternshis has documented several Jews from this region who adamantly assert that kosher pork was (and remains) an actual thing. One example comes from an interview Shternshis (labeled A.S.)

FIGURE 5.4. Postcard written in 1939 in Yiddish by Isaac Bashevis Singer to Melech Ravitch, stating, "Thank you very much. I am a 🐗" Melech Ravitch Archive, ARC. 4* 1540, Archives Department, the National Library of Israel. Image of signature used with the kind permission of the Isaac Bashevis Singer Literary Trust; photo by David Stromberg, used with permission.

conducted in Yiddish with Vladimir P. (labeled V.P), a Jew born in Odessa in 1922:

> [V.P.] However, we all liked *khazer* [pork]. We all liked *salo* [cured slabs of pig's fatback], pork, everything.
>
> A.S. Even your parents?
>
> V.P. Yes. My father had a special butcher, a *shoykhet* [ritual slaughterer], who slaughtered pigs. He ate it. Have you not heard of special Jewish butchers?
>
> A.S. Yes, but I have never heard of a *shoykhet* for pigs.
>
> V.P. Well, we had a special slaughterer who slaughtered pigs especially for Jews. He made kosher pork. Who knows how he did it, exactly.
>
> A.S. So, in your family, you ate it, right?
>
> V.P. Papa could not live without it. He had weak lungs, and doctors prescribed him to eat pork fat. Usually for lunch, when he came home from work, my mother fried some potatoes for him using salo. He ate it.
>
> A.S. Did you like it?
>
> V.P. Of course! It was delicious. Until now, I love Jewish food, the pork. If someone comes to visit me from Ukraine, I always ask them to bring some Ukrainian salo.[111]

While traditional Jewish interpretation would allow consuming pig for medical reasons, Vladimir P. testifies to something else. He refers to pork as "Jewish food" and believes that a ritual specialist can slaughter pigs in a manner that renders them kosher. He does not know how that works "exactly"; and neither do I. Shternshis notes that Vladimir P. was by no means alone in this belief, as she conducted several interviews in which Jews from this region make a similar claim.[112] Importantly, Shternshis observes that she only heard such claims from Jews who have moved away from their original home and not from those who remained. This leads her to conclude that this difference is not based on differing knowledge of kosher laws "but simply because they do not perceive the laws of kashrut as an important part of their Jewish identity."[113] For those like Vladimir P., who consider the observance of kosher regulations to be part of their identity, it matters to them that the pig that they ate was "kosher."[114]

"WE WON'T CALL IT SWINE FLU": JEWS AND THE PIG IN MODERN ISRAEL

It would not be an exaggeration to assert that I could write an entire book on the subject of laws regarding pigs in the modern nation-state of Israel; indeed, it has already been done. Before Daphne Barak-Erez was a justice on the Supreme Court of Israel, she was a law professor at Tel Aviv University who wrote a book on this very topic, titled *Outlawed Pigs: Law, Religion, and Culture in Israel*.[115] As Barak-Erez states at the outset,

> This book explores how the historical sensitivity of Jewish culture to pigs was incorporated into Israeli law. More specifically, it traces the course of two Israeli laws that sought to give concrete formulation to the abhorrence of pigs: the Local Authorities (Special Enablement) Law of 1956, which authorizes municipalities to ban the possession of and trade in pork within their jurisdiction, and the Pig-Raising Prohibition Law of 1962, which forbids pig-breeding throughout Israel, except for areas populated mainly by Christians. My focus will be on the processes that culminated in the adoption of prohibitions against pig-breeding and pork trading, and on the resistance they provoked. I argue that the controversies surrounding these issues provide a key to changing attitudes towards religion and tradition in Israeli society.[116]

Barak-Erez then goes on to demonstrate how pig-related legislation in Israel reflects larger debates and concerns throughout the relatively short history of the modern nation-state of Israel. For example, after the establishment of the State of Israel in 1948, there were meat and food shortages; so even among those (both religious and secular) who wished to ban pig, there was not a simple answer.[117] But in the 1950s and 1960s, as noted earlier, conditions were such that various legislation was passed.

Controversy ensued when legal cases began to challenge these laws, testing both their legality and popularity (with both changing over time). Barak-Erez expertly connects the dots wherein legislation and cultural concerns intersect in Israeli laws and judicial rulings. An excellent illustration of this comes from the case *State of Israel v. Shmukler* (1995). At issue was a municipal law in the city of Ashkelon that prohibited the sale of pork. In Judge Yitzhak's opinion on the case, he brings in material with which we are by now familiar:

> Why, then, has the pig been "picked on"? The reason is obviously not religious-halakhic. The reason is historical national. The pig became a symbol of abomination in the course of Jewish history, of the hatred of Edom, a symbol against the nations of the world that endangered the very existence of the Jewish people throughout history. The pig is an animal that possesses the external sign of ritual purity—a cloven hoof—but not the internal sign. It does not chew the cud. Externally, the pig looks pure, but it is actually not so. The pig, therefore, represents outside without inside, the symbol of hypocrisy and evil.[118]

Judge Yitzhak rejected the defendant's argument that a pig prohibition violated two of Israel's Basic Laws (Freedom of Occupation; and Human Dignity and Liberty). Why? Because of what the pig symbolizes. That alone, in his opinion, was legal justification for such legislation within the State of Israel.

The ground shifted in the pig debate in 2004, when several petitions related to various municipalities' pig laws resulted in a unanimous decision by the Supreme Court, in the case *Solodkin v. Municipality of Beth Shemesh*.[119] This case is worth our attention because the court's decision included a balancing test to assess whether a given municipality should rule to prohibit pig in order to protect those who are concerned with the symbolic weight of the pig or to permit pig in order to protect those who feel that a prohibition infringes on their individual liberties. First, the ruling states that a municipality can set different rules for different neighborhoods within a municipality; thus, pig sales could be banned in one part of a city but permitted in another. Second, the ruling offers an outline of a model analysis of three hypothetical neighborhoods: (1) in a neighborhood where the majority of the population supports prohibiting pig, a ban would be justified even though it infringes on individual liberties; (2) in a neighborhood where the majority of the population opposes prohibiting pig, a ban would not be justified because it disproportionately infringes on individual liberties;[120] and (3) in a neighborhood where opinion is split and cannot easily be divided geographically into separate pro- and anti-pig sections, decisions can vary (but legally can only ban if pig is reasonably accessible to those who want it). Any student of law can see that, as balancing tests go, this one opens more windows than it closes. On the one hand, this led to the state dismissing criminal charges against several butchers charged in the *Shmukler* case. On the other hand, the broad discretion now granted to municipalities in effect left in place the existing policy of the Ministry of Justice, which allowed variance based on similar local criteria. No one won a clear victory. *Solodkin* was simultaneously a decisive and indecisive decision. However, its ruling did weaken the kinds of claims made by Judge Yitzhak. The symbolic weight of the pig was not enough to infringe on an entire community's individual liberties, that is, unless a majority of the population consents.[121]

Analyzing these legal data, Barak-Erez concludes that, on the one hand, disputes about the legal implications of Israeli pig prohibitions in Israel indicate a decline in the symbolic status of such regulations; in short, "They tell the story of a tradition in a phase of change."[122] More importantly, I would argue, is that, on the other hand, "From another perspective, the public dispute concerning pig-related prohibitions reflects—even today—an identity discourse. Religious

Jewish society in Israel defines its identity through its adherence to the traditional characteristics of Jewish society. For secularists, however, rejecting the compelling nature of traditional prohibitions is part of the definition of their new identity, which is based on an 'adversary' approach to anything associated with religious coercion. In this sense, secular Jews in Israel also view the pig prohibition as symbolic, but in reverse: as standing for their opposition to what they perceive as religious coercion."[123]

The pig has not declined in symbolic value. If anything, it has increased. Therefore, we need to speak in terms of an evolution, not an erosion. While for religious Jewish Israelis, to ban the pig is a symbolic victory against religious oppression by non-Jews, now for secular Jewish Israelis, to permit the pig is a symbolic victory against religious oppression by religious Jews. In a manner analogous to the Sabbatians discussed previously, secular Jewish Israelis use pig to intentionally transgress Jewish law and, in so doing, to establish a new—and highly contested—Jewish identity.

The symbolic value of the pig for various Israelis continues to be front and center of pig-related discussion. Anything disapproved of can be compared to a pig. For example, when Rabbi Meir Yehuda Getz, the official rabbi in charge of the Western (or Wailing) Wall, voiced his disapproval of allowing women to actively participate in religious ceremonies there, he asserted, "a woman carrying a Torah is like a pig at the Wailing Wall."[124] Alternatively, publicly celebrating pig—and not just referring to pork using the common Hebrew euphemisms of "white meat" or "white steak"—utilizes the pig for another form of identity discourse. Thus, we see the unabashed publicity of the Israeli supermarket Tiv Ta'am selling pig products or the appearance of cookbooks by Israelis (and in Hebrew, the "Holy Tongue"), which celebrate embracing pig as part of a complex Jewish identity.[125] Further, Independence Day in Israel is a big day for the Israeli pig industry, as barbecues throughout the country perform identity on their grills, whether they feature kosher, nonkosher, or yes, even pig meat.[126]

Simple binaries of the pig as symbolic either of piety or of transgression are further complicated when we delve a little deeper. For example, in Tel Aviv—a city renowned for its secular identity—the first dim sum restaurant did not succeed until, among other things, it removed pig from its dumplings (though shrimp were allowed to remain).[127] Or take the case of perhaps the most controversial ham sandwich in the history of Israel: in 2005, an Israeli soldier was thrown in the brig for eleven days when he brought a ham sandwich for lunch.[128] Officially, the Israel Defense Forces (IDF) is kosher, and all of its provisions and mess halls must comply. But can a soldier bring their own pig-meat sandwich while on duty? After public outcry, the soldier's punishment was revoked, and IDF spokesman Brigadier General Motti Almoz clarified that, while the IDF will remain kosher, it will also keep out of its soldiers' private sandwiches. Officially, the symbolism of a pig-free Israeli military remains; but soldiers are, within limits, allowed to exercise their individual liberty.[129]

Pigs continue to both amuse and shock Israeli audiences, on all sides of the political, religious, and cultural spectrum. From Israeli kibbutzim (collective communities) that raise pigs to Israeli chefs publishing recipes for suckling pig on Yom Kippur, these stories generate symbolic meaning for those who are both pro- and anti-pig.[130] Pigs appear in surprising contexts, such as when we find that in 2009, Yaakov Litzman, Israel's deputy health minister, was unwilling to refer to the H1N1 public-health crisis by its popular name; instead, he declared, "We will call it Mexican flu. We won't call it swine flu."[131] Rather than risk religious/cultural offense and, concomitantly, preventing the Israeli public from taking the pandemic threat seriously, he renamed the influenza strain after its reputed country of origin.[132] Pigs also appear in unsurprising contexts, such as when the cartoonist Avi Katz drew on George Orwell's *Animal Farm* in order to critique Israeli politics. Below the iconic Orwellian quote of "All animals are equal. But some are more equal than others," Katz depicted six right-wing Israeli politicians (including then–Prime Minister

Benjamin Netanyahu) as disheveled pigs taking a selfie. Despite the well-known allusion to Orwell, and the conventions of political cartoons, Katz's use of pigs was seen as one step too far. He was fired; or, in human-resources parlance, he was a freelance cartoonist, "and based on editorial considerations, it was decided not to continue the relationship with him."[133] We expect this type of satirizing in the genre of political cartoons, but porcine jokes, unsurprisingly, are not always funny in Israel—except, of course, when they are (after all, the editors ran the cartoon in the first place!).

While the Mishnah famously declares that "a Jew may not raise pigs anywhere," pigs continue to raise concerns in the Holy Land almost two thousand later.[134] In these instances, the pig represents both those ancient traditions and subsequent historical events. More than just a package of "white steak" in a supermarket or a name for a pandemic pathogen, the pig embodies Jewish oppression and, for some, liberation.

"THERE WAS A GREAT CONSTERNATION": JEWS AND THE PIG IN MODERN NEW ZEALAND

The peripatetic journey of the pig has taken us across the globe, to both expected and unexpected locales. On this sojourn, we will make one last brief stop, in New Zealand—a location that (at least from my perspective) was not an expected destination.

Since pig was not a significant part of New Zealanders' diets, many Jews who wished to avoid eating pig in New Zealand were able to do so with relative ease. Such was the case for Jewish immigrants to Dunedin and Christchurch (on the Pacific Ocean–facing eastern side of South Island) in the mid-1800s.[135] But insignificant does not mean completely absent. Thus, we find a Jewish peddler in a small New Zealand town in 1863 who was served a breakfast of ham and eggs. Wishing to avoid eating the pig—but not ruin his chance at conducting business with the proprietor—the Jewish peddler was in quite the porcine pickle. He waited for his hostess to leave the room, and then "he threw [the ham] into the fire. In an instant it blazed and set fire to the chimney and there was a great consternation."[136] While extant records do not report what happened after the fire, it would seem that, at the very least, surreptitiously throwing pig in the fire to avoid eating it was not a general practice in New Zealand in the mid-1800s (and beyond).[137]

"ARE YOU GOING TO EAT PORK NOW, YOU BUM?": CONCLUSIONS

For the title of this chapter, I used a quote from the Yiddish poet Tsodek Dolgopolski, also discussed earlier, that "pigs represent for us a new problem."[138] Dolgopolski is joking. Pigs are an old problem—as old as the Hebrew Bible, in fact! But this old problem is also a new problem. As Jews navigate their lived reality, the pig continues to appear on their identity map. Time and again, we have seen the pig used as a means to mock Jews and Judaism, to represent Jewish identity in the form of abstaining from ingestion, and to represent a transgressive Jewish identity in the form of embracing ingestion. Depending on one's perspective, then, the pig can represent oppression, redemption, tradition, and/or innovation (and sometimes more than one of these at the same time).

We could multiply the examples cited earlier were we to scour the corners of the Earth. For example, if we spent time in the Caribbean, we would find Holocaust refugees who fled Europe and became pig farmers in Sosúa, Dominican Republic (though not all ate pig).[139] And if we ventured farther south, to South America, we would encounter Brazilian Jews who ponder their Jewish identity in relation to the Brazilian national dish, *feijoada*—"a thick black bean stew served with rice ... usually made with a combination of dried, salted, and smoked meats or sausage."[140] One Brazilian Jew named Felipe jokes about how, for some Brazilian Jews, *feijoada* symbolizes their embracing of certain Brazilian customs, which seem at odds with their Jewish identity: "One [Jew] runs into another and says,

'Are you going to eat pork now, you bum [*vagabundo*]?' I said, 'Yeah, today is Saturday, the day for *feijoada*! I love it!' Yeah, I say it. And I go eat *feijoada*. It's delicious in the winter."[141]

As the anthropologist Misha Klein notes, "The blending of Jewish and Brazilian practices, in spite of the contradictions, is especially potent in the consumption of *feijoada*, all the more so because it is traditionally eaten on Saturday, the Jewish Sabbath, further adding to the tension between Jewish and Brazilian expressions of identity."[142] To eat *feijoada* on the Sabbath is, simultaneously, to transgress Jewish practice and to assert a Jewish *and* Brazilian identity. In isolation, this practice makes no sense; but once considered in the larger narrative framework developed throughout our story, the dissonance resolves into harmony. We have heard variations on this melody before. And we shall hear them again in the final leg of our journey, where we turn our attention to the United States in the Modern Period.

6

"NO JEW EVER DIED REFUSING TO EAT SHRIMP"

Pig Polemics in the United States in the Modern Period

THE pig plays a prominent role in the story of how the United States shaped the American Jewish experience. Perhaps surprisingly, the pig also plays a prominent role in how the American Jewish experience shaped the United States. For example, one cannot tell the story of the rise of chicken consumption in the United States—from a rare, often seasonal animal protein to the most commonly consumed animal protein—without acknowledging the part that Jewish consumers played in this transformation of the American diet. As the historian Roger Horowitz notes, "Forbidden from eating pork by kosher dietary rules, New York's Jews were eager consumers of poultry in order to add variety to their diets and to have a special meal for Sundays [sic]. A 1926 Department of Agriculture study found that Jews accounted for 80 percent of the live poultry sales in New York City; with a Jewish population of two million by the 1930s, this was a substantial market."[1] The Jewish market proved important in propping up the nascent US poultry market, especially in the Delmarva Peninsula (at the intersection of Delaware, Maryland, and Virginia), which is now a major hub of chicken production in the United States.[2] And the reason that the Jewish market was so important was due to its avoidance of the pig.

In the final leg of our porcine journey, we explore the many ways in which the pig shaped the experience of American Jews and which American Jews shaped their lived experiences through interactions (avoidance, ingestion, humorous reference to, etc.) with the pig.

From the US frontier to the battlefront, from television sitcoms to humorous essays, and all points in between, American Jews have explored the contours of their identity with reference to the pig. Many Jews eat the pig (according to a recent Pew Research Center survey, 57 percent of self-identified American Jews do so); others do not; and still others sometimes partake.[3] But it seems as if all who do not, or do, eat the pig have something to say about what their porcine practice communicates about their American Jewish identity.

"AS KOSHER AS WE COULD": JEWISH IMMIGRANTS, FOOD, AND THE PIG IN THE UNITED STATES

With the exception of Native Americans, every human who has arrived on the shores of America—whether traveling aboard the *Mayflower* or in first class of a modern airplane; whether as a Pilgrim or from the Pale of Settlement—has been a recent immigrant. The story of American Jews, therefore, is one of immigration. Some of their patterns and narratives are similar to and overlapping with other ethnic and religious immigrant groups, and others are particular.[4] To understand the role that the pig performs in the story of the Jewish immigrant experience in the United States, we first discuss Jewish immigrants who spread across wide swaths of American territory and then focus on a particular case study of the Lower East Side of New York City.

We start far outside the Lower East Side of Manhattan because too often that narrative dominates and the American Jewish experience is read entirely through that lens. However, we have significant archival evidence for Jewish experience throughout the vast territory of the United States.[5] Many of these immigrants faced the harsh realities of frontier living. Rarely were there enough Jews to constitute a minyan—a prayer quorum that requires at least ten adults.[6] Religious practice, therefore, was difficult, at best. Further, procuring food in general was challenging, with starvation a very real threat. Obtaining kosher meat was often impossible.

There are numerous extant accounts of Jews struggling both to survive and to maintain kosher dietary laws. While many immigrant Jews simply discontinued keeping kosher (and others had not kept kosher prior to immigrating), there is significant evidence that immigrant Jews in the US South and on the frontier endeavored to keep kosher.[7] Many of those who traveled during the week and were able to return home for the weekend practiced what the historian Hasia R. Diner calls "situational kashrut." During the week, they would eat whatever food was available—even if it was pig—but come Friday, when they returned home, they would eat kosher food.[8] These narratives commonly reference avoidance of the pig. In particular, the pig is invoked often when compromise positions are staked out. For example, when Aaron Haas describes his childhood in circa-1850 Newnan, Georgia, he states, "While it was impossible to keep a kosher table, there was never a piece of hog in my father's house, nor was milk or butter ever on the table with meat."[9] Similarly, as Joe Dokovna discusses the menu on the farm that he grew up on near Wing, North Dakota, he recalls that, though far from "a kosher butcher shop, [they] never had pork or milk and meat together at the table. We tried to keep as kosher as we could."[10] Solomon Nunes Carvalho, traveling across the US West scouting a route for the transcontinental railroad, refused to eat porcupine—not because it was biblically prohibited in and of itself—but because it "looked very much like pork."[11] After immigrating from Germany to Milwaukee, Wisconsin, Sarah Thal and her family moved farther west to homestead in Nelson County, North Dakota, in the early 1880s. Describing that experience, she notes, "A newcomer must of course experience much embarrassment. My worst was one day [when] Mr. Mendelson brought in a crate of pork and asked me, a piously reared Jewess, to cook it. In time I consented."[12] As a young Jewish girl growing up in Albany, Indiana, at the turn of the twentieth century, Ruth Sapinksy had to explain the situation to her non-Jewish neighbors: "It was due to my 'church,' I made clear to the inquisitive, that our meat was never bought at the local butcher's. That Father killed our chickens with strict regard to certain religious regulations, and our meat, 'cow and not pig,' was delivered to us twice a week from Louisville."[13]

There are many more stories of Jewish immigrants to United States and their encounters with the pig.[14] What emerges from listening to them is the role that the pig plays in staking out an identity claim. In relenting to cook Mr. Mendelson's pork, Sarah Thal reimagines her identity as a pious Jewess and a North Dakotan homesteader. When Leon Schwarz's father arrives in antebellum Alabama and finds only pig to eat, the following exchange occurs: "As the Jewish peddler pitched in and ate heartily, the farm lady said to him, 'Mr. Schwarz, I am surprised to see you eat pork. I thought Moses ordered the Jews not to eat any hog meat.' Looking the table over, which contained nothing but hog meat cooking, Schwarz replied: 'Ah, madam, if Moses had travelled through Perry County, Alabama, he never would have issued such an order.'"[15] Schwarz is not denying what Moses ordered; rather, he observes that Moses wandered through a pigless desert outside of Egypt, not the pig-filled land of Perry County, Alabama. Since Mr. Schwarz is in the latter, he adjusts Mosaic legislation—and his Jewish identity—accordingly.

Concomitantly, when a Jewish immigrant who purports to keep kosher is accused of eating the pig, the resulting scandal portrays the presumed righteous as a hypocrite. Such was the case with Rabbi M. Klinkowstein in Denver, Colorado. On March 10, 1884, a local newspaper advertised kosher for Passover *matzah* being baked under the supervision of Rabbi Klinkowstein. It comes as a surprise, then, that, on June 1, 1884, Rabbi Klinkowstein was found guilty of eating pork and smoking on the Sabbath. The committee tasked with evaluating these accusations conducted a four-week investigation and voted twenty-one to eighteen in favor of his guilt. While the divided vote suggests that the story is far from straightforward, the accusations are shocking given that, on the previous Yom Kippur (on October 11, 1883), Rabbi Klinkowstein delivered a sermon that included a scathing rebuke of those local Jews whose stores remained open on "this sacred Sabbath of all Sabbaths, and who don't want it known they are Jews."[16] Much less surprising is that, in light of the committee's vote (and despite others in the community protesting the vote), Rabbi Klinkowstein left town.

There are also stories of Jews using pig to conceal their Jewish identity.[17] For example, in 1943, an anonymous letter was submitted to the *Jewish Daily Forward*'s advice column, "A Bintel Brief" (Yiddish for "A Bundle of Letters"). Claiming to hail "from a Western City," the author tells the story of a local dilemma. In the town resides "a man with an Irish name, who runs a large pork market."[18] In what sounds like the setup for a joke, the Irish pig dealer asks for a private meeting with the local Orthodox rabbi and surprisingly even declines the presence of a friendly Yiddish translator, since the rabbi speaks only a smattering of English. We soon find out why the Irish pig retailer claimed he "would manage to make himself understood."[19] It turns out that he is not an immigrant from Ireland but rather a Jew hailing from the same area in Europe as the rabbi (and had even known the rabbi's family before he immigrated in his youth!). When he came to the United States, he reinvented himself as a non-Jewish Irish immigrant, married a non-Jewish woman (from whom he had at first concealed his Jewish identity and who had died two years earlier), had two daughters, and became wealthy thanks, in no small part, to his business with pigs. Apparently, no one ever thought to question his Yiddish brogue. Now, in his late sixties, he wished to reengage with the Jewish community. He did not want to join the Reform community in town; instead, he wanted to become a member at the Orthodox shul. While he did not need to convert, since he was Jewish, the question became, Must he sell his profitable pig business in order to become a member in good standing? "The rabbi argues that as long as he has an income from the [pig] business he cannot become a member of the *shul*."[20] But the letter writer wants to know what the advice columnist thinks on this subject. While the advice columnist claims that an outsider cannot judge and generally defers to the local rabbi, another reader writes in to criticize the rabbi, asserting that "to demand that the man give up his pork market is a little too much to ask."[21] Rather, the rabbi should let the man join his community and then judge his sincerity. On all sides of the debate, the status of this pseudo-Irishman as a Jew is not the issue; rather, what may—or may not—prevent him from joining this Orthodox Jewish community is whether he continues to profit from pigs. After all, one can be a Jew who pretends to be Irish, but can one be a Jew who actually sells pigs?!

Perhaps the most famous case study of Jewish immigrants, food, and the pig in the United States involves another immigrant group and its food: solving the riddle of how, in the twentieth-century United States, Chinese food became the chosen food of the Chosen People.[22] The classic study of this historical development was published in 1993 by two sociologists: Gaye Tuchman and Harry Gene Levine. In their influential analysis, Tuchman and Levine identified three themes that they argue account for this culinary intersection and eventual culinary predilection. It is worth reviewing them.

The first theme is summarized by a term coined by the two sociologists, which has become well known in (both Jewish and non-Jewish) food studies since: "safe treyf."[23] "Treyf" is Yiddish for nonkosher food in general and pig in particular.[24] Chinese food was viewed by Jewish immigrants on the Lower East Side of Manhattan as "safe treyf" for a few reasons. First, Chinese immigrants settled around the same time and same place as Jewish immigrants—with sizable populations of both immigrant groups clustering in the Lower East Side toward the end of the nineteenth and beginning of the twentieth centuries. Thus, although they were seen as "foreign" (more on that later), Chinese immigrants were also familiar to Jewish immigrants. Second, unlike the dining establishments of other immigrant groups on the Lower East Side, Chinese restaurants did not feature religious iconography that triggered long-held fears. While an Irish or Italian restaurant, for example, might have a crucifix on the wall, a statue of the Virgin Mary, and/or images of Christian saints—which many Jewish immigrants associated with centuries of oppression and violence—Chinese religious iconography either was not understood as such or, even if it was, was seen as not weighed down with the same historical baggage. As Tuchman and Levine note, "However foreign Chinese restaurants might be, the decorations were *non-Christian*: They did not raise the issue of Jews' marginal position in a Christian society."[25] In that way, they were a safe(r) space.

The third reason is the most important one from the perspective of our topic: "safe treyf" refers to the ingredients, cooking methods, and language barriers encountered in a Chinese restaurant.[26] Here, it is helpful to break down the term "safe treyf" into its component parts. Chinese restaurants were "safe" for Jewish immigrants for several reasons. First, they did not have dairy on their menu. Therefore, the rabbinic prohibition against mixing milk and meat was not an issue.[27] This was helpful even for those Jewish immigrants who no longer kept kosher but for whom such combinations were still avoided due to a lifetime of acquired taste. Second, Chinese cooking often involves cutting, chopping, or mincing animal proteins. This culinary practice, coupled with the fact that dishes were often referred to by their non-English (usually Cantonese) names, meant that they appeared—so long as one did not ask too many questions—to be "safe" and not to necessarily violate kosher dietary taboos. Chinese restaurants were also "treyf" because not only was that cut, chopped, or minced-up meat not slaughtered according to kosher regulations, but it also might just be the ultimate treyf—the pig. While many Jewish immigrants who stepped into Chinese restaurants on the Lower East Side of Manhattan might not have been concerned with unambiguously violating kosher laws, many others were only comfortable if their actions were ambiguous. Chinese restaurants allowed them plausible deniability: Who was to say that their meat was pig? Of course, they could have asked, but doing so would make the uncertain certain. By not asking, they could dip their toe in the waters and venture into a new sea of cuisine, without fear of drowning. An important component of this, which is far too often underplayed, is the fact that Jewish immigrants who engaged in the practice of eating "safe treyf" *were transgressing without feeling transgressive.*[28] Yes, they were (probably) eating pig. But the doubt created via "safe treyf" allowed them to do so without feeling like they were completely abandoning long-held religious (and cultural) principles. Without this subterfuge, many probably would not have eaten Chinese food. We could playfully refer to this concept as "Schrödinger's pig," in that it allowed these Jewish immigrants to simultaneously eat the pig and not eat the pig. Therefore, we should not minimize the importance that "safe treyf" plays in this story.

The second theme identified by Tuchman and Levine is that eating in a Chinese restaurant was perceived as a performative act of cosmopolitanism by Jewish immigrants. Summarizing their argument, the culinary history writer Andrew Coe states, "Ordering a plate of chow mein showed sophistication, setting one apart from the Old World immigrants with the odors of the shtetl still clinging to their clothes."[29] While it might surprise modern readers that Chinese food—now a staple of shopping-mall food courts—was used to indicate worldly and sophisticated culinary knowledge, such was the case a century or so ago. In addition to demonstrating a cosmopolitan palate, the themes of "safe treyf" also play out here, in that immigrant Jews could imagine themselves as performing a mainstream white identity in a Chinese restaurant. Thus, in regard to "the Chinese restaurant, where the Lord has lifted the ban on pork dishes for the obedient children of Israel," Philip Roth writes,

> Why we can eat pig on Pell Street and not at home is because... frankly I still haven't got the whole thing figured out, but at the time I believed that it has largely to do with the fact that the elderly man who owns the place, and whom amongst ourselves we call "*Shmendrick*," isn't somebody whose opinion of us we have cause to worry about. Yes, the only people in the world whom it seems to me the Jews are not afraid of are the Chinese. Because one, the way they speak English makes my father sound like Lord Chesterfield; two, the insides of their heads are just so much fried rice anyway; and three, to them we are not Jews but

> *white*—and maybe even Anglo Saxon. Imagine! No wonder the waiters can't intimidate us. To them we're just some big-nosed variety of WASP! Boy, do we eat! Suddenly even the pig is no threat—though, to be sure, it comes to us so chopped and shredded, and is then set afloat on our plates in such oceans of soy sauce, as to bear no resemblance at all to a pork chop, or a hambone, or most disgusting of all, a *sausage* (ucchh!).[30]

Just as the "chopped or shredded" pork functionally passes as "safe treyf," Roth understands (through a clearly racist framework) the immigrant Jew to pass as "American" in a Chinese restaurant. But outside of this venue, the Jew sticks out from American white Anglo-Saxon Protestant society much like a pork chop, a hambone, or a pork sausage would appear on a kosher plate. Pretending to be American and not immigrant, patrician and not pig, kosher and not treyf, the pig once again indexes Jewish identity. This time, by misrecognizing the pig as "safe treyf," the Jewish immigrant can perform a more mainstream American identity and act cosmopolitan while eating Chinese food.

The third theme identified by Tuchman and Levine is one that does not get the emphasis that it deserves. They argue that, over time, eating in Chinese restaurants becomes a Jewish thing to do. While first-generation Jewish immigrants viewed this eating practice as performative cosmopolitanism, their children (and their children's children etc.) saw this simply as a Jewish eating practice. With each successive meal and each successive generation, "Chinese food had become, arguably, the ethnic cuisine of the American Jew."[31] Eating Chinese food was no longer a subversive act. Rather than functioning to transgress kosher laws without being transgressive and to subvert an immigrant identity for a more mainstream American identity, it simply became a thing that American Jews did (particularly on Christmas, but more on that later). And in so doing, it exemplifies why it is an excellent case study of Jewish immigrants, food, and the pig in the United States.

"NO PORK, YES OYSTER": THE PIG, "OCEAN VEGETABLES," AND REFORM JUDAISM IN THE UNITED STATES

On July 11, 1883, the Hebrew Union College in Cincinnati, Ohio, hosted a banquet to celebrate the ordination of the US college's first class of Reform rabbis. Later mythologized and (in)famously known as the "*Terefah* [nonkosher] Banquet," the menu for this gourmet feast included four biblically forbidden foods: clams, crabs, shrimp, and frogs.[32] It also violated other rabbinic dietary regulations by serving nonkosher meat and mixing milk and meat. Over a series of elaborate courses, each accompanied with its own wine or spirit (in accordance with notions of haute cuisine, French-inspired high cuisine then and still, to this day, popular among Americans as signifying high-class culinary convention), the diners who partook of this feast—and those who, according to reports, stormed out when they saw the menu—each made a statement about Reform Judaism's stance on Jewish dietary laws and, by extension, on Reform theology in general. The intra- and interdenominational consternation inspired, in part, by the *Terefah* Banquet eventually contributed to the bifurcation of American Judaism still evidenced today.

Lost in the haze of those who did—and did not—eat the clams, crabs, shrimp, and frogs was the fact that this transgressive meal did not transgress one particular biblical food taboo: pig never appeared on the menu.[33] The setting of this banquet is not incidental. As "America's leading antebellum pork processing center," Cincinnati rightfully earned the nickname "Porkopolis."[34] Therefore, the absence of pork in the city known to be "the very Hades of the swinish tribe" is worthy of note.[35] Though two years later, in 1885, the Reform movement would adopt the Pittsburgh Platform, which rejected "all such Mosaic and rabbinical laws as regulate diet," in general, early Reform Judaism did not violate this particular dietary prohibition.[36]

In fact, initial discussion about Reform Judaism's stance on non-kosher foods in the United States centered around two foods: pork and oysters, with the resulting general opinion that pork was prohibited but oysters were permitted. As a sea creature with neither fins nor scales, oysters fail the biblical kosher test.[37] They were, however, as Mark Kurlansky's popular book, *The Big Oyster: History on the Half Shell*, has demonstrated, tasty, affordable, popular, considered healthy, and, as an added bonus, an aphrodisiac.[38] These factors led Rabbi Isaac Meyer Wise, founder of Hebrew Union College, to refer to oysters as "ocean vegetables." Further, he argued, "There can be no doubt that the oyster shell is the same to all intents and purposes as the scales to the clean fish, protecting against certain gases in the water"; thus, he permitted their ingestion.[39] No such fanciful reinterpretation occurred for pork. Indeed, while Rabbi Wise would eat oysters, he would not eat pig—though that did not stop him from keeping two pigs on his farm to consume leftovers. (Playfully, he named one pig Kosher and the other pig Treyf.)[40] The Reform rabbi and American Jewish historian Lance Sussman aptly summarized this "widespread opinion" as indicative of a "'no pork, yes oyster' viewpoint."[41]

The embrace of oyster was on display three months after the *Terefah* Banquet, when two members of Hebrew Union College's first ordination class joined together to host a joint wedding party. Summarizing the menu, Rabbi Sussman notes, "A 'no-pork' dinner was served, including fried and scalloped oysters, lobster salad, and cold buffalo tongue, to mention but a few of the many courses provided."[42]

For a variety of reasons, Reform Judaism emended its official stance two years later at the convention that ultimately produced the Pittsburgh Platform. By rejecting "all such Mosaic and rabbinical laws as regulate diet," Reform Judaism now officially promulgated a "yes pork, *and* yes oyster" policy. But the delay suggests the tension between the legacy of more than two millennia of historical baggage embodied in the pig and Reform Judaism's interpretation of Judaism in the post-Enlightenment world of the modern United States. Leaders of Reform Judaism were willing to serve various biblically nonkosher foods at their rabbinic ordination ceremony and at various other public events, but it took further deliberation before they crossed the line represented by the pig. In a motif that appears numerous times over more than two thousand years, for a Jew to eat pig embodies the ultimate rejection of Jewish belief and practice. So it was not without serious deliberation that Reform Jews placed pork on their plate, alongside their oysters. For them, however, this represented not a complete rejection of Jewish belief and practice but, rather, a rejection of a particular model of Jewish belief and practice. After all, these culinary debates were unfolding at ordination ceremonies and weddings of Reform Jewish rabbis and at official conventions of the Reform Jewish movement and not at secular enclaves rejecting any notion of religious practice or belief.

In sum, by saying yes to pork, they were not saying no to Judaism; rather, they were saying no to one manifestation of Judaism and yes to another, new manifestation.

"EATING HAM FOR UNCLE SAM": JEWS, PIG, AND THE US MILITARY

Jews have fought on behalf of the United States in every major war in the country's history, from the American Revolution through Operation Enduring Freedom / Operation Iraqi Freedom. A major component of all warfare is logistics: assuring that personnel, troops, equipment, and supplies—including food—are readily available. Wars are won or lost based on which side is better with accounting. After all, if you run out of bullets with which to fill your soldiers' guns or food to fill their bellies, then you cannot fight.[43] Logistics in battle intersects with Jewish practice when an American Jewish soldier is confronted with a common dilemma: to eat the pig or to refrain.

We have documented evidence for this porcine dilemma at least as far back as the Civil War.[44] The Union soldier Nathan Cohen recalls being offered ham by a non-Jewish German woman whose home he was staying in during the war: "I hesitated at the ham, but

FIGURE 6.1. A "Hebrew Volunteer" during the Civil War sketches his perception of pig-centric military rations. *New-York Illustrated News*, September 9, 1861. Courtesy of Manuscripts and Special Collections, New York State Library, Albany, NY, used with permission.

my appetite got away with my religion and I cleaned up."[45] Those Jewish Union soldiers who could not eat pig without compunction faced difficulty, as rations tended to be pig-heavy. This dilemma is illustrated quite literally in figure 6.1, in which a "Hebrew volunteer" demonstrates how he views the quartermaster's food supplies: namely, as chock full of pig. Of course, many Jewish Union soldiers were willing to eat pig, with varying degrees of comfort.[46] Others might have been willing to do so but were squeamish about publicizing this information. For example, in 1862, Joseph C. Levi described his diet at Camp Belgar (outside Baltimore), which consisted of "bread, coffee and pork for breakfast, coffee, pork and bread for dinner, and pork, bread and coffee for tea"; he then equivocated, "perhaps as a good orthodox, the less I say on the subject the better." While he still considered himself to be an Orthodox Jew, Levi felt that he had no choice but to "adapt [him]self in this, as in other things, to existing circumstances."[47] Nathan Cohen, Joseph Levi, and so many of their fellow Jewish Union soldiers "regarded [their] daily pork ration as taking [their] (treyfe) medicine for Uncle Sam."[48]

Jews fought on the other side of the Civil War, as well. And during their battles, they also had to fight against the Evil Inclination tempting them to eat pig.[49] Painting a picture of one such wartime porcine encounter, Shari Rabin writes, "During the Civil War, Confederate soldier Edwin Kursheedt depleted the food supply that his sweetheart had given him, and was left with army rations of 'bacon + crackers.' Writing to her, perhaps on the same table where he ate, he confessed, 'I enjoyed the latter, but have not made up my mind to partake of the former.'"[50] Kursheedt lost perhaps the battle (against bacon) and definitely the war (against the Union).[51]

During World War I, the Jewish Welfare Board argued that, in order to strengthen morale, "men should [not] be furnished with food which is abhorrent on conscientious or religious grounds," though it acknowledged that "in the actual line of battle," Jewish law "declared for many hundreds of years that religious laws may be set aside in defense of one's country."[52] At that time in the country's military history, however, dietary (and other religious) accommodations were handled on a case-by-case basis. Writing about one such individual exception, the historian Ronit Stahl notes, "One sensitive officer notified Chaplain Louis Egelson (Jewish) that 'he would order the substitution of other food for me on the occasions when pork or ham was served. This he did voluntarily without the slightest intimation on my part.'"[53] This "sensitive officer" was the exception, not the rule, as the Jewish Welfare Board was not successful in its lobbying for kosher food for Jewish American soldiers fighting in World War I.

Writing about Jewish soldiers during World War II, the historian Deborah Dash Moore states, "Getting over the pig was the first hurdle that Jews confronted in their transformation into military men."⁵⁴ The role of the pig in embodying the transformation of American Jews to GI Jews is playfully asserted in a popular contemporary basketball cheer:

> Ikey, Mikey, Jakey, Sam
> We're the boys that eat no ham.⁵⁵
> We're all in the Army now
> So we're eating ham for Uncle Sam.⁵⁶

One such GI Jew was Artie Gorenstein, who in 1944 entered the Army after completing his first year at the Teacher's Institute at Yeshiva College. He wrote home to his parents that, on the first day of basic training, he had to decide whether he would be like Ikey, Mikey, Jakey, and Sam. Staring at his plate, which among other things featured "ham'n'eggs," he first ate everything but the pig.⁵⁷ He then reports, "Hesitated a minute and remembered the five long hours until lunch." Thus, he decided to eat the pig, which was "horrible": but "with the help of the coffee I swallowed it much as one would aspirin."⁵⁸ In doing so, he joined the band of brothers: GI Jews who ate ham for Uncle Sam.⁵⁹

Another GI Jew who confronted pork in the mess hall immediately upon enlisting in 1944 was Paul Steinfeld. He came prepared to eat ham for Uncle Sam. So when he was served a pork chop, he told himself, "You gotta learn to live with this stuff." It was only when a pad of butter was placed by a server on top of his pork chop that he had reached his limit.⁶⁰ "Steinfeld 'had trouble not vomiting.' He had girded himself to face down the pork chop. But the butter, as he politely put it, 'really violated my sensitivities.'"⁶¹

Of course, not all GI Jews ate pig. For example, Chaplain Aryeh Lev would often forgo the meal when rations included pig. As one of his colleagues, the Lutheran chaplain Herman Heuer, recorded more than once in his personal diary in 1945, "Poor Lev is taking a beating at meals."⁶² Whether over the rumbling of explosions in the heat of battle or the grumbling of an empty stomach at breakfast during basic training, American Jewish soldiers confronted the pig. "At that critical moment, Jewish G.I.s had to decide whether they wanted to stand out among their fellow soldiers by eating so differently or to swallow this most unkosher food as a sign of fellowship and patriotism."[63] It is telling that, yet again, the symbolic line in the sand—between inclusion and exclusion—was the pig and not other nonkosher foods.

"SHRIMP IS TREYF, BUT PORK IS ANTI-SEMITIC": THE PIG IN JEWISH AMERICAN LITERATURE

Jewish American authors grapple with their dual identity—American and Jewish (or Jewish and American?)—in a variety of literary forms and using a diverse range of metaphors and symbolism. By now, we should not be surprised to discover that the pig appears often, sometimes as a brief aside and other times as the star of the show.[64] There are far too many instances to cover completely in this section. This is especially true because pigs are sometimes mentioned briefly in passing, a terse aside that communicates much. For example, in the author (and scholar) Dara Horn's novel *In the Image*, the only mention of the pig comes in a scene where a character is flipping through cookbooks in a Jew's kitchen: "the chapter on pork obviously untouched."[65] This is contrasted with notes written by the Jewish amateur chef in other cookbook chapters, showing interaction with the recipes. This one line tells us much about the character's practice and identity. As I have argued throughout, exhaustively cataloguing all such mentions of the pig is not necessary; the main contours can be mapped out with representative examples.

The masterpiece (if I may be so bold) of reflection on Jews, pig, and identity in American Jewish literature is the humorist David Rakoff's essay "Dark Meat."[66] Besides the many clever jokes, this essay references the Pittsburg Platform, the *Terefah* Banquet, and even an 1890 Yom Kippur Ball in Philadelphia that, though it did not come to fruition, was to feature pig on its menu.[67] I cannot quote every joke from Rakoff's rumination on pig and American Jews (or, according to him, scientific name *"Hebreo baconophagis americansis"*).[68] In short, he speaks to what he deems a universal truth: "that between Jews and pork there is no greater love."[69] He then turns to a question that both frames his essay and explains why I have such abundant love for this work: "We are a questioning people. Why shouldn't something as beyond-the-pale forbidden like the eating of pork become normative among people who fully and proudly identify as Jewish?"[70] Rakoff proceeds to answer his own question. For him, eating pig is a transgressive act that simultaneously subverts and affirms Jewish identity. On the one hand, it is a break with the past: "Pork served as the ultimate demarcation from the hidebound small-mindedness and superstition of the shtetl."[71] He admits that taste plays a role in this, as well, noting, "Any revolution that includes a good carbonara is an awfully easy rampart to storm. It certainly helps that pork chops are so delicious."[72] On the other hand, the focus on the pig is a continuation of the past into the present: "Among the many tenets of *kashrut*, it is the proscription against pork that sticks in the mind, for both Jews and Gentiles. Shellfish is nowhere near as freighted as pork. Many a Dungeness devotee would never dream of touching swine. Rabbi X has a colleague, also a prominent and respected cleric, who explains himself with, 'I'll eat shrimp. No Jew ever died refusing to eat shrimp. But pork, never. Shrimp is *treyf*, but pork is anti-Semitic.'"[73]

This balancing of rupture and continuity is precisely what we have seen various Jews articulate when they choose both to eat pig *and* to mark that ingestive act as a practice that affirms their Jewish identity. Or, in Rakoff's own words,

> And yet, with all of this, I almost never feel more Jewish than in that moment just before I am about to eat pork. Allow me to horrify kosher readers when I draw a parallel between that instant and the custom of breaking a glass at a Jewish wedding, the perfect illustration

of the Jewish worldview.[74] In this sober evocation of the destruction of the Second Temple in 70 A.D. is a reminder that all joy houses the Newtonian capacity for an equal and opposite sorrow. As a Jew Who Eats Pork, extolling the boundless perfection of the baby pig at NY Noodletown at the corner of Bowery and Bayard necessarily requires a simultaneous split second of acknowledgement along with my blithe rhapsody that this is meat ineluctably bound up with my grim history. Otherwise, I'd just be a guy eating pork.[75]

Rakoff's final line drives the point home: sometimes a pig is just a pig. Without the long history covered in the previous pages of this volume, he would "just be a guy eating pork." But as "a Jew Who Eats Pork," the act of eating pig is a bite-sized moment of sorrow and joy, of shattering glass and putting the broken pieces back together, and of transgression and affirmation.[76]

Another instance of pig eating as acknowledgment of Jewish history and identity relates to a practice that I promised earlier to discuss further: eating Chinese food on Christmas. This practice made a brief appearance at a 2010 US Senate hearing for a Supreme Court nomination. When the future justice Elena Kagan was asked where she was on Christmas Day 2009, she replied, "You know, like all Jews, I was probably at a Chinese restaurant." Senator Charles Schumer (D-NY) then explained this tradition to his Senate colleagues.[77] We have already explored the historical associations between American Jews and Chinese food. All of those reasons combine with the sense of nonbelonging of being Jewish in a supposedly secular country in which Christmas is a federal holiday. To reestablish a sense of belonging, a common American Jewish practice developed of eating Chinese food on Christmas.[78] While some Jews order in, many go out to a restaurant to publicly celebrate with fellow Jews. For many Chinese restaurants, especially in areas with significant Jewish populations, Christmas is by far their busiest day of the year.[79] Many of these Jews choose to go to kosher Chinese restaurants; others go to nonkosher Chinese restaurants but do not eat meat; still others go to nonkosher Chinese restaurants and eat meat but do not eat pig; and finally, others go to nonkosher Chinese restaurants and eat pig. All of these Christmas diners are making a plate-based statement about their Jewish identity.

With this framing in place, we are now ready to explore "*Erev* Christmas [Christmas Eve]," a Yuletide parody written in 1993 by Bruce Marcus and Lori Factor.[80] The title itself begins the parody, as *erev* is Hebrew for "evening" and refers to the day before a Jewish holiday. This wordplay marks Christmas Eve as a legible Jewish holiday. Thus, it opens, "'Twas the night before Christmas, and we, being Jews, / my girlfriend and me—we had nothing to do."[81] The poem begins with a common Christmas-poem opening. But instead of a quiet house, we encounter two bored Jews. Unlike their Christian neighbors, these American Jews are left out of the fun. What to do? "And while all I could do was sit there and brood, / my gal saved the night and called out 'Chinese food!'"[82] With this inspiring (and, the reader is expected also to acknowledge, obvious) suggestion, they get ready and depart for Chinatown. Once there, we learn, "in search of a restaurant: 'Which one? Let's decide!' / We chose 'Hunan *Chazer*,' and venture inside."[83] Their choice of (fictional) dining establishment communicates much. Hunan is a region in China known for its spicy food. For this reason, "Hunan" commonly appears in many Chinese restaurant names. *Chazer*, as we know by now, means "pig." When they walk into "Hunan Pig," they are expressing their identity as American Jews who eat Chinese food on Christmas and who do not follow kosher laws. The titular "Pig" does double work here: simultaneously signifying an embracing of and transgression from Jewish practice. Ironically, the pig also identifies the Chinese restaurant as a Jewish space.

Dietary taboos are flung asunder as the poem details the smorgasbord of nonkosher dishes, including (but not limited to) squid, shrimp, and pig. After stuffing themselves, they are served fortune cookies. And what prophetic insight does the fortune cookie contain? "But my fortune was perfect; it summed up the mood / when it said: 'Pork is kosher, when it's in Chinese food.'"[84] This is not factually correct. But the spurious fortune conveys a truth for many American Jews. Eating Chinese food on Christmas is a widespread American Jewish practice. And while eating pig is a transgressive Jewish practice, eating pig at a Chinese restaurant on Christmas is understood, jokingly and somewhat seriously, as a Jewish practice. In this complex framing, it can be considered kosher. Even if it is not. Hopefully, by now this both makes sense and does not. Such is the riddle of Jews and the pig.

Pigs pop up in prose and in poetry, in historical fiction and nonfiction, in award-winning novels and in detective fiction, and in novels written in the US South, short stories in the East, and all other literary genres and points of the compass.[85] In short, you can probably find Jews and the pig in every section of the US bookstore. To prove that assertion, we will conclude by discussing the pig and Jewish identity in an unexpected genre: children's books.

Pigs are popular animals in children's literature, and not just those who are little and travel in teams of three. For example, there is a Peppa Pig Hanukkah book.[86] However, while Peppa and George learn about and celebrate the holiday with Granny and Grandpa Pig, the fact that they are *pigs* is not discussed in any way, shape, or form.[87] In contrast, starting with its title, *Baxter, the Pig Who Wanted to Be Kosher* places pigs and Jewish identity at the forefront of its plot.[88] The book opens at a bus stop in front of Max's Delicatessen (which is clearly marked as a kosher food establishment), where Baxter meets a Jew who tells him about the Sabbath (Shabbat). Baxter thinks about the Sabbath all week long and then returns to the bus stop on Friday to talk further with the man who introduced him to the Sabbath. While he cannot find that man, he finds another Jew at the bus stop. Baxter asks him if he knows anything about Sabbath dinner; and when the man answers in the affirmative, Baxter inquires, "Will you tell me how I can be part of it?" Baxter, of course, wants to partake as a diner, not as the dinner, but the Jew is confused and replies, "YOU? A pig? Part of Shabbat dinner? That's impossible!" It is only then that Baxter learns that he is not kosher. But the Jew leaves before answering Baxter's deceptively simple question, "What's kosher?" The reader knows what is not kosher: pig! But Baxter does not, so he goes shopping and discovers pickles marked "KOSHER." He spends the next week eating kosher pickles and drinking kosher pickle juice. He then returns to the same bus stop, where he finds a Jewish woman, and inquires, after he has consumed so many pickles, "Do you think *I'm* kosher yet?" Sadly, the answer is no. He then goes to the store and spends the week eating kosher challah (a bread consumed on the Sabbath and holidays). On Friday, he returns to the bus stop and meets the old man who first introduced him to the Sabbath. Baxter greets him and says, "I'm glad you're here! I've learned so much—all about pickles and challah! What do you think? Am I kosher yet?" The man is rightly surprised. Why would a pig want to be kosher? Anyway, it is not possible. "But a pig is a pig is a pig. It's too bad you aren't a cow. *Cows* are kosher!" Baxter spends the next week pretending he is a cow. He returns to the bus stop, and finding no one, he feels dejected. But then along comes Rabbi Rosen. She asks sad Baxter if she could help him.[89] "Oh I only wish you could!" laments Baxter, "But I fear it's hopeless. 'A pig is a pig is a pig.' I'll *never* be kosher." Rabbi Rosen replies in surprise, "Why on earth would you want to be kosher?" Baxter's answer summarizes the dramatic irony of this story: "I want to be kosher . . . so that I can be part of Shabbat dinner." Again, Baxter desires to be the diner, not the dinner, but the other characters think he is asking the opposite. Rabbi Rosen clarifies the matter when she asks him, "But . . . why would you want to be eaten?" And with that, Baxter is finally able to clarify, stating, "Eaten?! Me?" Baxter looked up sharply. "Who said anything about getting eaten? I want to see the candles gleam and glow and dance. I long to lift my sweetest voice in song! Isn't that what Shabbat dinner is all about?" Rabbi Rosen laughs, as she finally gets the joke that we, the readers, have known all along: Baxter wants to be "kosher" as in Jewish, not be "kosher" as in served for a Sabbath meal. The story has a happy ending, but what matters to us is that this children's book is one extended joke about pigs and Jewish identity. It is funny that a pig wants to be kosher. And while he cannot be kosher as in being served on the Sabbath table, he *can* be kosher as in sitting around the Sabbath table. If Baxter were a camel, a rock badger, or a hare, the joke would not be as funny. The fact that it is a *pig* who wants to be kosher is what gets the most laughs.

"THE FOLLOWING YOM KIPPUR, I HAD BACON": EATING PIG OFF THE PATH

While we have just explored the pig in modern US literature by and about Jews, there is an interesting subset of porcine literature that is worthy of note: namely, the role that the pig plays in Jewish memoirs. In particular, I focus on a specific genre of memoir: autobiographies of Jews born Orthodox (especially ultra-Orthodox) who make the often painful choice to break from the religious, cultural, and social world of their upbringing and to venture out into secular society.[90] The popularity of such works suggests a growing fascination by both Jews and non-Jews with the choices made by those who leave, and those who remain within, these insular communities.[91]

Colloquially, the process of leaving the Orthodox world is referred to as going "off the *derekh*" (or, for short, OTD). *Derekh* means "path" or "way" in Hebrew and refers to the path on which one walks in accordance with normative rabbinic law (*halakhah*, in Hebrew, a term that also refers to walking on the proper legal path). Those who go OTD have decided with full knowledge and intention to take the path not taken.[92] And, as Robert Frost famously told us, that has made all the difference.

An example that is simultaneously typical and atypical of the genre of OTD memoirs is Abby Chava Stein's *Becoming Eve: My Journey from Ultra-Orthodox Rabbi to Transgender Woman*.[93] Assigned male at birth, Abby grew up in an ultra-Orthodox, Hasidic family. She struggled to conform to rigid gender binaries in her community, to the point of receiving ordination in the exclusively male rabbinate, marrying a Hasidic woman, and conceiving a child. However, this life took an enormous toll on her physical, emotional, and spiritual well-being. Eventually, Abby leaves her community and most of her family behind, to build a new sense of community, faith, and identity.

The pig plays a key part in her first steps off the *derekh*. As she remembers,

> The Saturday after that was the first time I used my phone on Shabbos [the Sabbath], breaking the prohibition against using electricity on the day of rest.
>
> The next fast day—the Fast Day of Esther [right before the Jewish holiday of Purim]—I ate a tuna bagel.
>
> The following Yom Kippur, I had bacon.
>
> I'd begun a two-year process in which I first rejected everything Jewish and then later found my way back, on my own terms. I found my gender identity in my own way, too.
>
> Today I am proudly Jewish, and proudly transgender.[94]

While Abby's tale is atypical in its focus on transgender identity, she conforms to the OTD memoir genre in using ingestion of the pig to signal her departing from the path. Notice that she first breaks the Sabbath rules against using electricity and then eats on a fast day. However, (a) she eats a kosher meal, and (b) the fast day is one of the minor fasts. It is not until Yom Kippur—the Day of Atonement and the most major fast day on the Jewish calendar—that she describes herself as eating bacon. To eat bacon on Yom Kippur is the epitome of breaking from tradition.[95] The theme of eating pig on Yom Kippur as a statement of Jewish transgression is one that we have encountered before and transcends this genre. It is a practice that simultaneously expresses rejection of Judaism while concomitantly reinforcing a Jewish identity. After all, eating pig on any other day just does not have the same heretical zing; yet, marking Yom Kippur as the holiest day of porcine transgression brings one closer to, rather than farther from, a Jewish identity.

OTD memoirists regularly reference their fascination and eventual first contact with the pig in all its culinary forms. I would argue that it has fast become one of the required elements of this genre: author's back story, emerging doubts, first taste of the pig, eventual break with their community, and then reconciliation of their new identity. Memoirists encounter the pig in haute cuisine and in fast food establishments, but they always encounter the pig.

Examples of both experiences come from memoirs of two authors raised in Hasidic families in and around New York. Deborah Feldman's first culinary encounter with the pig came in a fancy Manhattan restaurant, where her cultured (and non-Jewish) friend Polly orders her prosciutto.[96] After initially becoming nauseated at the thought of eating the pig, Feldman remarks,

> It's funny, I say to Polly; most Hasids who go off the path just go to McDonald's for a burger, but I'm eating gourmet *treif* [nonkosher] cuisine. "That's how you do it, though," she says. "Even when you break the rules, you do it with pizzazz."[97]

Shortly after, Feldman—whose story is dramatically reimagined in a Netflix miniseries—declares, "I don't want to be a Hasid anymore."[98] Feldman's encounter with Italian ham symbolizes her readiness to break from tradition.

Shalom Auslander's first culinary encounter with the pig occurs in a much more lowbrow dining establishment: the Snack Shack at the town pool in Ramapo, New Jersey. At the pool, a hungry Auslander watches as his non-Jewish friend Vinnie consumes a pork hot dog:

> Vinnie stood beside me, piling his pig dog high with sauerkraut and thin-cut pickles. I stared, openmouthed, as he flipped his hair back, cleared a path to his mouth, and took a bite. It was as if he'd never even heard of Leviticus 11:7.

>   —What's the matter, kid? asked Vinnie.—Never seen a dude eat a dog before?
>
>   It was a pig I'd never seen a dude eat before.⁹⁹

Screwing up his courage, Auslander's choice of pig meat is not fancy Italian prosciutto but an ordinary Slim Jim:

> This was what it was like to be one of them—the people who drove by us as we walked to synagogue on Saturday, the people who watched TV on Friday night, the people who could eat sticks of meat, who lived with Ramapo-pool-type freedom every blessed day of their un-Chosen lives. I closed my eyes, took a deep breath, and shoved as much of the Slim Jim into my mouth as I could, coiling it up inside my mouth like a pig-flavored garden hose, forcing the last few reddish brown inches with the tips of my impure, trembling fingers as I tried in vain to squeeze my lips shut.¹⁰⁰

On that fateful day at the Ramapo pool, Auslander fails to keep his lips shut and ends up regurgitating his hastily consumed first bites of the pig. But that does not stop him from continuing to frequent the Snack Shack, where he becomes a regular purchaser of Slim Jims.¹⁰¹

What these and the growing number of OTD memoirs teach us is that—in yet another context—ingestion of, or abstention from, the pig indexes Jewish identity. As Reva Mann stared into the mirror to gaze at her transforming identity, she writes, "I would see myself, hot bacon and egg sandwich in hand, and realize just how far away from home I had strayed."¹⁰² While the path might be pig-free, once one wanders off the *derekh*, the pig is readily available. The connection between the pig and departing from the path is so tangible that, when four unrelated Orthodox persons in New York City in the early 1990s were found to have recurrent seizures and brain lesions caused by the pork tapeworm *Taenia solium*, researchers immediately went to work on this medical mystery. After thorough investigation, infectious-disease experts concluded that the source of infection was not the secret ingestion of pig by Orthodox persons; rather, the source of the infection was traced to two domestic employees who, having recently traveled from Latin American countries where the pork tapeworm is endemic, worked in the homes of these Orthodox Jews. But given the strong association between eating pig and departing the path, this study was deemed worthy of publication in the prominent medical journal the *New England Journal of Medicine*.[103]

In forms ranging from bacon to prosciutto and even to Slim Jims (and beyond), OTD memoirs feature the pig as symbolic of key moments of transgression.[104] To decide to eat the pig is to cross a line, a line that demarcates the outer boundary of the path. It is for this reason that the pig is a key element of OTD memoirs.

"DYNAMITE HAM": JEWS AND THE PIG IN AMERICAN POPULAR CULTURE

Trotting out the pig is a common shtick in humorous moments involving Jews in American popular culture. In many of these instances, the pig is used to index Jewish identity and to contrast it with Christian (pig-eating) identity. For example, the pig is often served as a meal in television and movie scenes that feature Jewish and non-Jewish interdating. In the 1972 pilot episode of the television sitcom *Bridget Loves Bernie*, for instance, we learn of the blossoming love between Bernie Steinberg and Bridget Theresa Mary Colleen Fitzgerald. Their full names are chosen to clearly communicate their respective Jewish and Catholic identities, which is why—upon sharing them with each other—they declare in unison, "I think we have a problem." They are in love already before they realize that their marriage would be an intermarriage. After Bridget meets Bernie's family (which owns a Jewish delicatessen and catering service) over an awkward family meal, Bernie is introduced to Bridget's Catholic family. Her family was not expecting a Jew, and in an attempt to mitigate (or highlight?) the awkwardness of this unexpected guest, they serve everyone else at the table the planned ham dinner but offer Bernie salami instead.[105] Obviously, who gets to eat pig—and who does not—communicates who is not, and who is, a Jew at the table. While we never discover whether Bernie would actually eat ham, Bernie and Bridget end up eloping. When Bridget's mother learns that her daughter has disappeared (but before discovering the marriage), she laments, "Oh, it's all my fault! I served ham and drove her out of the house!"[106]

The *porcus classicus* of interdating pig dining scenes appeared five years later. In Woody Allen's 1977 film *Annie Hall*, the Jewish comedian Alvy Singer dates the eponymous (and decidedly not Jewish) Annie Hall. When Alvy visits Annie's family in Chippewa Falls, Wisconsin, for an Easter dinner, we are not surprised to find ham on the table. After all, it is Easter. But the fact that it is both Easter *and* there is Easter ham simultaneously serves to highlight both Alvy's Jewish identity and Annie's non-Jewish identity. Otherwise-innocuous statements therefore take on deeper levels of signification. Thus, when Annie's mother compliments Grammy on her cooking by stating, "It's a nice ham this year, Mom," we are meant to understand it differently than when Alvy declares, "It's dynamite ham." Grammy—whom Alvy asserts "is a classic Jew hater"—seems displeased with Alvy's remark because it reminds her of his Jewish identity. Though the scene continues to mark their contrasting Jewish/non-Jewish identities in other ways, the pig at the beginning makes all the difference.[107]

The cinematic trope of pig and Jewish identity at the table is so well known that it can make an appearance even when the diners are neither Jewish nor dating. In Quentin Tarantino's 1994 Academy Award–winning film *Pulp Fiction*, two hitmen are eating breakfast at a diner when the following exchange occurs:

> **VINCENT:** Want some bacon?
>
> **JULES:** No man, I don't eat pork.
>
> **VINCENT:** Are you Jewish?

JULES: Nah, I ain't Jewish. I just don't dig on swine, that's all.
VINCENT: Why not?
JULES: Pigs are filthy animals. I don't eat filthy animals.
VINCENT: Bacon tastes good. Pork chops taste good.

When Vincent, played by the white actor John Travolta, discovers that Jules, portrayed by the African American actor Samuel L. Jackson, refrains from ingesting pig, he immediately inquires whether Jules is Jewish. As an African American, Jules is (statistically speaking) far more likely to be Muslim than Jewish.[108] Since both Muslims and Jews do not eat pig, we need to ask why Vincent suspects that Jules's dietary practice derives from his adherence to Judaism and not Islam. Perhaps Jules's habit of quoting Ezekiel 25:17, a pseudo-biblical passage, prior to executing someone influences Vincent's question. However, I would argue that this joke relies on the historical associations between pig and Jewish identity. Muslims may not eat pig, but it is funnier to presume that the patron who profanes the pig is a Jew. Further, given Tarantino's penchant for cinematic intertexts, the Jew-who-does-not-eat-pig dining scene makes this breakfast between fellow assassins both familiar and foreign, simultaneously conforming to and subverting the trope.

Jews and pigs appear in a variety of other contexts and genres, on both the big and small screen.[109] Sometimes the pig is not eaten but is an extended metaphor, as is the case in *To Dust* (2018). In this film, a Hasidic Jew named Shmuel is distraught over the death of his young wife. Trying to understand what happens to her body after her burial, Shmuel befriends a community college professor (played by Matthew Broderick). Shmuel ends up buying a dead pig from the backdoor of a Chinese restaurant and then stealing a live pig from a pig farm in order to conduct a "scientific" experiment to learn about body decomposition. While Jewish identity is at the forefront of this film (e.g., when Shmuel meets an African American security guard, she, after hearing his story, declares, "Jesus loves you"), there is never any hint that Shmuel wants to eat or interact with the pig in any manner other than to understand the physical decay of his wife's body. All of his pig-related sins are nonculinary. In this manner, *To Dust* is not of the same genre of *Leon the Pig Farmer*. Instead, *To Dust* navigates mourning and loss, both poignantly and humorously, by using the pig as a compass to guide Shmuel (and the audience) through grief. Without ever appearing on his plate, the pig marks Shmuel's Jewish identity.

In the reality television show *Hogan Knows Best*, we also find a reference to Jewish identity by means of the pig. In a 2006 episode titled "Koshermania," the former professional wrestling superstar Hulk Hogan and his family have just moved to a new neighborhood in Florida, which they discover has a large observant Jewish population.[110] As they learn more about their neighbors and about Jewish practice in general, the audience comes to find out that the Hogan family does not know the meaning of the term "kosher" (though Hulk Hogan continuously asserts that it means "pickles"). At one point, Hulk's son, Nick Hogan, declares, "'Kosher' means 'Jewish.'" Hulk responds, "'Kosher' means 'Jewish?' . . . Like 'sausage' means 'Italian'?" Kosher signifies Jewish identity, and sausage signifies Italian identity; and they are mutually exclusive. This statement also suggests that—as one presumes about reality shows—the cast knows more about the situation than they are letting on. Hulk and Nick Hogan eventually learn about kosher rules, but not before more hilarity ensues.

Beyond television and movies, where Jews and the pig appear both explicitly and tacitly, we also find numerous references to the pig in Jewish identity in other forms of popular culture.[111] One of my favorite examples comes from the satirical newspaper *The Onion*. An article published on September 30, 1998, boldly declares in its title, "Jewish Elders Lift 6,000-Year Ham Ban."[112] The story claims that the World Rabbinical Council voted to end the Jewish pig prohibition. In reality, this vote never happened, and this council does not exist. But the article and the newspaper in which it appears are written to make the audience laugh and not to report actual facts. The article details the reactions of various Orthodox Jews who, after a lifetime (and generations) of abstention, can now go hog wild eating the pig. The reason this entire premise works is because one cannot image a bunch of Orthodox Jews remaining faithful *and* faithfully eating the pig. Once again, we should reflect on how much less funny the joke would be if the headline were to read, "Jewish Elders Lift 6,000 Year Camel Ban."

"ONCE IN A WHILE, I ALSO ENJOY A HAM SANDWICH": SITUATIONAL KASHRUT, KOSHER STYLE, AND THE PIG IN THE UNITED STATES

As the old joke goes, a Jew immigrating to the United States from Europe was stopped by a US Customs official. Looking through his luggage, the official inquired why the man had five sets of gold teeth. The Jew explained that he was an observant Jew who would not eat milk with meat; therefore, he needed one set of gold teeth for when he ate a dairy meal and another set for when he ate a meat meal. Puzzled, the customs official replied that that explained why he would have two sets, not five. The Jew then added that two additional sets were required for Passover, when he could not eat leaven and therefore needed an additional dairy and meat set of gold teeth, which could not be used at any other time of the year. Still puzzled, the customs official replied that that explained why he would have four sets, not five. Sheepishly, the Jew then confided, "True, but every once in a while, I also enjoy a ham sandwich."[113]

This joke exemplifies the concept of "situational kashrut," discussed earlier.[114] While that is the term used by Hasia Diner to refer to Jews who observe kosher laws when possible but are willing to eat nonkosher foods in certain contexts, other scholars and writers refer to the same phenomenon using a variety of other similar terms, including "selectively treyf," "selective kashrut," and so on.[115] This is what Jewish peddlers on the frontier often practiced; it is the practice of Reform Jews who ate oysters but not pig; it is also what many American Jews who ventured into Chinese restaurants practiced. Another manifestation of this phenomenon is "kosher style," wherein certain elements of kosher practice are followed but not others. Perhaps meat and milk are not mixed, but the meat is not certified kosher. Perhaps the food is not kosher but is considered ethnically or generically "Jewish" (the delicatessen is the most often cited exemplar).[116] Or, often, the element that makes it "kosher style" is the absence of pig. Writing about this phenomenon, the historian Jenna Weissman-Joselit observes, "The gastronomic equivalent of ethnicity, 'kosher-style' enabled its adherents to practice kashruth 'without pain or effort' by disentangling the food from the traditional restrictions governing its use, a Judaized version of having your cake and eating it too."[117]

In many ways, these culinary conceptions are akin to the modern culinary category of "flexitarian"—that is, one who is mostly vegetarian but who will eat some meat from time to time. Just like kosher style, the definition of flexitarian depends on who is practicing it. Whatever we term it—situationally kosher, kosher style, and so on—these culinary practices are about navigating the world, between tradition and innovation. For some Jews, eating a bagel is a Jewish practice of nostalgia.[118] For others, they refuse to eat nonkosher food due to their own religious practice.[119] And in between, there is a wide variety of American Jews. As usual, the pig plays an outsized role in the conversation. For many kosher-style diners and dining establishments, the pig is a leap too far, and hence, they might serve nonkosher meat but not the pig. Other American Jews are willing to eat the pig, provided it is in certain cuisines (e.g., Chinese food) or locations (e.g., outside the home).[120] For still others, they might like foods that they perceive to be ethnically Jewish, but the allure of the pig is a siren call of symbolic transgression—and they are seeking that very culinary transgression. These are the American Jews who hunger for the "culinary apostasy" of the bacon-wrapped *matzah* ball (a dish actually available on some menus).[121] In an apt comparison, the journalist Sue Fishkoff asserts that, for this group of

Jewish diners, "pork is to Jews like sex is to Catholics—a guilty pleasure that provokes sheepish grins and whispered giggles."[122] Even when venturing far beyond tradition, one tradition tends to stick around longer than others: the tradition of not eating pig (even if, ironically, they *are* eating it in order to symbolize their own complex Jewish identity).

"PORK TOUCHED KOUFAX'S PITCHING HAND": CONCLUSIONS

On October 6, 1965, Sandy Koufax refused to pitch in Game 1 of the World Series. Despite the importance of the championship series, Koufax—the greatest left-handed pitcher in Major League Baseball history—decided not to take the mound for the Brooklyn Dodgers because the game fell on Yom Kippur. Many Jews fast on Yom Kippur, the Day of Atonement; some do not; some even eat pig on that day, as we have seen before on several occasions. In a protest that is equally famous and mythologized in American Jewish history, Sandy Koufax asserted his Jewish identity by benching himself on Yom Kippur.[123] While this story has a happy ending (for the Dodgers at least, as they eventually won the 1965 World Series against the Minnesota Twins), there is a less-famous Koufax controversy that brings together many themes discussed earlier: "Four decades after the fact, two best-selling Jewish authors, Scott Turow and Mitch Albom, engaged in a heated polemic about the significance of a ham sandwich Koufax allegedly was seen eating in the hotel elevator in Minnesota that week. Albom's friend, a rabbi's son still a young man in 1965, was apparently still devastated at having seen pork touch Koufax's pitching hand. Turow responded indignantly: 'Who's to say what is Jewish enough? Who's to say what a Jew is?'"[124] Does one sandwich undermine Koufax's enduring legacy as a symbol for American Jewish identity? Does it matter that the pig that God prohibited touched the pitching hand that God gave Koufax? The answers are less important than the questions. By now, we are unsurprised to see a ham sandwich generate enduring debate about Jewish identity.

For over 275 years, we have documented history of interactions between Jews and the pig in the United States.[125] Indeed, Jews negotiated the pig in America even before the founding of the country in 1776. In these myriad moments, Jews expressed their evolving identities as Jewish Americans, or American Jews. Porcine metaphors proved so popular that they were deployed even when the pig was otherwise absent. For example, during the 1902 kosher meat riots in the Lower East Side of Manhattan—which, as one might surmise, refers to an incident in which Jews (especially women) rioted over the price of kosher meat—a local newspaper, commenting on how scarce kosher meat was during the riots, declared that it "is likely to be as scarce around Essex Street as ham sandwiches."[126] They also appear when the limits of "Jewish" identity are stretched, such as in recent debates about inmates in US prisons who want a kosher diet for reasons that may (or more often may not) have to do with a sincerely held belief in Judaism. In these debates, the pig is just one piece of the complex puzzle, but it is an important piece nonetheless.[127]

Concluding the final leg of our porcine journey, we reflect on what Walter Sobchak, a character in the Coen brothers' 1998 movie *The Big Lebowski*, refers to as "three thousand years of beautiful tradition from Moses to Sandy Koufax." While Moses would be surprised to hear about the pig's long and strange trip, Sandy Koufax would probably be less so. After all, by the time Koufax arrived on the scene, the pig packed more of a punch than the lefty's famed fastball. That being said, as we shall see in our story's conclusion, the pig has at least one more curveball to throw.

CONCLUSION

"Thank You Very Much. I Am a 🐷":
Arriving at the Tail of Our Tale

After tracing the long and winding path of the pig across space and time, we should not be surprised when our path takes yet another unexpected twist; or, to continue the metaphor that concluded chapter 6, to discover another porcine curveball even after we step away from Sandy Koufax's God-given-and-possibly-pork-touching left hand. And that is just what we encounter in a recent kosher controversy.

Following the company's success with various plant-based, nonmeat "meat" products, in 2021, Impossible Foods released a new vegetarian product: Impossible Pork. Given that the ingredients were basically the same as its previous plant-based products, the company was surprised when neither its halal nor its kosher certification agencies would certify Impossible Pork. While Impossible Beef and other vegetarian products including Impossible Sausage remained certified as halal and kosher, it proved impossible to certify Impossible Pork. Why? "'The Impossible Pork, we didn't give an "OU" [kosher certification] to it, not because it wasn't kosher per se,' said Rabbi Menachem Genack, the CEO of the Orthodox Union's kosher division. 'It may indeed be completely in terms of its ingredients: If it's completely plant-derived, it's kosher. Just in terms of sensitivities to the consumer . . . it didn't get it.'"[1] Reading between the lines, we see that, by Rabbi Genack's own admission, Impossible Pork is technically kosher. Its ingredients and method of preparation all accord with the modern kosher standards of the Orthodox Union. But it does not pass the kosher smell test.

Taken in isolation, this legal decision does not make sense. First of all, other products that also would fail the kosher smell test remain certified as kosher, from Impossible Sausage to Bacon Bits.[2] Second, there is an almost-one-hundred-year history of pork-substitute products being certified as kosher in the United States. For example, in the 1930s, "beef frye" was all the rage. Beef frye was a product designed to emulate bacon from snout to tail—that is, from its look to its taste and smell. When it arrived on the scene, kosher consumers would stand outside the windows of delicatessens to watch the novel kosher product being sliced. Commenting on this culinary, cultural, and religious phenomenon, the historian Jenna Weissman Joselit states, "Ultimately, beef frye's value to the kosher consumer was as much symbolic as gustatory; it, too, held out the very real and tantalizing possibility that the observance of kashruth posed no barrier to participation in the wider world, at least in a culinary sense. After all, even kosher Jews could now eat bacon!"[3] As food technology continued to advance, fake pig products were routinely certified as kosher—provided that their ingredients and method of preparation accorded with modern kosher standards.[4] The desire for the American Jewish consumer to participate in American society more broadly proved key in this development. As the historian Jeffrey Gurock argues in regard to another famous fake-pig-but-still-certified-as-kosher product,

> Even items that looked patently treif—such as "bacon bits" made from soybean—graced the tables of the pious. Cynics might wonder where and how these punctilious Jews acquired a taste for that particular nontraditional addition to a tossed salad. Perhaps that supermarket selection gained its popularity from its hosts' and hostesses' desires to provide gentile or unkosher Jewish friends or business associates with tastes to which they were accustomed. The tradition of culinary substitution to help aspiring observant Jews feel comfortable inviting

others into their homes without the fear of committing the "sin" of appearing uncultured has its own long and distinguished history.[5]

Bacon bits, beef frye, and other similar kosher fake pig products allow American Jews to simultaneously perform their dual identities: as both observant Jews and Americans. Modern-day American Jews can look to their parents, grandparents, great-grandparents, and perhaps even great-great-grandparents and find them eating fake pig products certified as kosher in the United States.

So what's the beef with Impossible Pork? It would seem that the stumbling block for this product, which looks and tastes so much like the pig, is the unambiguous word "pork." Declaring "pork" kosher just did not feel right—even though it is not really pork. This feels a bit like another instance of "safe treyf," in that products labeled "bacon" or "sausage" or "frye" can pass the kosher smell test, but "pork" cannot.[6] Rabbi Genack himself admits that this is the case: "'We've been inculcated for millennia' against eating pigs, Genack added. 'This is something that's been verboten and that we don't eat. It takes time for the person to absorb that this is synthetic, (that) it's not real pig.'"[7] Unlike fake "bacon" or fake "crab"—products routinely certified as kosher—fake "pork" is beyond the pale. To truly understand this perplexing ruling, we need to contextualize it within the more-than-three-thousand-year history of Jews and the pig. It is only then that we understand, for some Jews, the impossibility of Impossible Pork.

DOES THE PIG STAND ALONE?

The time has come to answer a question that vexes any historical inquiry: Is this case study exceptional? Thus, we must ask, Is the story of Jews and the pig unique? Having spent almost two decades pondering this question, I have reached the conclusion that the short answer to this question is yes. But it is worth taking a moment to give a slightly longer answer.

At first blush, one could argue that we could look at other objects or practices and their relationship to Jews and Judaism across a similar geographical and temporal span and cover much of the same territory. We could even do so with food as the object of study. For example, I myself wrote a short essay titled "A Brief History of Jews and Garlic," which would fit this bill.[8] Yet, while this might be so in the abstract, when we drill down to the details, we would discover that the sheer volume of data pales in comparison to that regarding the pig. Focusing on the garlic example, the essay in question was ten pages long. Though it certainly could have been longer, it would never approach book length. But, to play on the wording of Ecclesiastes 12:12, the conversation about pigs is without limit![9] As the preceding pages have demonstrated, there is more than sufficient material on Jews and the pig to write a book.

Even more so than the volume of relevant historical data is the fact that the pig has been singled out for over two millennia. During this time, both Jews and non-Jews have continued to look toward the pig to discuss Jewish and non-Jewish identity. These metaphors both include and extend beyond mere consumption. As we have seen, the pig has embodied enemies of the Jews (e.g., Rome) and Christian vices, for example.[10] In this manner, the pig accords with a famous mishnaic statement by Ben Bag Bag: "Turn it over, and turn it over [again], for all is in it."[11] While that sage was referring to Torah, the same could be said for the pig. Everyone who has turned to the pig has found both embodied and metaphorical expressions of Jewish and non-Jewish identity therein. There is a reason that the Nobel-laureate Yiddish author Isaac Bashevis Singer often used the pig (and not the camel) as part of a cheeky signature. Thus, when we saw earlier that he wrote the Yiddish poet Melech Ravitch a postcard and signed off with the phrase "Thank you very much. I am a 🐖," Singer's scribble was but one more example of the singularity of the pig (see figure 5.4).[12] Others may appear on the stage, but the pig hogs the spotlight.

As we have seen, time and again, both Jews and non-Jews have found the pig to be exceptionally useful to support their larger arguments about Jewish and/or non-Jewish identity and practice. This has been the case whether we are in the first or the twenty-first century, whether we are in England or its former colonies, whether the authors are pious or irreverent Jews. So is the story of Jews and the pig unique? I contend that the answer is yes and has been so for more than two millennia. As I argued early on, starting in the Second Temple Period, there began to be something special about the pig. This book has told the story of how the pig came to mean so much and, ultimately, how it developed into an exceptional historical case study in Jewish and non-Jewish identity. While there are many pretenders to the throne, the pig does indeed stand alone.

"BLOT OUT IMAGES OF GIRLS AND PIGS": THE JEW AS OTHER AND THE OTHER WHITE MEAT

This book has argued that both Jews and non-Jews have turned to the pig to discuss and set the boundaries of both Jewish and non-Jewish identity for over two millennia. Given the exceptionality of our case study, though this chapter concludes our conversation, it by no means concludes the story. Jews and pigs continue to pop up; indeed, they even make headlines. For example, in a highly publicized September 2022 front-page story in the *New York Times* about public funding and Hasidic schools in New York, one might be surprised to find the pig—that is, unless you have read this book.[13] And where does the pig appear in this story? Amid discussion of censorship of learning materials: "Secular textbooks [in Hasidic boys' schools] are either censored with black marker to blot out images of girls and pigs and words like 'library' and 'college,' or specially printed to omit such content altogether."[14] As early as the Classical Rabbinic Period, we have seen rabbinic censoring of the word "pig," so this practice has a long history. And the fact that girls and women are also censored fits with various gendered aspects of our story discussed throughout, from the Roman women with whom Rabbi Aqiba refuses to interact to the Pig Faced Lady and beyond. Thus, while the front-page story may contain many revelations about modern public funding for religious education in the United States, the fact that Jews would censor images of the pig is not really news. For Hasidic Jews who wish to adhere to what they perceive to be Jewish tradition, censoring the pig is certainly a venerable and well-attested tradition.[15]

While many Jews continue to avoid the pig (even to the point of censorship), others continue to embrace the pig as a means to transgress and, in so doing, to express a new conception of Jewish identity. Going forward, I expect these practices to endure, with the pig being used to imagine Judaism and Jewishness in a variety of novel ways. Concomitantly, I expect some Jews and Jewish communities to respond to these practices with condemnation, ranging from mild rebukes to vitriol and even violence. And while this subject is not just academic, it is also academic. For example, the archaeologist Max Price points out that another scholar uses his scholarship to critique those Jews who have advocated eating pig:

> But beneath the thin veneer of decolonialist rhetoric, Schorsch's argument smacks of a reactionary attack intended to brand those who eat and enjoy pork—and, worse, show no shame in the process—as transgressors. Dolled up in academic garb and disguised as an appeal to the liberal-minded, it is simply another rehashing of the argument that Jews who eat pork are sellouts to the majority, traitors ingesting the identity of the Hellenistic/Roman/Christian/Western "other." Those who make such arguments defy the anthropological reality of cultural hybridization. They arrogantly see themselves as the gatekeepers of identity, judges of who is and who is not a "real" Jew or Muslim.[16]

Rather than apologize for or critique these practices, I have sought to explain them. In my view, these Jews should be understood as transgressing as a means of expressing; their rejection is a form of acceptance, and hence, it is a key part of the conversation. This type of transgression that ultimately reinforces one's identity, too, has a venerable history, and I see no reason to expect it to disappear from the narrative as the saga continues.

The pig will continue to play a significant role in the conversation about Self and Other. In a fortuitous coincidence, the National Pork Producers Council's famous advertising slogan for pork is apt: "Pork—the Other White Meat."[17] Whether one is a partaker or an abstainer, pig is indeed the Other white meat. Pigs will continue to appear in conversations about Jews, Judaism, Jewish identity, and the rhetoric, beliefs, and practices of others in relation to Jews, Judaism, and Jewish identity. If history has taught us anything, it is that we should expect the presence or absence of pig from one's diet to be laden with meaning for many years to come—both in This World and in The World to Come (where, of course, pig will be kosher).

ACKNOWLEDGMENTS

THE fact that I have been working on this project for nearly twenty years means that I have a lot of people to thank for help along the way; it also means that there is a high degree of likelihood that I will forget to thank someone who is deserving of acknowledgment. For those I neglect to mention, I apologize.

Through the years, I have been fortunate to present various parts of this book's argument at several conferences and universities. My very first pig talk was at a graduate student conference at Yale University in 2005; and thanks to an invitation by Gabe Rosenberg, I returned to Yale again in 2015 to give a talk at the wonderful Agrarian Studies conference "Pig Out: Hogs and Humans in Global and Historical Context." Pigs were the subject of my job talk in 2008 at the University of Wisconsin–Madison, and I have spoken about them on several other occasions at the university since. Pigs have played main or supporting roles in talks I have given at the annual conference of the Society of Biblical Literature. Recently, I have given pig talks at the University of California–Berkeley (thanks to Duncan MacRae) and the University of South Carolina (thanks to Erin Roberts and John Mandsager).

I wish to acknowledge the many librarians and archivists who have made this research possible. First and foremost, I must thank the librarians at the University of Wisconsin–Madison, who are too often anonymous engines behind the well-oiled machine that is Interlibrary Loan. No matter how esoteric, oddball, or based on fragmentary information my request, they searched the four corners of the world and found my pig references. I simply could not do my job without their amazing skills. In addition, I thank Dana Herman, Gary P. Zola, and Joe Weber at the Jacob Rader Marcus Center of the American Jewish Archives; Elizabeth Jakubowski, senior librarian at the Manuscripts and Special Collections unit of the New York State Library; Marcus Mordecai Schwartz and Havva Zellner at the Library of the Jewish Theological Seminary of America; Adam Corsini at the Jewish Museum London; and all of the phenomenal librarians and archivists at the various archives where I sought image permissions, additional information, or even just leads on the pigs I was chasing down.

I am fortunate to have a group of colleagues who not only tolerate my love of pigs but also actually listen to me when I talk about them. I wish to acknowledge Febe Armanios, Beth Berkowitz, Sarah Bond, Catherine Bonesho, Jonathan Brumberg-Kraus, Nathanial DesRosiers, Boğaç Ergene, David Freidenreich, Gregg Gardner, Rachel Harris, Ross Kraemer, Steven Larson, Kevin McGinnis, Steve Nadler, Michael Naparstek, Saul Olyan, Nora Rubel, Michael Satlow, Michal Bar-Asher Siegal, Daniel Ullucci, Arthur Urbano, and Luke Whitmore. In addition, the following colleagues helped me find particularly difficult-to-locate pigs: Rachel B. Gross, Paweł Maciejko, Adam Mendelsohn, David Stromberg, and Jeffrey Yoskowitz.

At the University of Wisconsin–Madison, I have an embarrassment of riches in terms of generous and kind friends and colleagues. In particular, I would like to acknowledge Susan Ridgely, for helping me sharpen my ideas and my kid's hockey skates; Tony Michels, for regularly adding insight over lunches at Chinese restaurants; Sunny Yudkoff, for introducing me to several important Yiddish pigs; and Judith Sone, for listening to my pig updates most mornings on our daily commute. I also thank all of my fellow Badgers, who are far too numerous to name.

Helping navigate numerous administrative hurdles are Gwen Walker and David Pettersen in the Mosse-Weinstein Center for Jewish Studies at UW-Madison. In particular, I want to thank David, who handles all of the finances and thus helped me procure all of the random books I needed. I promise that every single one of them either ended up in the book or helped shape ideas found herein. I also want to thank the Center for Jewish Studies for providing me with research funds. Every year I benefit from the amazing resources of the Belzer Professor in Classical Judaism; and for the term of 2019–2024, I also benefited from the generous support of the Max and Frieda Weinstein-Bascom Professor of Jewish Studies.

Support for initial stages of writing this book was provided by the Office of the Vice Chancellor for Research and Graduate Education (VCRGE) at the University of Wisconsin–Madison with funding from the Wisconsin Alumni Research Foundation (WARF).

Like everything in life, this book was derailed and delayed by the pandemic. Many of the people just mentioned helped me personally and professionally make it through those difficult years. In addition, I want to thank my writing group: Debra Scoggins Ballentine, Tracy M. Lemos, and Karen B. Stern. We finished a coedited project together at the very beginning of the pandemic and then realized that we could support each other as colleagues, parents, humans, and scholars during this impossible time. Our virtual meetings were equal part group therapy and writing session. I would not have been able to restart writing without them; and when my confidence or energy faded, they were always there to pick me up. I also want to acknowledge the labor of Isabelle Szerenyi. When the pandemic began, you went from providing a few hours of child care to being a part of our family's bubble and then of our family. Thanks to your amazing job as virtual kindergarten coteacher and friend to our son, I finally was able to restart writing this book in the summer of 2021.

Everyone at NYU Press has been amazing to work with. In particular, Jennifer Hammer has been an enthusiastic supporter of this project.

These past few years especially have highlighted the importance of friendship networks to help us all survive and thrive. In addition to those people mentioned earlier, I would like to thank Jennifer Pruitt and Mark Hammond; Daniel Kapust and Eunsook Jung; Jamie

Gaffke and Ruth Vater; Tova and Elias Walsh, cofounding members of the Madison Jewish Family Collective; Mike Naparstek, Rob Peyton, and Mitch the Drummer for helping me keep my garage-band dreams alive; all the parents and kids on the Van Hise walking school bus; and Casey Poole and all the members of the Polar Caps community. I especially want to thank Stan Zipper and Ross Wolfson, who remind me who I was, who I am, and who I can be.

For support and encouragement, I think my family: Mom, Ian, and Lisa; Aunt Debby and Avi; Dad, Rose, and Michael; Aunt Elaine; Ron and Eugenie; and Sarah, Scott, and Maceo.

Deserving of their own paragraph are my wife, Valerie, and my son, Josiah. Val tolerates my constant reply to almost any question: "Would you like to hear a relevant fact about Jews and the pig?" She also reminds me, "It's a good thing that *you* love the rabbis." She challenges me in all the best ways. I am a better person for having spent time with her. And over the past few years, we have spent *a lot* of time together. She inspires me every day. Josiah also inspires and challenges me every day. Over the past few years especially, he has taught me how to remain positive during times of crisis. His sense of humor and wit often make me laugh, and his insight into life regularly astonishes me. Whether watching him read a book or skate across the ice, I am in awe of how he creatively navigates life. Thanks to both Val and Josiah, I am getting better at setting limits on work, in search of the work-life balance—or, as we refer to it in our house, the work-hockey balance.

While I was finishing this book, two of my role models in life passed away. Uncle Rom, z"l, was larger than life. When I was a kid, he was both my uncle and my hero, as he would swoop into town in his Hawaiian shirts and take us on adventures. As an adult, I got to know his more philosophical and introspective side. There are so many conversations I am glad that we had and so many more that I wish we did have. May his memory be a blessing.

I dedicate this book to the memory of Harold "Fess" Blau, z"l. To say that Fess was my stepfather is to understate the role he played in my life. He taught me my multiplication tables and how to tell a good joke, gave me my first driving lessons, and picked me up from high school jobs and after-school activities. As I state in the dedication at the front of this book, he read every word I ever wrote. Even from his hospital bed, he shared his thoughts on drafts of various chapters in this book. After he passed, I found it impossibly hard to keep writing certain sections, especially about Yiddish, when I knew that I could no longer send him a quick email to share with him what I had just found out. I miss him every day. May his memory be a blessing.

NOTES

INTRODUCTION

1. On the historical development of this principle, see S. Cohen 2000, 263–307.
2. As with all religious identities, defining Judaism has a complicated history. For an accessible historical survey, see Satlow 2006.
3. Kornblut 2006. In a scene in Michael Chabon's Pulitzer Prize–winning novel *The Amazing Adventures of Kavalier & Clay*, a Jewish character denies that he had a "relapse" back into Jewish practice by asserting, "I eat a pork chop every day" (2000, 585).
4. The map metaphor is drawn from Satlow 2006, 8–9; in turn, Satlow draws this metaphor from the work of Jonathan Z. Smith.
5. Though this is just an idiomatic expression, Easter eggs are briefly noted in chapter 5.
6. Kreiner 2020, 17.
7. While I constantly refer to pigs as embodied animals, unless it is directly relevant, I rarely discuss specific details about the biology and/or evolution of these nonhuman animals themselves. For more on these topics, see, e.g., Essig 2015; Mizelle 2011; Price 2020; B. Weiss 2016.
8. Berkowitz 2018, 13.
9. My usage of the verb "attend" here is intentional, informed by the scholar of religion and animal studies Aaron Gross (2015, 13–15). For example, Gross notes, "By this verb I mean simply attention to animals in roughly the same manner scholars train themselves to be attentive to gender, sex, race, or theological nuances. I specifically choose the term *attending* because it contains within it the word *tending*, which can mean both tending flocks and a kind of mental attention" (2015, 13, original emphasis).
10. Berkowitz 2018, 13.
11. Berkowitz 2018, 14.
12. For a broader discussion of the historical development from Judean to Jew, see S. Cohen 2000.
13. Leviticus 11 and Deuteronomy 14 repeat much of the same material, with the latter being the more concise and probably earlier text. On the relevant redactional issues, see J. Milgrom 1991, 698–704.
14. Fish: Leviticus 11:9–12; Deuteronomy 14:9–10. Fowl: Leviticus 11:13–19; Deuteronomy 14:11–18. On ancient debates about the meaning of biblical food laws, see Rosenblum 2016b.

15 Leviticus 11:3; Deuteronomy 14:6. Throughout this book, unless otherwise noted, all translations from original languages are my own.
16 Leviticus 11:4–6; Deuteronomy 14:7. Neither the rock badger nor the hare actually chews the cud, but the constant movements of their jaws led the author(s) of these texts to presume that they did. In reality, they lack *both* criteria for ingestion.
17 See Leviticus 11:4–6.
18 See Deuteronomy 14:7.
19 The fact that the Hebrew Bible only prohibits ingestion (and not breeding and/or commerce) of the pig is noted in Daphne Barak-Erez's discussion of pig laws in the modern nation-state of Israel (2007, 4, 15, 136n4) and in the discussion thereof in chapter 5.
20 For a recent analysis of the mentions of pig in Isaiah, see Rhyder 2023, 230–235.
21 Isaiah 65:2, 4. On Isaiah 65:4, see Blenkinsopp 2003, 272 (also, on the slight emendation of this text, see 267ng).
22 Isaiah 66:4.
23 Isaiah 66:3.
24 In Blenkinsopp's translation and commentary, he twice refers to this passage as "extremely elliptical" (2003, 292nf, 297).
25 Blenkinsopp 2003, 272.
26 Isaiah 66:17.
27 Some emend the text to change "abominable things" to "swarming creatures," which are explicitly tabooed in Leviticus 11:29 (see Blenkinsopp 2003, 309–310nc). Either way, the food would be biblically forbidden, since abominable foods are not permitted for ingestion (see, for example, the formulation in Leviticus 11:11). Mice are explicitly forbidden in Leviticus 11:29.
28 Proverbs 11:22. Here I follow the translation of Michael Fox (2009, 539).
29 In this section, I draw on the commentary in Fox 2009, 539–541.
30 Fox 2009, 540. This lack of insight would accord with how at least one rabbinic text uses this verse as a prooftext; see Mishnah, *Avot* 6:2.
31 Fox 2009, 540.
32 This metaphor proved useful more than two thousand years later, when Eli Yishai, a member of the Israeli Knesset, expressed his disproval of a pig-related Israeli Supreme Court ruling (in the *Solodkin* case, which is discussed in chapter 5) by describing the decision as "a jewel in a swine's snout" (Barak-Erez 2007, 100).
33 Proverbs 12:4. Translation based on Fox 2009, 547, with slight modification.
34 My usage of the word "final" is based neither on chronology nor on placement in the biblical canon (after all, Psalms immediately precedes Proverbs in the present order of the Hebrew Bible). Rather, it refers to my own organizational schema of the texts, which is intended for ease of presentation of the evidence to the reader.
35 Psalm 80:13–14. Translation based on the Jewish Publication Society (JPS) translation, with emendation (see Berlin and Brettler 2004, 1373).
36 For example, see Deuteronomy 28:49; Ezekiel 17:3; Habakkuk 1:8; Obadiah 1:4; Lamentations 4:19. The eagle is also used in the positive metaphorical sense in Isaiah 40:31. For references to how scholars have interpreted animal metaphors in the Hebrew Bible in relation to biblical dietary rules, see Rosenblum 2016b, 17–18.

37 For a summary of many of these theories and their problems, see Rosenblum 2016b, 15–18 (though I did not comment on this theory therein, another recent theory that I find unpersuasive for similar reasons is in Ruane 2015; similarly, I find the theory advanced in Rhyder 2023 unpersuasive, though it is perhaps the most nuanced approach toward the data I have seen in recent years). For a critique of the ecology theory, see Kreiner 2020, 168; and for a critique of the hygiene theory, see Price 2020, 99–101. For a relevant discussion about various theories that addresses Islam's pig taboo, see Armanios and Ergene 2018, 22–26.

38 Max Price (2020) levels this same criticism. For a recent attempt to resist monocausal explanations, see Rhyder 2023, 241.

39 A useful summary of the evidence is Price 2020. Also see Darshan 2022; Hesse and Wapnish 1997; Lev-Tov 2003; Rhyder 2023, 224–225, 229, 238. For studies about pig bones and Jewish identity from later periods and locations, see, e.g., Dunne et al. 2021; Price 2020, 190.

40 For the explicit prohibitions of these animals, see Leviticus 11:4, 13, 17; and Deuteronomy 14:7, 12, 16.

41 For other instances of removing pigs when children's toys or books are translated into Hebrew, see Barak-Erez 2007, 25.

CHAPTER 1. "ALL WHO EAT IT AGREE"

1 Please continue reading to discover why I prefer to use the term "cultic practice" here rather than "religion."

2 Psalm 137:4. This Psalm, including this verse, is quoted extensively in the popular reggae song "Rivers of Babylon" (written and first recorded in 1970).

3 A now classic starting point is S. Cohen 2000. For a concise summary of the various issues, including a comprehensive bibliography, see Satlow 2013.

4 I first wrote about this concept in Rosenblum 2016b, 117–118 (also see Rosenblum 2019b, 42). Therein, I used the phrase "Swine and Signified." However, one of the anonymous reviewers for this book felt that that phrase was nonintuitive and suggested that I instead refer to this as "The Signifying Swine." I have decided to adopt their suggestion and wish to acknowledge my intellectual debt to them, though due to anonymity, I cannot publicly acknowledge them by name.

5 See D. Kraemer 2009, 31; Rosenblum 2010c, 102.

6 See Grantham 1996; Hesse and Wapnish 1997; Lev-Tov 2003; and Price 2020. For the presence of pig bones in a cave at Masada being used by some scholars to identify skeletal remains as non-Jewish, see Magness 2019, 195 (for additional references, see 227n24); Zias 1998, 2000.

7 See Rosenblum 2010c, 96–97. Scholars refer to this region during this time period as "Palestine." This scholarly convention reflects the fact that the region was then under Roman rule, which is important for numerous historical developments and events (as we shall see). However, it should not be interpreted as making any statement about modern nomenclatures or geopolitics.

8 As I noted in the introduction, we need to continuously remind ourselves that we should not presume that, in any time or place, all Jews avoid (or do not avoid) the

pig. Jews, like any ancient or modern community, engage in a variety of practices and should not be assumed to be monolithic.

9 For references to scholarship on these conversations, see Rosenblum 2016b, 30n5.

10 See Schäfer 1998, 69. I will not discuss every specific text here; instead, I focus on significant examples. For a fuller treatment, see Rosenblum 2016b, 30–35; Schäfer 1998, 69–77.

11 Erotianus, *Vocum Hippocraticarum Collectio cum Fragments*, F33 = *GLAJJ*, 1:446. For nonspecialists, I want to take a moment to explain what has become a scholarly convention in my field. When there is a Greek or Latin reference to Jews or Judaism referred to in the now-classic M. Stern (1974) 1998, the convention is to cite that reference, as well. I also will use the translations cited therein, where readers can find the full information on each translation (usually taken, and sometimes modified, from the corresponding Loeb Classical edition). The abbreviation *GLAJJ* stands for Menahem Stern's title, *Greek and Latin Authors on Jews and Judaism*.

12 Arrianus, *Dissertationes*, 1:22:4 (*GLAJJ*, 1:542). For more context on this statement, see Rosenblum 2016b, 31–32; Schäfer 1998, 69–70.

13 Plutarch, *Quaestiones Convivales*, 4.5 (*GLAJJ*, 1:550, 554). In this section, I often provide two page numbers in *GLAJJ*, the first of which indicates the page number on which the Greek text appears and the second of which indicates the page number of the translation. For the full ethnographic explanation, see Plutarch, *Quaestiones Convivales*, 4.4:4–6:2 (*GLAJJ*, 1:550–557). For discussion, see Grottanelli 2004; Rosenblum 2016b, 32–33; Schäfer 1998, 72–74.

14 Plutarch, *Quaestiones Convivales*, 4.4:4 (*GLAJJ*, 1:550, 554). The same term appears in 5:1 (*GLAJJ* 1:550, 555).

15 Grottanelli 2004, 63, italics in original. My comments in this section summarize and interact both with his commentary on each category (see especially 63–78) and with my previous work on this topic (see Rosenblum 2016b, 32–33).

16 Plutarch, *Quaestiones Convivales*, 4.5:2 (*GLAJJ*, 1:551, 555). Grottanelli 2004, 63–70, offers parallels to other ancient texts.

17 Plutarch, *Quaestiones Convivales*, 4.5:2 (*GLAJJ*, 1:551, 555). Plutarch offers similar examples from Egyptian and other cultures (e.g., field mouse, lion, ibis, hedgehog). Other authors note that Egyptian priests refrained from eating the pig: e.g., the Jewish historian Josephus (37–ca. 100 CE) includes this fact in his defense of Jews against Apion, who, among other things, denounces Jews for not eating the pig. See Josephus, *Against Apion*, 2.137–142.

18 Plutarch, *Quaestiones Convivales*, 4.5:2 (*GLAJJ*, 1:551, 556). Further, he claims that Jews abstain from eating the ass and the hare because they honor these animals; see Plutarch, *Quaestiones Convivales*, 4.5:2–3 (*GLAJJ*, 1:551–552, 556).

19 Quoted in Origen, *Against Celsus*, 5.34 (*GLAJJ*, 2:255, 285).

20 Plutarch, *Quaestiones Convivales*, 4.5:3 (*GLAJJ*, 1:552, 556). Grottanelli 2004, 70–74, offers parallels to other ancient texts. The Rabbis also note a potential connection with pigs and skin ailments, though not in the same manner as Plutarch. See Babylonian Talmud, *Qiddushin* 49b (and, according to Rashi, referenced on Babylonian Talmud, *Shabbat* 129a–b).

21 For discussion of skin ailments in the Hebrew Bible, see Olyan 2000, 45–47.

22 Tacitus, *Historiae*, 5.4:1 (*GLAJJ*, 2:18, 25). For more on this text, see Rosenblum 2016b, 33–34. The first words of this quote provide the title for this section. This theme briefly reappears in early modern Europe; for a brief discussion, see Deutsch 2012, 180–181; Efron 2001, 199 (and, for a rejection of health reasons for the pig taboo, see 69); also see Teplitsky 2022, 329.
23 Porphyry, *De Abstentia*, 1.14 (*GLAJJ*, 2:433–434); cp. Jerome, *Contra Iovinianum*, 2.7, who offers a roughly similar reason for a pig taboo (though not in regard to Jews).
24 Grottanelli 2004, 74–77, offers parallels to other ancient texts. Also see the famous speech by Jules in *Pulp Fiction* (1994); I discuss this movie in chapter 6.
25 Plutarch, *Quaestiones Convivales*, 4.5:3 (*GLAJJ*, 1:552, 556).
26 For example, see Philo, *Special Laws*, 4.101. Similarly, see Schäfer 1998, 240n42.
27 Plutarch, *Quaestiones Convivales*, 4.5:3 (*GLAJJ*, 1:552, 556). Grottanelli 2004, 77–78, offers parallels to other ancient texts.
28 Schäfer 1998, 77 (and, in general, see 77–81).
29 While I focus on Latin satirists here, I should note that Plutarch records a satirical comment reportedly uttered by the Roman orator Cicero, in which Cicero makes a snarky pun via wordplay and the association between Jews and pig avoidance. See Plutarch, *Vita Ciceronis*, 7:6 (*GLAJJ*, 1:566); and, for discussion, S. Cohen 2000, 180–181; Rosenblum 2016b, 36–37.
30 Petronius, *Fragmenta* 37, line 1 (*GLAJJ*, 1:444).
31 See Rosenblum 2016b, 36; Schäfer 1998, 77–79.
32 Juvenal, *Saturae*, 6.157–160 (*GLAJJ*, 2:99–100). For discussion of Juvenal here, see Rosenblum 2016b, 37; Schäfer 1998, 79–81.
33 Juvenal, *Saturae*, 14.98–99 (*GLAJJ*, 2:102–103).
34 Macrobius, *Saturnalia*, 2.4:11 (*GLAJJ*, 2:665). Further, see Rosenblum 2016b, 37–38; Schäfer 1998, 81.
35 Menahem Stern notes, "This joke, based on the play of the Greek words υἱός [son] and ὗς [pig], loses its piquancy in the Latin translation" (1998, 2:666). There is another connotation for the Greek word ὗς, namely, referring to female genitalia; however, I do not think that is in play here. For general discussion, see Golden 1988, 1–2.
36 Paul Roth 2014, 49.
37 Philo, *Special Laws*, 4.101 (trans. Colson 1939, 69).
38 In general, see Philo, *Special Laws*, 4.100–102; and Rosenblum 2016b, 52–53. For a recent consideration of what Philo's discussion about kosher laws teaches us about ancient emotion, see Mermelstein 2022, 357–363.
39 Philo, *Embassy to Gaius*, 361 (trans. Colson [1962] 2004, 181).
40 Philo, *Embassy to Gaius*, 361 (trans. Colson 2004, 181).
41 See Rosenblum 2016b, 46–76.
42 This section draws on my earlier work. See Rosenblum 2016b, 38–45; and especially 2019b.
43 The first explicit story about the Hanukkah miracle of one cruse of olive oil lasting for eight days is reported in the Babylonian Talmud, *Shabbat* 21b. The Books of the Maccabees do not contain any such narrative, though they do have *a lot* to say about the pig.

44 Peter Schäfer argues that "the image of the founder" refers to a marble statue of a bearded Moses seated on an ass (1998, 55–62, especially 58–59).
45 Diodorus Siculus, *Bibliotheca Historica*, 34/35.1.3–4 (*GLAJJ*, 1:182–183).
46 Clearly, the irony that his xenophobic actions force this renunciation of their reputedly xenophobic practices is lost on him. Further, see Rosenblum 2010c, 101–102; Schäfer 1998, 67.
47 For discussion, see Rosenblum 2010c, 102–107.
48 For relevant discussion, see Rajak 2000. Also see Moss 2014. Although Moss rightfully questions the veracity of early Christian martyr narratives, she seems to readily accept those of the Maccabees, including instances of pig-related Jewish martyrdom (see especially 48–52). I argue that Moss's skepticism of later Christian narratives should extend to earlier Jewish ones, as well. As an added benefit, extending this skepticism to the Maccabean pig-related Jewish martyrdom texts would further strengthen Moss's overall argument.
49 Rajak 2000, 128–129.
50 I omit from discussion two texts that some people might consider relevant. First, in 1 Maccabees 1:47, Antiochus Epiphanes orders the construction of altars, on which pig and other unclean animals shall be sacrificed. Lacking from explicit mention, however, is forced consumption of the pig. Second, 1 Maccabees 1:62–63 summarizes the events discussed here but never explicitly discusses forced ingestion of the pig; rather, it references unclean food, which may or may not equate with the pig. For a different perspective on this material, see Rhyder 2023, 235–240. I am not entirely convinced by Rhyder's overall argument and, in particular, find her argument in regard to 1 Maccabees and the function of pig as metonym therein to be a stretch (see 235–236).
51 On the differing conceptions of the basis of law in this text, see Hayes 2015, 110–111; and for a consideration with regard to ancient notions of emotion, see Mermelstein 2022, 353–357.
52 4 Maccabees 5:8 (in general, see 5:6–13). All translations of 4 Maccabees are from Anderson 1985.
53 4 Maccabees 5:8–9. For Eleazar's self-defense, see 4 Maccabees 5:14–38.
54 See Leviticus 11:7; Deuteronomy 14:8. In a personal communication, Daniel Ullucci pointed out that here, "the persecutor's absurdly obtuse inability to comprehend the position of the martyr is a characteristic of the genre going all the way back to Plato's *Apology*. The ease of escape highlights the principled stand of the martyr. This is critical to the story. There is nothing glorious about just getting executed."
55 4 Maccabees 5:13. As we shall see in chapter 2, the Rabbis would probably agree with Antiochus Epiphanes in this particular circumstance.
56 4 Maccabees 6:14–15.
57 I am influenced here by the wording of Mermelstein 2022, 355.
58 E.g., see 4 Maccabees 14:11–16:25. On the construction of masculinity in this text, see Moore and Anderson 1998; and on the gendering of emotions in this text, see Mermelstein 2022, 355–356.
59 On the emotion of anger as gendered as female in regard to this text, see Mermelstein 2022, 356.

60 4 Maccabees 8:5. On the biblical concept of friendship and how biblical notions of friendship are received in the Hellenistic Period, see Olyan 2017.
61 4 Maccabees 8:7 (in general, see 8:4–11).
62 4 Maccabees 8:29–9:9.
63 4 Maccabees 17:7.
64 Commenting on some of these graphic details, which I omit, Candida Moss observes, "The culinary undertones of the scene invoke ideas of barbarism and cannibalism. . . . The implication is that the people forcing others to eat pork have other, darker appetites" (2014, 51). I agree with Moss that these graphic details can be read as part of a rhetoric of dehumanization. This is a further example of the utility of the concept of animality, discussed in the introduction.
65 I admit that this is a bit of an overstatement. My aim is not to completely dismiss history but rather to highlight the discursive function of such claims. Over time, these stories become endowed with cultural power, hence their widespread and enduring transmission. Less important than the kernel (more or, as I have come to believe, probably less) of truth beneath these stories is how the rhetoric shapes the way that these narratives impact, and are impacted by, subsequent texts and events. My skepticism about the veracity of many of the pig-related claims in Maccabees is shared by Honigman 2021, 244–245, 249–50; and Schäfer 1998, 66–69.
66 See Lincoln 2014, 1–3.
67 Philo, *Flaccus*, 96 (in general, see 95–96); trans. Colson (1941) 2001, 355–357.
68 R. Kraemer 2012, 256 (and, in general, see 256–257). Though I retain Kraemer's wording of "perhaps," I have become increasingly convinced that this more likely than not refers to violent rape.
69 Philo here is also excusing these particular women for being in the marketplace; for a discussion of this issue, see R. Kraemer 2012, 256–257.

CHAPTER 2. "A JEW MAY NOT RAISE PIGS ANYWHERE"

1 For a brief introduction to the Rabbis, with references to additional resources, see Rosenblum 2020, 16–35. In general, I capitalize "Rabbis" because the term refers to a distinct group. Unlike the generic term "rabbi," which refers to "my teacher" in Hebrew, "the Rabbis" should be treated like a proper noun.
2 The classical rabbinic corpus—which spans several centuries and the distance between Palestine and Babylonia—should not be considered a unified whole. However, given the symbolic weight that the pig takes on, the pig is a matter of interest across the classical rabbinic corpus. Were this a more technical volume, I would spend more time parsing more of these details. For our present purposes, I will note what I think is relevant for the broader argument. For readers interested in this information, please consult the references cited in subsequent notes.
3 Rowling 1999, 298.
4 Babylonian Talmud, *Berakhot* 43b. "Hang" is perhaps a pun, as the Aramaic word for "hang" (תלה) is similar to the Aramaic word תלתא, which is a species of date palm.
5 For more on Rav Pappa and the beer business, see Rosenblum 2020, 74–75, 144–146, 175.
6 More specifically, the proverb seems to suggest that a pig, when offered a clean and delicious food item around its neck, will continue to roll around in mud and get

dirty when it need not do so. The connection between the pig and dirt is discussed further later.
7   Discussed in the introduction. For "that kind," see *Ecclesiastes Rabbah* 7.12.1, discussed later in this chapter. Additional references to pig as "that thing" include, e.g., Babylonian Talmud, *Shabbat* 110b (on this text, see Har-Peled 2013, 30; Mokhtarian 2022, 16–18); Babylonian Talmud, *Pesahim* 76b; and references in this section.
8   For a brief discussion and references, see Rosenblum 2020, 250–254. For more on medicine in rabbinic literature, including discussion of bloodletting, see Mokhtarian 2022; Preuss (1978) 2004.
9   Babylonian Talmud, *Shabbat* 129a.
10 Babylonian Talmud, *Shabbat* 129a–b.
11 Let alone, who is who?
12 Babylonian Talmud, *Qiddushin* 49b (also cited by Rashi on Babylonian Talmud, *Shabbat* 129b). Pigs, plague, and linguistic avoidance make a brief reappearance in chapter 5, when we discuss the "swine flu" in modern Israel.
13 See Rashi on Babylonian Talmud, *Shabbat* 129b, discussed further later in this chapter. The Hebrew term *tzara'at* is commonly—and incorrectly—translated as "leprosy." While it clearly refers to some form of skin ailment, the symptoms do not match up with Hansen's disease (popularly known as leprosy).
14 Saul Olyan rightly points out that, in biblical texts, skin disease functions much like a physical disability and thus reflects the associated social stigmatization (2008, 54–56). The connection between pigs, skin disease, and "that thing" also appears on Babylonian Talmud, *Ketubbot* 61a–b. For further discussion on this topic, see Har-Peled 2013, 28–30.
15 Rashi on Babylonian Talmud, *Shabbat* 129b. Rashi attributes the text's second *davar aher* to skin disease explicitly transmitted by pigs (citing Babylonian Talmud, *Qiddushin* 49b).
16 Babylonian Talmud, *Avodah Zarah* 36b. For a parallel text, see Babylonian Talmud, *Shabbat* 17b.
17 For discussion, see Rosenblum 2020, 239–242.
18 Elsewhere, even the word "sex" itself is glossed as "that thing." See Babylonian Talmud, *Berakhot* 8b, where this occurs despite the fact that the text is praising a group's modesty in sexual relations.
19 Fear is not the only reason not to name something; hatred is also a reason. Writing in the eighteenth century, the German Hebraist Johann Jacob Schudt argues that Jews "hate the pig so much that they do not even call it by its name" and explicitly references the Hebrew term *davar aher* (Diemling 2015, 133).
20 "Pig" was used euphemistically in ancient Greek to refer to female genitalia. See Golden 1988.
21 Babylonian Talmud, *Pesahim* 3b.
22 Except when it is. As discussed later, sometimes humor is used to highlight the fraught nature of the pig. It is notoriously difficult to make blanket statements about rabbinic literature. One thing and its opposite can both be true, even when they stand in direct tension and contradiction with each other. Thus, I can state that "the

pig is no joking matter" here and a little while later show instances when it is a joking matter. This is not a bug but a multivocalic feature of rabbinic literature.
23 For discussions of this history, see, e.g., Bakhos 2007; G. Cohen 1967; Har-Peled 2013; Simkovich 2018, 2019. One anonymous reviewer of an early version of this book asked me to clarify the extent to which I rely on Har-Peled's scholarship for my discussion about the identification of Rome with the pig. While I cite Har-Peled's work, it did not influence the underlying argument because three years before Har-Peled's dissertation was completed (2013), I published an article (Rosenblum 2010c) in which I made this precise argument; and I was not aware of Har-Peled's work until after he defended his dissertation.
24 Genesis 25:22.
25 Genesis 25:23.
26 For more specifics, read the whole biblical story, starting in Genesis 25:19 and continuing on through Genesis 36.
27 Genesis 35:9–10.
28 Genesis 35:11–12.
29 Genesis 36:6, 8.
30 See Psalm 137:7.
31 1 Maccabees 5:65.
32 Jerusalem Talmud, *Ta'anit* 4:8, 68d. For additional references, see Simkovich 2018.
33 Though Betar was the last holdout, the more well-known final battle was at Masada. See Magness 2019.
34 *Midrash Tanchuma, Bereshit* 7.
35 "Puts forth" is clearly a pun: מפשט means "puts forth," and משפט means "justice"; therefore, the Hebrew reader will recognize that the actions of the pig / The Pig are the inversion (and perversion) of justice. The version of this text that appears in *Leviticus Rabbah* 13:5 refers to this "Evil Empire" as "the Empire of Edom."
36 Similarly, see Rosenblum 2010c, 109. The metaphor of the pig seeming to be kosher on the outside but corrupt and/or hypocritical at its nonkosher core will appear in several other contexts over the course of our story. Some, but by no means all, of these instances refer to this text. In many cases, though, it is more likely that it was an obvious, embodied metaphor that occurred to various people over the years and thus arose independently.
37 For further discussion of *Leviticus Rabbah* 13:5, see Har-Peled 2013, 169–176; Rosenblum 2016b, 118–120.
38 See the discussion of the children's book *Baxter, the Pig Who Wanted to Be Kosher* (Snyder 2010) in chapter 6.
39 Price 2020, 160.
40 *Avot d'Rabbi Natan* A4, 69–73. Cp. *Avot d'Rabbi Natan* B7, 3–11.
41 However, see Babylonian Talmud, *Gittin* 56b, which contains a detailed story in which Vespasian returns to Rome and leaves Titus in charge. Upon taking over the Second Temple, Titus graphically defiles the Holy of Holies. Titus eventually gets his just deserts, in the form of a gnat flying into his nose and painfully picking away at his brain until he dies. Almost two millennia later, Titus receives his proper credit in a Yiddish play. Written in 1932 by Yeheskil Dobrushin, *Mitn ponim tsum khazer*

(Turn your face toward the pig) notes, "It is written in the Gemorah [Talmud] that our wise men forbade us to raise pigs because the tsar Titus took a pig and threw it against the walls of our Temple. Then the earth was shaken five hundred miles around this place" (as quoted and translated in Shternshis 2006, 84).

42 Part of the confusion might be due to the fact that Titus succeeded his father as Roman emperor upon Vespasian's death.
43 All quotes in this paragraph are from Jerusalem Talmud, *Berakhot* 4.1, 7b (= Jerusalem Talmud, *Ta'anit* 4.8, 68c).
44 For additional rabbinic texts on this theme, see Rosenblum 2010c, 102–107.
45 Kreiner 2020, 133. For the story, see Virgil, *The Aeneid*, 8.26–65.
46 This coin was minted in 77–78 CE, so the events were still fresh in their minds.
47 Kreiner 2020, 133.
48 The short story, "The Adventure of Silver Blaze," was first published in 1892 and was then collected in *The Memoirs of Sherlock Holmes*, a volume readily available on the internet, e.g., at https://archive.org.
49 *Pesiqta d'Rav Kahanah* Supplement 3:2. For notes, references, and parallels, see Rosenblum 2015, especially 70, from which I base my translation and much of my commentary.
50 On what that slander might have referred to, see Rosenblum 2015, 70–71.
51 For example, see Babylonian Talmud, *Berakhot* 61b (which refers to Rome as "The Evil Empire"). However, I do not consider this text to be evidence of pig-related Jewish martyrdom because there is no explicit (nor, in my opinion, implicit) connection to that practice in this text.
52 Rubenstein 2018, 433.
53 For further discussion of the rhetoric of disgust in this text, see Mermelstein 2022, 364–367; Rubenstein 2018, 432–434; S. Stern 1994, 64.
54 On the sexualized pun contained in this expression in Hebrew, see Rosenblum 2015, 74.
55 On this point, see Rubenstein 2018, 434; Schofer 2005, 111.
56 In fact, it is a common scribal error—a fancy term for an ancient typo—to mistakenly write a ו (*vav*) too short, so that it looks like a י (*yod*), or vice versa.
57 See Rosenblum 2010b.
58 I made this precise point earlier in Rosenblum 2015, 73–74.
59 For discussion, see D. Boyarin 1999.
60 4 Maccabees 6:14–15, discussed in chapter 1.
61 In this section, I draw on my previous work in Rosenblum 2019b.
62 See Babylonian Talmud, *Sanhedrin* 74a (cp. Babylonian Talmud, *Yoma* 85b). Similarly, Islam prohibits the pig but allows consumption of the pig in cases wherein one is forced by necessity to ingest it. For example, see the following verses from the Qur'an: 2:173, 5:3, 6:145, 16:115; and the brief discussion in Armanios and Ergene 2018, 13–14.
63 See Mishnah, *Yoma* 8:5.
64 Mishnah, *Yoma* 8:5, continues on to discuss a sick person who craves food on Yom Kippur. In that case, they are fed on the advice of experts, or if no experts are around, they are fed based on the sick person's own self-assessment. However, only the first case of the pregnant woman is relevant to the porcine matter at hand.
65 Literally: "If her mind becomes settled."

66 Babylonian Talmud, *Yoma* 82a. The text continues on to explain why those are the three exceptions to the rule.
67 This can get a little trickier if the pregnant woman is the daughter or wife of a priest. But the text presumes that the meat would be prohibited for the woman to ingest, or else why would it be a matter of concern?
68 The Hebrew word for "fat" here (שומן) refers to the permitted fat of animal. There is another Hebrew word that refers to the prohibited fat of an animal (חלב). These terms are clearly juxtaposed, for example, in Mishnah, *Keritot* 4:1.
69 For discussion of how this text functions within the wider narrative history of Elisha ben Abuya (Aḥer), a famous sinning sage, see Har-Peled 2013, 85–90. And for discussion of how this story influences medieval Jewish law, see Baumgarten 2007, 138; and the discussion in chapter 3.
70 For a brief but healthy dose of skepticism, see Schwartz 2014, 96–97.
71 Here I draw on my earlier research on rabbinic hand-washing rituals (Rosenblum 2018).
72 A *maneh* is a unit of currency. As one of the largest coins in their monetary system, this is some costly meat.
73 *Numbers Rabbah* 20:21. Translation from Rosenblum 2018, 84–85, with modification. On this text, also see S. Stern 1994, 57.
74 The eighteenth-century German Hebraist Johann Jacob Schudt reports a roughly comparable contemporaneous anecdote. See Diemling 2015, 136–137.
75 On this situation, also see Babylonian Talmud, *Avodah Zarah* 18b; and for brief discussion, see D. Boyarin 1999, 73; Rosenblum 2019b, 45n39.
76 *Ecclesiastes Rabbah* 7.12.1. Translation from Rosenblum 2019b, 45. Here I draw on that earlier work (especially 44–47).
77 I say literal here because, although the term "prestidigitation" often refers to general sleight-of-hand tricks, the etymology of the term comes from two words, meaning "quick/nimble" and "finger."
78 I should note that there are occasions, albeit rare, wherein the pig is mentioned and there appears to be no significant stigma. For example, see Babylonian Talmud, *Avodah Zarah* 20a–b, where the pig does not seem to have any more signification than donkeys or birds.
79 I remind the reader that my aim throughout is to offer representative examples rather than an exhaustive catalogue. Therefore, not every example (of both primary and secondary sources) will be discussed or referenced.
80 This is a central point of Marvin Harris's famous, though problematic, argument in regard to the biblical pig prohibition. In general, see M. Harris 1998, 67–87. Further, many linguistic expressions mark the pig as especially dirty. For example, in English, a "pigsty" is a mess, and an extremely pleased person is as "happy as a pig in shit." For discussion, see Mizelle 2011, 140–141.
81 *Ecclesiastes Rabbah* 1.2.1. The same verb that appears in *Genesis Rabbah* 65:1 (discussed earlier) for "put forth" appears here, further connecting the toddlers' actions to that of pigs.
82 Babylonian Talmud, *Berakhot* 25a. Ancient connections between pigs and excrement were also noted in chapter 1. Further, the belief that pigs would eat anything—no

matter how repugnant—appears to underlie a statement on Babylonian Talmud, *Shabbat* 155b, that "no [creature is] richer than a pig."
83 Jerusalem Talmud, *Berakhot* 2:3, 22a.
84 Mishnah, *Bava Qamma* 7:7. For a brief assessment of the evidence for Jewish involvement in pig production in Roman Palestine, see Safrai 2014, 172–173. The text literally says "Israelite" rather than "Jew." Commenting on this wording, Beth Berkowitz astutely observes, "The power of the pig to differentiate Jews from others may explain why the Kaufmann and Parma manuscripts of the Mishnah at that point introduce 'Israelite' as the subject of the sentence (and shift the subject to the more generic *adam* ['person'] in the subsequent law restricting dogs)" (2018, 136–137).
85 In an anomalous tradition, Babylonian Talmud, *Sanhedrin* 93a, explains the absence of Daniel from a certain point in the narrative of the biblical book of Daniel by claiming that he was not present because he was off exporting Alexandrian pigs from Egypt to Babylonia. While one could quibble about whether exporting/importing pigs falls under the umbrella of raising pigs, I believe this text focuses more on explaining Daniel's absence from a key miraculous moment in the book of Daniel than on the business of pigs. It even seems to express respect for the fact that, in its understanding, Daniel sneaked Alexandrian pigs out of Egypt with their wombs intact, when local rules prevented that from occurring (to maintain a monopoly on breeding such pigs or, in the words of Rafael Neis, "a violent form of patent" [2023, 102]). On the requirement to remove the wombs of Alexandrian pigs prior to their exportation, see Mishnah, *Bekhorot* 4:4; Babylonian Talmud, *Sanhedrin*, 33a.
86 Babylonian Talmud, *Menahot* 64b; Babylonian Talmud, *Bava Qamma* 82b; Babylonian Talmud, *Sotah* 49b. For another context that mentions the prohibition against Jews raising pigs, see Babylonian Talmud, *Nedarim* 49b (cp. *Ecclesiastes Rabbah* 8.1.4; Jerusalem Talmud, *Pesahim* 10:1, 37c; and Rosenblum 2020, 60–63, which includes additional references).
87 Babylonian Talmud, *Shabbat* 155b.
88 See Mishnah, *Bava Qamma* 7:7, discussed earlier. And for excellent analysis of this passage, see Berkowitz 2018, 132–138. On Jewish views toward the dog throughout history, see Ackerman-Lieberman and Zalashik 2013.
89 Babylonian Talmud, *Mo'ed Qatan* 24a.
90 As discussed earlier, this would not be the only rabbinic connection between pigs and sexual activity.
91 Rashi on Babylonian Talmud, *Mo'ed Qatan* 24a.
92 For example, see Babylonian Talmud, *Pesahim* 111a.

CHAPTER 3. "THE PIGGISH TALMUD"

1 Further, these labels represent a European—and Christian—bias. For example, when viewed from the perspective of Islam, this period is often referred to as the Islamic Golden Age, due to a flourishing of, among many things, mathematics, science, theology, philosophy, and economics. Given that most of the material we focus on in this chapter is from Europe, I confess that a certain amount of this bias is reflected here. I refer to some material beyond this focus, but for a variety of reasons

(time, space, scholarly expertise, lack of knowledge of Arabic, etc.), I must leave the story of Islam and the pig for another scholar to tell.

2. Fuller treatment of this period can be found in many of the sources that I cite throughout this chapter.
3. An interesting work to read for broader background, and in conversation with this entire book, is Nirenberg 2014.
4. For discussion, see Rosenblum 2016b, 77–85 (especially 81–84).
5. Matthew 7:6 (cp. Gospel of Thomas 93); Luke 15:11–32. All New Testament translations are from the NRSV, as found in Levine and Brettler 2011. The phrase "do not throw your pearls before swine" has quite the afterlife, becoming a popular English idiom and even serving as the title of a syndicated cartoon (*Pearls Before Swine*). For a brief summary of pigs in New Testament texts, see Kreiner 2020, 16.
6. For the full story, see Mark 5:1–20 (cp. Matthew 8:28–34; Luke 8:26–39). The afterlife of this narrative is discussed in chapter 4, where we consider Shakespeare's use of this New Testament story.
7. Mark 5:7–9.
8. Mark 5:9.
9. Mark 5:11.
10. Mark 5:12.
11. Mark 5:13.
12. Mark 5:14–20.
13. Roman military buffs will quibble with this round number, which is why I have included this note. A legion is a Roman military unit with various subunits that, with some variability, total between approximately forty-two hundred and six thousand men. Therefore, I roughly split the numerical difference.
14. See Lawrence M. Wills's commentary on Mark, found in Levine and Brettler 2011, 69. On "gerash," Wills had previously noted on the same page that "Gerasa may evoke Heb 'gerash,' which means expel, and was used in some of the biblical accounts of God driving the nations out of the land (Ex 23.28), as here the swine, unclean animals, are driven out."
15. Kreiner 2020, 133. For the reverberation of this text beyond the New Testament, see Kreiner 2020, 182–183, 187–195.
16. In general, see Rosenblum 2016b, 140–157, especially 146–153.
17. See Nirenberg 2014.
18. *Epistle of Barnabas* 10:1–3. Translation from Ehrman 2003, 47 (Greek on 46). On this passage, also see McGowan 2021, 110.
19. For references, see Rosenblum 2016b, 149.
20. For example, John Chrysostom points out that such moral lessons are imparted in churches; but "Jews" who do not spend time in churches end up acting like gluttonous pigs (see *Discourses against Judaizing Christians*, 1.4.1). If only they went to church, they would know to skip the sin and eat the swine.
21. Augustine, *Reply to Faustus the Manichaean*, 30.3. Earlier in this same tractate (6.7), Augustine has an extensive explanation of how he views the Old Testament pig prohibition: it is about metaphorical avoidance of sins and vices and *not* about literal avoidance of the mammal.

22 Kreiner 2020, 157–158. For relevant documents in English translation, see Marcus and Saperstein 2015, 40–48, especially 43–46.

23 Price 2020, 163. In his endnote on this quote, Max Price claims, with reference to my earlier work, that "Rosenblum neglects, or at least underplays, the importance of the feedback in Roman-Jewish relations" (240n112). I take Price's critique seriously and thus here wish to highlight this feedback loop.

24 For an accessible translation of some of these texts, see Elliott 2005, 46–122; and sources cited later in this section. Authors also filled in the gaps in the biography of Mary, Jesus's mother. See Vuong 2019.

25 Bodleian MS Laud Misc. 108, 1027–1050. Translation from Pareles 2019, 222. On these traditions, see Pareles 2019 (which, given my lack of knowledge of Middle English, especially informed my discussion herein); Fabre-Vassas 1997, 89–94; Shachar 1974, 13–14; and Steel 2011, 188–189. Also see Trachtenberg 1983, 51–53.

26 Both Pareles 2019 and Steel 2011, 188–189, pay particular attention to this rhetoric of dehumanization.

27 Fabre-Vassas 1997, 94.

28 It is both a stretch and not really a stretch to allude here to the famous line from John 1:14, "And the Word became flesh and lived among us."

29 Other contemporaneous narratives intentionally play on alleged cannibalistic desires of Jews eating Christian children and, in at least one example, refer to the roasted child as "my piglet." See the thirteenth-century English story *The Passion of Adam of Bristol*, discussed in A. Boyarin 2021, 177–178. The claim that Jews will not eat pig because they consider them to be brethren continues into the modern period. For example, see Felsenstein 1995, 137, 291–292n40.

30 John 8:58.

31 Dunne et al. 2021. For other zooarchaeological studies of pig bones in later periods, including one on sixteenth- to eighteenth-century Jewish households in Amsterdam, see Price 2020, 190.

32 Pun intended, as the pig is a nonruminant animal; ruminant animals regurgitate as part of the ruminant process.

33 Kisch 1970, 275. In general, see Fabre-Vassas 1997, 126–127; Kisch 1970, 275–287; and Shachar 1974, 14.

34 Kisch 1970, 277. For some of the medieval German texts involved in the Jewish Oath, see Kisch 1949, 51–53, 61–63, 68, 70–72, 87–88, 97–98, 104, 120–122, 142–144, 159, 199, 218, and 253–254.

35 *Schwabenspiegel*, L 263, G 215. Translation from Kisch 1970, 278 (full text on 278–279).

36 Babylonian Talmud, *Shevuot* 38b.

37 *Sachsenspiegel*, fol. 221v. For the original text, see Kisch 1949, 51. Here, I combine and slightly modify the translations of Kisch 1970, 282; and Shachar 1974, 76.

38 I would argue that this fact is alluded to in the *Schwabenspiegel*, L 263, G 215, when it later states, "And so help thee the five books of Moses; / And that, so thou eatest something, thou wilt become defiled all over" (translation from Kisch 1970, 278).

39 Shachar 1974, 14. In a connection to the previous example, the earliest extant version of the infancy story of Jesus transforming Jewish children in an oven into nonhuman animals reports that they emerged not as pigs but as goats. See *The Arabic Infancy*

Gospel, 40:1–2 (for translation, see Elliott 2005, 106). My comments earlier about how to understand the replacement of goats with pigs apply equally here.

40 The classic study of the *Judensau* is Shachar 1974. Shachar's work greatly informs my discussion in this section. More recently, see Wiedl 2010.
41 On the gendered implications of this image, see Fabre-Vassas 1997, 108.
42 Shachar aptly summarizes this as "the symbolic equation of greed = pig = greedy person = Jew" (Shachar 1974, 21).
43 Bynum 2020, 160–161. Here, Bynum clearly summarizes the argument of Shachar 1974.
44 Shachar 1974, 4.
45 For brief reflections on the long legacy of this image, see Bynum 2020, 160–162; Geller 2018, 33–40; and Loewen 2015, 226–227.
46 Lipton 2014, 16. For more on the Jewish hat, see Lipton 2014, 16–54; Kisch 1970, 186–187, 206–207, 283, 284, 286, 297–299.
47 Shachar 1974, 2–3.
48 Shachar 1974, 31, identifies the Wittenberg *Judensau* sculpture as the first identifiable image where this transformation is explicit.
49 My description and analysis of this image are greatly informed by Shachar 1974, 34–35. This image is also briefly discussed in Fabre-Vassas 1997, 99.
50 Jay Geller describes this act as "engaging in anilingus" (2018, 36). In other *Judensau* images, Jews drink urine. This association then influenced some later claims in Germany that Jews wanted to become doctors so they could handle urine as part of their "alleged urophilia activities" (Efron 2001, 52–53).
51 On the common claim that Jews smell, see Rosenblum 2019a, 149–151.
52 Shachar 1974, 35.
53 The Wittenberg *Judensau* was the subject of a 2022 German lawsuit in which a German Jew argued that it was antisemitic and should be removed from the church and moved to the Luther House Museum. The German Federal Court of Justice (BGH) ruled against the plaintiff and found that the *Judensau* could remain in situ. I thank Claire Kilgore for informing me about this lawsuit.
54 In general, see Shachar 1974, 30–31, 43–51; Bynum 2020, 160–162; Loewen 2015, 21, 226–228; and Nirenberg 2014, 260.
55 Nirenberg 2014, 260. On 534n22, Nirenberg credits himself with coining the term "Papensau." To the best of my knowledge, this claim is correct. On this image, also see Shachar 1974, 56–57.
56 I rely on the translation of Shachar 1974 in this section. For each reference, I note the page numbers in his text both for the original Latin and for his English translation. In general, see Shachar 1974, 45–48, 87–88.
57 Translation from Shachar 1974, 46–47, 87n239.
58 Translation from Shachar 1974, 47, 88n239. The theme in both this quote and the previous one were riffed on in a subsequent text cited by Shachar 1974, 50–51, 89–90n264.
59 Shachar 1974, 42–44.
60 See Shachar 1974, 42 and plate 38b. Though the person is not explicitly identified as a Jew, another reference to the greed–Jew–pig–money bag connection is found in Dante's *Inferno* (17:64–66), when a usurer is described as having an image of a

pregnant sow on his coin purse. The connection between usury, a pig symbol, and a Jew seems obvious enough so as not to require explicit mention in the text that the usurer is a Jew.

61 See Shachar 1974, 62 and plate 56b.
62 Shachar 1974, 62.
63 See Shachar 1974, 62–64. For another example of this phenomenon, see Geller 2018, 39, which discusses a 1783 German text in which pigs' tails and supposed Jewish physiognomy are compared in what amounts to an extended phallic joke.
64 For those who are interested, the decree expelling Jews from Spain was issued on March 31, 1492, and Columbus set sail on August 3, 1492.
65 It is worth noting here that the first Jews to come to the Americas (including the first Jews to settle in the Dutch colony that became New York) were Sephardic Jews whose ancestors were directly impacted by the Spanish expulsion of Jews in 1492. See Leibman 2013; Sarna 2019, 1–61.
66 If you are interested in learning more about Columbus and pigs, see Essig 2015, 119–129.
67 To learn more about the history of Jews in medieval Iberia, see Ray 2013. The absence of pig was noticeable even prior to the arrival of Islam on the scene. For example, the fifth-century Christian historian Sozomen notes that Arabs, like Jews, refrain from pork (see 6.38.10–13; for discussion and reference, see S. Cohen 2000, 164–165).
68 Maimonides is not alone in this claim. For references to Muslim authors, see Price 2020, 188–189.
69 Maimonides, *The Guide for the Perplexed*, 3.48. Translation from Pines 1963, 598, original emphasis. Compare Jerusalem Talmud, *Berakhot* 2:3, 22a, discussed in chapter 2. In the chapter in which this appears, Maimonides is making an argument on the basis of reason for various biblical dietary laws, including the pig taboo. The full chapter can be found in Pines 1963, 598–601.
70 See J. Kraemer 2008, 490n76.
71 *Cantiaga* 85. Translation from Kulp-Hill 2000, 110. On this *Cantiaga*, see Patton 2012, 160 (and on the illuminated manuscripts of the *Cantiagas*, see 135–169).
72 Montoro, *Poesía* #98. Translation from Wertheimer 2009, 102. On Montoro in general, see Wertheimer 2009, 98–103. Montoro is not alone in using pig to display his newly Christian identity. Jewish and Muslim converts to Catholicism in fifteenth- and sixteenth-century Spain would commonly display a piece of ham or pork as *medallas*, medals or badges to signify their "true" Christian identity. See J. Williams 2019, 28. In a work of historical fiction, the author David Liss discusses how, while first- and second-generation Conversos "made a point of showing they were not Jews by eating pork," for some later generations, things were different: "It is but one of the foods we eat, one we ate when we were children, and which, perhaps, reminds us of better days. It is ironic, do you not think, that pork should be the meat most likely to produce nostalgia in one of my kind?" (2014, 194–195).
73 Wertheimer 2009, 98–103, especially 102, claims that the suspicions of Montoro's colleagues about his religious sincerity were well founded. Other, non-Converso fifteenth-century Spanish poets referred to the connection between Jews and pigs. For a brief discussion, see Nirenberg 2014, 234–235.

74 I say "relatively neutral" because the absolutely neutral term would be completely unmarked: that is, "Christian."
75 Roth 1992, 28. Also see Fabre-Vassas 1997, 119–125; Nirenberg 2014, 244; Roth 1992, 27–28, 96, 384n11.
76 Marranos were blamed for various theological, social, and even physical illnesses. For example, when syphilis arrived in Italy in the sixteenth century, Jews in general—and Marranos in particular—were blamed for its spread. See Stow 2001, 59.
77 See Roth 1992, 110–116; Marcus and Saperstein 2015, 198–204. One common method for punishing medieval Jews was hanging them upside down—a method used for both pigs and Jews; see Fabre-Vassas 1997, 125–128.
78 For additional examples, see J. Williams 2019, 32, 93, 97–98, 102–108, and 108–114 (I separate this latter case because, interestingly, it involves an accusation that a Converso would eat pig but eschewed snails, claiming that this avoidance was for reasons of taste and citing consumption of pig as proof that he did not practice Judaism; he simply hated snails). For a contemporary (but polemical) account of pre-Inquisition Converso food behaviors, which includes reference to pig avoidance, see J. Williams 2019, 91–92.
79 See J. Williams 2019, 93.
80 In general, see Fabre-Vassas 1997, 129–159. Especially graphic examples appear in images associated with the story of Simon of Trent, some of which feature Jews wearing badges with pigs on them and/or that feature images of a martyred Simon alongside the *Judensau*. For discussion, see Fabre-Vassas 1997, 130–136; Shachar 1974, 36–37. On the life and afterlife of the Simon of Trent story more broadly, see Teter 2020 (references to pig in that volume can be found on 186–187, 189, 216, 267). Additional examples can be found in A. Boyarin 2021, 23, 177–178; and for additional references from the early modern period, see Felsenstein 1995, 149–150.
81 See Fabre-Vassas 1997, 120–121, 290 (where she references another term for this nonpig product: *borifarro de marrano*). A similar term is used in twentieth-century Russia, where porkless sausage is referred to as "Jewish sausage"; see Estraikh 2018, 119–121. For additional references to Jewish (and Muslim) pig-free sausages around the globe, see G. Allen 2015, 73–74, 96–97. The connection between pig and accusations of the blood libel continues. For examples from eighteenth-century England, see Felsenstein 1995, 149–150.
82 See Roth 1992, 179–180; 400n7; Fabre-Vassas 1997, 119–125. For examples of how modern fiction authors use this connection (especially as part of historical fiction), see Liss 2014, 11, 112, 134, 194–195, 273; Morris 2019, 19, 21, 24–25, 117, 120, 172, 212, 217, 223, 275, 276, 279, 298–299. Also see the Converso backstory in the cookbook by Genie Milgrom (2019, 92–93) about Tia Paulita's fake pork *chuletas* (*chuleta* is Spanish for "pork chop"). Finally, an interesting example of a Converso using pigs to hide his true identity is Hernando Alonso, who hid in plain sight: he was a wealthy pig farmer in Mexico City; that is, until October 17, 1528, when he was the first colonizer burned alive at the stake in the New World by the Inquisition for his perceived heresy. See Kritzler 2008, 41–43.

83 For example, see Bentley 2014; Jung 2015; Schiebinger 2004. For ancient rabbinic discussions, see Rosenblum 2016a; and for early Christian conversations, see Penniman 2017.
84 As with most things rabbinic, the full answer to whether young children are allowed to eat nonkosher food is a little more complicated, but please accept this brief summary for our present purposes. To be clear, once children reach the age of religious majority, they are obligated to follow rabbinic dietary regulations.
85 *Min* is a Hebrew term that can refer to either a kind/category (as in a type of food) or a heretic (especially in medieval Judaism referring to a Christian). The text clearly has both meanings in mind here. For a similar reading, see Baumgarten 2007, 227n103.
86 *Sefer Or Zaru'a* 4: no. 146. Translation from Baumgarten 2007, 138.
87 This regulation is asymmetrical, as Jews are forbidden to serve as wet nurses for Christian children. For discussion, see Rosenblum 2016a, 167–172.
88 For ancient rabbinic discussion about this speculation relevant to the pig, see Har-Peled 2013, 85–90.
89 This text is almost certainly based on the earlier tradition found in the Jerusalem Talmud, *Hagigah* 2:1, 77b. The wordplay and euphemism of "that kind" here clearly calls to mind the *davar aḥer* discussion in chapter 2.
90 Text from Fabre-Vassas 1997, 145 (for a later version of this tale, see 99). For further analysis and additional pig-related examples, see Trachtenberg 1983, 144–146; Har-Peled 2016.
91 Text from Fabre-Vassas 1997, 145; also see Trachtenberg 1983, 145–146. I cannot cover every supposed plot of Jews to kill Christians, as texts on that topic are unfortunately voluminous. To offer but one other example, in a seventh-century narrative written in Armenian, Jews are accused of killing two pigs and using their blood to defile the Islamic sanctuary on the Temple Mount in an attempt to frame Christians for doing so; see *The Armenian History Attributed to Sebeos*, 43 (translation in Thomson, Howard-Johnston, and Greenwood 1999, 102–103). On this text, see Freidenreich 2022, 40–44 (with discussion of this passage on 43). I thank David Freidenreich for this reference.
92 While these themes continue in subsequent chapters of the book, I had steeled myself by then. It was in writing this chapter that I had to learn how to do so, which is why I consider it the most emotionally difficult one to write.
93 Price 2020, 186.
94 Kreiner 2020, 159, original emphasis. For Kreiner's analysis of this process, see 159–203.

CHAPTER 4. "SAV'D HIS BACON"

1 A relevant discussion of these, and other pertinent, issues can be found in Goldstein 2017, 67–93; also see Goldstein 2014.
2 Shakespeare 2003, 84 (act 1, scene 3, lines 26–30). I have previously used this quote as the epigraph for a chapter; see Rosenblum 2010a, 185. So too, Maria Diemling uses this scene as an epigraph in the introduction to an article on Jews, Christians, and the pig (2015, 115).

3   As we discussed in chapter 3, "usurious" and "Jewish" often function (sadly, unto this day) as mutually interchangeable adjectives. This association further explains an observation made by David Goldstein that, in *The Merchant of Venice*, the first two things we learn about Shylock are that he practices usury and that he does not eat pig (2017, 68).
4   There is a brief reference to this presumption in Christopher Marlowe's late sixteenth-century play *The Jew of Malta*, in which Barabas refers to "these swine-eating Christians" (act 2, scene 3, line 12).
5   Goldstein 2017, 69 (my understanding of this scene is informed by 68–71).
6   Goldstein 2017, 69, original emphasis.
7   For the full story, see Mark 5:1–20 (cp. Matthew 8:28–34; Luke 8:26–39); and the discussion thereof in chapter 3.
8   For example, Samuel Johnson omitted this line from his edition. See Goldstein 2017, 69.
9   Goldstein 2017, 70.
10 Goldstein 2017, 70. On the trope of the devil and Jews, see Trachtenberg 1983 (with brief reference to *The Merchant of Venice* on 31, 106). Though one could read another layer into this by noting the fact that Jesus is a Jew, I do not think that Shakespeare meant to add that ingredient to the mix here.
11 Shakespeare 2003, 91 (act 1, scene 3, line 90).
12 This reverberates throughout the play. As Goldstein notes, "The word 'devil' occurs fourteen times in the play, nine of them in relation to Shylock, and all of those occur after his use of the term in reference to 'the Nazarite.' Even in those other contexts, . . . the term 'devil' reflects back upon Shylock's use of it" (2017, 70).
13 Goldstein 2017, 71. For additional relevant references, see Felsenstein 1995, 126–127.
14 In this section, I draw extensively from the research of Mampieri 2020; and Michelson 2022, 1–6, 264–266. On the identification of Corcos here, see Mampieri 2020, 362–363. I thank Rachel B. Gross for bringing Michelson's scholarship to my attention.
15 On this route, see Mampieri 2020, 367; Michelson 2022, 1. Mampieri notes that this was the location of the Roman Jewish cemetery from the sixteenth century through 1934 (2020, 367n64). The historian Kenneth Stow notes in his study of the sixteenth-century Roman Ghetto both that Rabbi Corcos was "the most influential rabbi of the entire Roman Ghetto period" and that he was a party pooper for lambasting the popular custom of having fun parties on the evening before a boy's circumcision (2001, 104–105).
16 Sometimes the language was actual Judeo-Italian, and other times it was an invented mishmash of Italian and Hebrew words (and sometimes both). On Judeo-Italian, see Rubin 2017.
17 Mampieri 2020, 352 (and, on the genre as a whole, see especially 352–353). There is a phallic dimension to the humor, playing on circumcision, as noted by Fabre-Vassas 1997, 112–119 (and, for more on the *giudiate*, also see 243).
18 For additional references to such practices, see Stallybrass and White 1986, 53–56; Tseëlon 2001, 28–29.
19 See Mampieri 2020, 358–360 (on Roman Carnival violence against Jews in general, see 358–362). Flora Cassen notes that the day often ended with the ritual death of a

Jewish convict and that "in Venice, pigs were chased through the street and stoned" (2018, 40).
20 See Fabre-Vassas 1997, 162.
21 See Fabre-Vassas 1997, 162 (which also notes that, in the mid-fifteenth century, the fee was raised to thirty florins; the fee was paid by each synagogue in the papal states, so it added up to quite a significant sum); Mampieri 2020, 359–360.
22 Fabre-Vassas 1997, 162.
23 Fabre-Vassas 1997, 162.
24 See Mampieri 2020.
25 The Italian text that asserts this claim is found in Mampieri 2020, 373 ("E si crede la prima Giudiata in Roma"). I base my own translation on the translation of this passage in Michelson 2022, 3n7.
26 See Mampieri 2020, 351–352.
27 For those who are interested, the "*sic*" points to the fact that his name was actually Melchiorre Palontrotti. On this historical figure, see Mampieri 2020, 353–358.
28 Regarding "teacher," instead of Italian, here Palontrotti transliterates the Hebrew word *morenu*—meaning "our teacher."
29 For another example of a non-Jewish author knowing the Hebrew word for pig, see the discussion in Diemling 2015, 133, about Johann Jacob Schudt.
30 For the Italian text, see Mampieri 2020, 373. The translation is from Michelson 2022, 3n7 (with modification).
31 Italian: Mampieri 2020, 375; English: Michelson 2022, 3 (with modification). The Hebrew *ra'* is transcribed as "rangh" as per characteristics of Judeo-Roman. See Mampieri 2020, 365; Michelson 2022, 4n10.
32 My use of "fate" here is not just metaphoric. Originally, the Hebrew term *mazal* referred to an astrological sign and to the heavenly constellations. This extends to the notion of fate—the destiny written in the stars.
33 There are rabbinic traditions that the pig, and other nonkosher foods, will be kosher in The World to Come, but these traditions are not found in that particular tractate of the Talmud. For discussion, see Rosenblum 2017. I believe the reason for choosing this tractate was probably because Avodah Zarah (= "Idolatry") discusses various idolatrous practices and thus was the funniest tractate to use as the butt of this joke. The fact that the reference is inaccurate is less important than the comedic purpose it serves. For a contemporaneous English claim that pig will be kosher in The World to Come, see Felsenstein 1995, 137; and for a German one, see the discussion in Deutsch 2012, 181.
34 Italian: Mampieri 2020, 375. English: Michelson 2022, 4 (with modification and with reference to Mampieri 2020, 367–368).
35 While this may be true of The World to Come, in This World, Italian Jews usually substituted goose for pig in recipes. For discussion, see Toaff 2011, 55–69.
36 I agree with Mampieri (2020, 368), that this is how the phrase "Eat pig without any respect" should be understood.
37 Mampieri 2020, 370. Similarly, see Michelson 2022, 5.
38 Michelson 2022, 5.
39 Felsenstein 1995, 132.

40 Voltaire, *Candide*, chap. 6. I thank Monica Kleinman for reminding me of this reference. For an eighteenth-century quip comparing Voltaire, Jews, and pigs, see the discussion in Felsenstein 1995, 127 (and for additional references to this topic in general, see 127, 289n18).
41 The claim of pig as an excellent meat as part of Jewish pig polemics has a venerable history, going back as far as the Second Temple Period. See 4 Maccabees 5:8; Philo, *Flaccus*, 96; and discussion thereof in chapter 1.
42 I have confirmed my transcription by comparing it to that of Felsenstein 1995, 132–133.
43 There are other texts, however, that directly state that Easter ham symbolizes the body of Christ. See Fabre-Vassas 1997, 252–256, especially 253; and the discussion of pig on Easter later in this chapter.
44 For further analysis of this verse and illustration, with additional references, see Felsenstein 1995, 132–137. Felsenstein's work was especially helpful in formulating this section.
45 Endelman 1999, 114.
46 Endelman 1999, 114. Additional references to texts and incidents can be found in Felsenstein 1995, 134–135; and for these, and other, uses of the pig to mock Jews referenced in the work of Johann Jacob Schudt, see Diemling 2015, 135–136.
47 Felsenstein 1995, 135. Clearly the focus on Jews' beards genders this violence. That being said, there is evidence from 1824 of a Jewish woman being forced to eat pig. See Endelman 1999, 114–115 (discussed in chapter 5). And there is evidence of a young girl in 1930s Ukraine being bullied by non-Jewish kids who attempt to smear pig fat on her lips (see Shternshis 2015, 18–19). There are earlier instances that involve violence via bacon fat. For an example from Spain in 1465, see J. Williams 2019, 77.
48 This sentiment continues to resonate long after. For example, if we cross the Pond and jump ahead more than one hundred years, we learn of a Jewish Union soldier who, while recovering from war injuries in a hospital, reports that he is mocked by a convalescing Christian solider thusly: "Haloo, thou unbelieving son of Abraham, hast thou got a piece of pork at length into thy clutches? No! Well, then, it were better that thou hadst, for until thou eatest swine's flesh, thou never canst be saved" (as quoted in Mendelsohn 2022, 168; for original citation, see 296n143).
49 For a historical overview of Jewish Emancipation, see Sorkin 2019. Given its five-century history, this theme obviously reverberates beyond the boundaries of the Early Modern Period. Additional discussion appears in chapter 5.
50 As is my usual caveat, I cannot address every reference in detail. For an additional example, see the excerpt from Gotthold Ephraim Lessing's German play *The Jews* (written in 1749 but published in 1754), which casually mentions that Jews do not eat pig (scene 21; in Mendes-Flohr and Reinharz 1995, especially 63).
51 The reference to Shakespeare in the previous sentence was not just a segue; rhetoric explicitly drawing on Shakespeare's *The Merchant of Venice* was utilized throughout debate leading up to, during, and after the passage and repeal of this act. For discussion, see Shapiro 1996, 195–224; Shapiro 2000; Felsenstein 1995, 181–182.
52 Text from Mendes-Flohr and Reinharz 1995, 27; for the full text of the bill, see 27–28; and for additional texts related to the naturalization of Jews in England, see 10–17, 21–22, 146. For further discussion of "The Jew's Bill," see Felsenstein 1995, 187–213.

53 Text from Mendes-Flohr and Reinharz 1995, 27.
54 As quoted in Shachar 1975, 354.
55 Shachar 1974, 63. Similarly, in antiquity, Greek and Roman authors routinely noted three Jewish practices: circumcision, Sabbath observance, and pig avoidance (see the brief discussion thereof in chapter 1).
56 I take the label for this poem as "doggerel" from Endelman 1999, 90.
57 From the 1753 anthology *A Collection of the Best Pieces in Prose and Verse, against the Naturalization of the Jews*, 77; as quoted in Shapiro 1996, 210–211.
58 Clearly there is also a punning association here between the common claim that Jews clipped coins and the much-better-attested claim that Jews practiced circumcision (a.k.a. clipping of the foreskin). On the connection between early modern British discussions of the Jewish pig taboo and the Jewish ritual practices of circumcision, see Felsenstein 1995, 123–157 (with coin clipping specifically referenced on 140–142). Jews, pelf, and treachery are further connected in a 1753 English print titled "The Grand Conference or the Jew Predominant." In addition to including various common antisemitic tropes, this print features the following line amid a poetic verse: "As JUDAS did for pelf betray our Lord." For discussion of this print, see Felsenstein 1995, 207–208, original emphasis.
59 My phrasing purposefully serves to highlight the association between The Pig and empire—whether Roman or British.
60 Shapiro 1996, 210.
61 Felsenstein points out that these lines allude to the popular contemporary ballad "The Roast Beef of Old England" (1995, 203).
62 This is also furthered by the reference to "Jonathan's jobbers." Jonathan's Coffeehouse was a well-known seventeenth- and eighteenth-century meeting place for people involved in London's evolving financial markets. In fact, it was the original site of the London Stock Exchange. Brokers and jobbers would trade stocks, a relatively new concept that then (as today) could spell boom or bust for the local and global economy. This is another not-so-subtle way that the poem connects Jews with the financial ruin of the perceived once-great (and, it should be noted, pure) nation. For a modern historical novel (set in this time period) about Jonathan's Coffeehouse, jobbers, and Jews, see Liss 2004b (for a joke about Jonathan's Coffeehouse, jobbers, Jews, and circumcision, see 82; and on Jews and the pig, see 24, 112, 118, 150, 259, 323). Liss also wrote a historical fiction novel discussing early stock markets in seventeenth-century Amsterdam and Jews; see Liss 2004a (on the pig, see 143, 217, 269–277, 317). On the intersection between pig, Jews, and coffee, see Liberles 2012, 56, which concisely summarizes debates about whether pig fat was added to coffee; and the brief discussion of the eighteenth-century German print that features the Frankfurt *Judensau*, titled "The Jewish Coffee House," in Shachar 1974, 65 and plate 61a. And while we are on the subject of Frankfurt, for another pig controversy in eighteenth-century Frankfurt (involving baking Jewish bread in the same oven as Christian egg-and-ham quiche), see Diemling 2015, 122–123.
63 Shachar 1975, 337.
64 Shachar 1974, 63.

65 My description of this image draws on Shachar 1975, 346. According to Alfred Rubens, whose collection this image is found in, this image measures 2 7/8 × 4 1/8 inches (1954, 36).
66 Shachar 1975, 346, states that similarities between the two caricatures suggests that both should be identified as Gideon. I err on the side of caution here and prefer to view this as suggestive but not definitive.
67 On this image, see Shachar 1975, 346–347, plate 24; Shapiro 1996, 218.
68 See Felsenstein 1995, 212–214.
69 For additional examples of how pig polemics played into discussions after the repeal of The Jew's Bill, see Felsenstein 1995, 136.
70 For discussion of some of these images, see Shachar 1974, 63. On the stereotype of Jews and peddlers, see Shachar 1975, 337, 363; Geller 2018, 36. Felsenstein also notes that when the pig says "Buy Buy my Pork," it is "ironically mimicking the familiar street cries associated with Jewish peddlers and itinerant traders" (1995, 203).
71 Fabre-Vassas 1997, 247. For pig as part of Catholic identity in a different context (namely, in modern India, from the perspective of chef Vimala Rajendran, mainly in relation to the surrounding Muslim community but also in regard to Jews), see B. Weiss 2016, 205–212, especially 206–207.
72 This custom goes back at least to the Medieval Period. See Fabre-Vassas 1997, 247.
73 Translation from Fabre-Vassas 1997, 248; on this text, see 247–249; and on Easter pig traditions in general, see 233–257.
74 Scholem 2016; Tokarczuk 2022. Tokarczuk won the Nobel Prize in Literature in 2018. For a scholarly study of Frank, see Maciejko 2011.
75 The fact that these conversions were also necessary to save their lives (a.k.a. their bacon) was, for obvious reasons, downplayed by both these figures and their followers.
76 My understanding of ritual inversion throughout this section is influenced by the theoretical work of Bruce Lincoln (2014, 142–159).
77 The consumption of leavened bread is forbidden on Passover (see, e.g., Exodus 12:15). As discussed in chapter 2, there is a long history of Jews referring to pig as "the other thing." In the Hebrew text quoted here, pig is never referred to by name, only by the euphemism "the other thing." I thank Paweł Maciejko for sharing a copy of the Hebrew text with me and for answering some technical questions about this material.
78 Maciejko 2011, 32. Here Maciejko relies on the report of Jacob Emden, *Sefer shimush*, 20r–v (the reference on 274n49 to "5v, 6v" is a typo).
79 See Maciejko 2011, 33.
80 See, e.g., Exodus 12:15.
81 Karl Marx is reported to have placed Easter pork on matzah and eaten it. See Fabre-Vassas 1997, 233. I discuss this sandwich further in chapter 5.
82 For discussion and references, see Rosenblum 2020, 67–72.
83 See Mishnah, *Hullin* 8:4.
84 In addition to this intentional practice, the casual nonobservance of this food taboo was viewed by at least some outsiders as a critique that calls the person's entire moral character into question. For example, the eighteenth-century Christian

Semitics scholar Johann Michaelis once declared, "When I see a Jew eating pork, which is an affront to his religion, I know that I don't trust him because I do not know what's in his heart" (as quoted in Liberles 2012, 112). Michaelis also claimed (citing Johann Andreas Eisenmenger's earlier work) that Jews derogatorily referred to non-Jews as "Pork Devourer" (*Schweinefleischfresser*), which he viewed "as illustrative of the contempt with which Jews hold Christians" (Geller 2018, 250n25).

85 In Tokarczuk's Nobel Prize–winning novel, she effectively uses Frank and his community's ingestion of pig to convey key elements of their practices and beliefs. For example, see Tokarczuk 2022, 673, 491, 483, 311–309 (page numbers are reversed, as the book starts on 965 and counts backward to 2).
86 For the relevant document, see Marcus 1999, 316 (and, more broadly, see 314–319); also see Maciejko 2011, 144–145. Tokarczuk includes discussion of this in her novel (2022, 460).
87 See Maciejko 2011, 145–146.
88 This suggestion was made to me by Paweł Maciejko in a personal communication.
89 As quoted in Felsenstein 1995, 150. For a brief comparative study of this antisemitic ditty—which was popular across the globe, from London to Cincinnati, Ohio; to Adelaide, Australia; and beyond—see Sarna 1982.
90 Shachar 1974, 62. Jews and pigs are blamed both for epidemics and for their cures. One hundred years later in Hamburg, cholera broke out. For both the 1892 and 1902 outbreaks, Russian Jewish immigrants were blamed, with one German newspaper asserting, "Russia may wish to keep its infected Jews to itself, just as it may its infected pigs" (Efron 2001, 257).
91 On the highway tax, see Felsenstein 1995, 128; the reference to the highway sign is found on 289–290n22.

CHAPTER 5. "PIGS REPRESENT FOR US A NEW PROBLEM"

1 See chapters 3 and 4, in which several examples of this tradition are discussed.
2 William Blake, "The Everlasting Gospel," lines 208–211; as quoted in Felsenstein 1995, 137; for references, see 291n39.
3 Felsenstein 1995, 136.
4 On this image, see Felsenstein 1995, 129–132. While I draw on Felsenstein's work here, I offer a different interpretation of what we learn from the interaction between the Jew and the Pig Faced Lady.
5 Griskin is a lean cut of meat taken from the pig's loin.
6 Felsenstein argues that "his beard [is] erect to define his state of arousal" (1995, 130)—but I am not sure if that is intentional or is drawn that way just to keep his beard out of the way of her hand in the image. If intentional, it further highlights the sexual tension; and if unintentional, then it certainly does not diminish the sexual tension already so palpable in the image and words.
7 This is a delightful pun, as "gammon" can mean both to deceive/hoodwink/flatter/cajole (verb) and the haunch of a pig (noun). Further, it can refer both to smoked or cured ham or to the flesh between a human's buttock and thigh. All of these meanings can coexist simultaneously in this statement, for comedic and bawdy purposes.

8   Regarding "plagued," for example, there are the antisemitic (and demonstrably false) connections between Jews and plague, the occasional claimed connection between plagues and pigs as a historical rationale for the Jewish pig taboo, etc. On rare occasion, the association works the other way: by eschewing the pig, Jews avoid plague. For example, see the 1854 publication of the Reverend Charles Richson's sermon (originally delivered, in shorter form, on April 30, 1854, in the cathedral of Manchester, England), which features notes by physician John Sutherland and, taken together, argues that the Old Testament pig taboo prevents various diseases and plagues. For discussion, see Hart 2007, 175–179. Also see Teplitsky 2022, 329. Additionally, as is discussed later in this chapter, there is a connection between pigs' ears and antisemitic stereotypes, which might have been part of the joke in the wording of this engraving.
9   For example, see Felsenstein 1995, 128–129.
10 Endelman 1999, 114–115. In general, I draw on Endelman's description of events in this paragraph.
11 As quoted in Endelman 1999, 115.
12 Further, at other times, there are repetitions of accusations from the past. Since we have discussed this in previous chapters, I will not address this topic much here. To offer one example, in Maria Edgeworth's 1817 novel *Harrington*, she repeats the common claim of the Jewish blood libel. In her story, one character frightens a child by telling the tale of a Jew who pretended to sell pork pies—but in reality, he peddled pies made from the flesh of little children! For reference and discussion, see Felsenstein 1995, 150.
13 Coincidentally, Aby Belasco's involvement in an 1824 boxing match is part of another case study of Jews and food in England, namely, the history of fish and chips. See Panayi 2022, 31, 115 (and for a reference to pig and antisemitism in the history of Jews and fish and chips, see 115–116).
14 See Endelman 1999, 220. Boxing was quite popular among lower-class Jews in England. For discussion, see Endelman 1999, 219–223; and for a historical novel that greatly draws on this phenomenon, see Liss 2004b.
15 For discussion, see Diner 2001, 84–145.
16 Orwell (1933) 2021, 132.
17 It might be a stretch, but I do note that the only other explicit mention of pig consumption in the novel involves two large rats eating a ham. See Orwell 2021, 105. Some of these themes may be at play in a later incident in British politics, wherein Labor Party leader Ed Miliband was mocked for a face he made while eating a pig sandwich. The pig puns in headlines and news stories about the Jewish politician's pig-sandwich-eating face wrote themselves, but the extent to which this was overt antisemitism is up for debate. For discussion, see Delman 2015; Greene 2020, 112. I thank Duncan MacRae for this reference.
18 Directed by Vadim Jean and Gary Sinyor. You may quibble with my claim that this is the single best film on this topic on the grounds that it is the *only* film on this topic. However, in 2017, *Holy Lands*, directed by Amanda Sthers and based on her book (2019) was released. (I discuss the book and movie later in this chapter, in the section on France.) That film did not supplant *Leon the Pig Farmer* in my own personal

19   ranking. To my knowledge, these are the only two full-length films whose plots center around Jewish identity and pigs. I leave aside documentaries (though I discuss one documentary about pigs in Israel later in this chapter). I also do not count *To Dust* (2018) as a member of this small genre, for reasons I discuss in chapter 6.
19   To the best of my knowledge, this is a made-up location. For an academic discussion of the role that infertility plays in *Leon the Pig Farmer*, see Sternberg 2015.
20   The film does not seriously grapple with the fact that, regardless of whose sperm was in the test tube, Leon's biological mother remains Judith Geller, a Jew (whose name, probably on purpose, means "female Jew" in Hebrew). From a rabbinic legal standpoint, then, Leon is most certainly Jewish. But if the film ruminated on that (pun intended), it would not have allowed for the comedy of error that is Leon's sojourn to the Chadwicks' pig farm.
21   Many of these scenes involve slapstick comedy. Writing about similar instances in modern French films about pig and Muslim identity in France, Nicole Beth Wallenbrock refers to these kinds of scenes as "the camp-horror treatment" (2015, 112). I discuss Wallenbrock's scholarship further later in this chapter.
22   Again, I will not spoil the ending, but I must remark that the rabbis in the film do not offer what I think is clearly the correct answer (on well-attested biblical and rabbinic grounds) to what amounts to a straightforward and relatively easy question. The answer, in my opinion, is "no"—but you must watch the film to find out what is the question.
23   Solomons 2011. Full disclosure: there is no connection between myself and Mr. Rosenblum (or Natasha Solomons), but I must confess that when I discovered the title of this book during a search, I immediately put it on the top of my "to read" pile.
24   On the complex history and dynamics of Jews changing their names in modernity, see Fermaglich 2018.
25   Solomons 2011, 221–222 (on pig, also see 135, 314). While we will not discuss this novel in detail, reading it, I was strongly tempted to interpret the character of the Dorset woolly-pig (e.g., see 137–138) as a metaphor for Jews.
26   E. Harris 2013, 56 (and for more on the pig, see 200, 232, 336–337).
27   This enduring connection to Judaism comes especially from his mother, as is exemplified in the subtitle to Ainsztein 1964: "The Jewish Background of Karl Marx: His Mother Strongly Opposed Conversion."
28   As quoted in Fabre-Vassas 1997, 233. I checked this quote against the source from which Fabre-Vassas quotes (Ainsztein 1964, 16; see Fabre-Vassas 1997, 357n1, for the reference). The 1964 reference contains slightly different punctuation than Fabre-Vassas's version. I decided to default to the 1964 source in general but retained Fabre-Vassas's introduction of quotation marks for direct speech, as I believe it made the story clearer to read. I also modified the transliteration of *matzah* (from the original of *matza*), for the sake of consistency throughout this book.
29   As opposed to the famous "Hillel Sandwich," named after the ancient sage Hillel, who, over two thousand years ago, reputedly made a sandwich out of *matzah* and bitter herbs as part of the celebration of Passover. For discussion, see Babylonian Talmud, *Pesahim* 115a. This story is included in the standard *Haggadah*, part of the ritual observance of Passover unto today.

30 While Fabre-Vassas uses the quote about Marx to introduce a chapter, she does not concretely make this obvious connection, merely noting that *matzah* and pork "stand in contrast to one another" (1997, 233).
31 She was reluctant at least at first. After more than fifteen years, however, she reportedly became a devout Lutheran. See Ainsztein 1964, 16.
32 Geller 2018, 36–37; Geller continues to discuss these postcards in more detail on 37–39.
33 See Geller 2018, 37.
34 Shachar 1974, 64.
35 Efron 2001, 243. While Freud famously forbade his wife, Martha Bernays, from lighting Sabbath candles, there is at least one pig-related story from their past: Freud found it objectionable "when Bernays was unwell on vacation and she checked with her mother about whether she could eat ham rather than just deciding what she thought was good for her health and what 'tastes good to her'" (Bailey 2023, 52, 30). In my research, I found at least one other instance of pig-related fisticuffs. Living in post–World War II Vienna, the prominent photojournalist Harry Weber tells a story of when his non-Jewish wife "punched an 'older woman' who had called Weber a *Saujud* (Jewish pig) one night" (Bailey 2023, 180).
36 It was also used on a more mundane level, to mock private figures. Of the many examples I could offer, here is but one: in a divorce proceeding under the Third Reich, on November 4, 1938, the divorcing couple's neighbors testified to "hearing a wife call her husband a 'Jewish pig'" (Bailey 2023, 129; Bukey 2011, 103).
37 Shachar 1974, 64. In German: "Schlag tot den Walther Rathenau / Die gottverdammte Judensau."
38 In Mendes-Flohr and Reinharz 1995, 684 (full text on 684–685). Shachar also noted that "Aryan" women who married Jews were treated to the same kinds of porcine abuse as Walther Rathenau (as well as violence; 1974, 64). Nazi rhetoric about Jews and pigs also extended to notions of pig breeding and eugenics. For discussion, see Saraiva 2018, 101–106.
39 Decades later, the artist Art Spiegelman (literally) drew on his parents' history of surviving the Holocaust (1986, 1991). Spiegelman depicted Jews as mice, German Nazis as cats, Polish non-Jews as pigs, etc. When Polish Jews pretended to be non-Jews, they wore pig masks (e.g., 1986, 64, 125, 136–141, 144, 146, 149, 152–155). While some people (albeit often with an ideological agenda) criticized Spiegelman for flattening all Polish people into pigs (= Nazis and/or Nazi sympathizers), Spiegelman does grapple with the issue that not all Polish people were complicit (see, e.g., 1986, 37; 1991, 28). The pig as Other clearly functions within these graphic novels but is not developed much beyond the obvious signification of the pig as potential and/or actualized dangerous Other (nor, for that matter, is the Jewish taboo against consuming pig; see, e.g., 1991, 61).

The vitriolic association between Jews and pigs continues in neo-Nazi rhetoric. This is briefly noted in Rakoff 2010, 88. It also continues in other contexts. For example, in a concert in Belgium in 2013, the musician Roger Waters incorporated Nazi symbols and a pig-shaped balloon with a Star of David on it to criticize the modern state of Israel. While I will not comment on his intentions here, the inclusion of Nazi symbols and a pig-shaped balloon clearly (in my opinion) crosses the line into the realm of antisemitism. I thank Karen Stern for this reference.

40 For but one of the many examples of both the previous and the present scenarios of Jewish pig eaters during the Holocaust, see Ackerman 2008, 103, which describes the ironic situation of a Christian pig farmer (and zookeeper) resisting the Nazis by sneaking food from a pig farm into the Warsaw Ghetto to feed pig to Jews.

41 Foer 2010, 17 (for the full story, see 15–17).

42 While I cannot tell the story of every German Jew and their relationship with the pig, I also cannot resist slipping in one more story. Fleeing Nazi Germany, the Jewish Assyriologist Benno Landsberger found an academic position in Turkey. He loved food and especially enjoyed pig's feet. In Ankara, Turkey, he frequented the only delicatessen that sold pork products. The lack of pigs for sale was obviously due to Muslim rather than Jewish sensibilities. See the recollections by Hans G. Güterbock in Shils 1991, 274 (and on Landsberger in general, see 267–275). I thank Seth Sanders for this reference.

43 A quick porcine aside: many Reform Jews and members of the European scientific community in the nineteenth and twentieth centuries discussed the pig prohibition from the perspective of dietary and epidemiological benefits (often attributing the taboo's origin to these factors). For brief discussion, see Efron 2001, 69, 199; Zalashik 2018, 166, 172–173.

44 In Mendes-Flohr and Reinharz 1995, 263 (full text on 262–265).

45 In Mendes-Flohr and Reinharz 1995, 263.

46 As we should expect, there was a range of German Jewish practices with regard to pig ingestion. For additional references, see Kaplan 1991, 72, 79; 2018, 245–246.

47 See Geller 2018, 37–39 (the Rothschild poster is on 38). The Rothschild family features prominently in antisemitic conspiracy theories unto today.

48 Fabre-Vassas 1997, 97.

49 Fabre-Vassas 1997, 98.

50 Fabre-Vassas 1997, 98–99 (references on 337n2; on the pig's ear in general, see 97–102).

51 See Armanios and Ergene 2018, 246–247 (for further context, see 226–227, 239); also see the brief mention in Diemling 2015, 134.

52 On the term "culinary nationalism" in this context, see Wallenbrock 2015. For a larger treatment of the role that Jewish avoidance of pig plays in political discourse in modern France, see Birnbaum 2013.

53 Sfar 2005; Sthers 2019. In 2017, Sthers's novel was released as a major motion picture, titled *Holy Lands*. Sthers both wrote the screenplay and directed the film.

54 Wallenbrock 2015, 110. Also see the brief discussion in Armanios and Ergene 2018, 226–227.

55 Koltun-Fromm 2020, 152 (on this graphic novel in general, see 152–167; on the restaurant scene that I discuss in detail, see 163–167).

56 Both quotes are from Sfar 2005, 116.

57 Sfar 2005, 116.

58 Sfar 2005, 116 (we first meet the dog on 111). It is interesting to contrast this to a scene from an American comic about a Muslim superhero: Kamala Khan, a.k.a. *Ms.*

Marvel, who is pig-curious but does not act on this curiosity. For discussion, see Koltun-Fromm 2020, 104–108.

59 Sfar 2005, 117. This panel is reproduced in Koltun-Fromm 2020, 165.
60 "Forlorn and beaten" from Koltun-Fromm 2020, 163; the rabbi's dialogue from Sfar 2005, 117.
61 Sfar 2005, 117. This panel is reproduced in Koltun-Fromm 2020, 165. The panel adds a note: "*Blessing for non-kosher food." However, normative rabbinic law prohibits reciting any blessing on nonkosher food. The one exception would be nonkosher food consumed due to danger to one's life, an exception that it would be a major reach to apply to the rabbi's existential crisis here.
62 As the food is drawn as a nondistinct pile of yellow mush, I cannot assert with certainty whether it was the pig or any of the other nonkosher dishes that he ordered that crossed his lips at this defining moment.
63 Koltun-Fromm 2020, 164.
64 To use the language of the scholar of religion Bruce Lincoln, this is an act of symbolic inversion. However, as Lincoln rightly notes, "To be sure it is a powerful act to turn the world upside down, but a simple 180-degree rotation is not difficult to undo. An order twice inverted is an order restored, perhaps even strengthened as a result of the exercise" (2014, 159). Blessing the forbidden meal allows the rabbi to easily reinvert his symbolic inversion the next day, restoring order.
65 This is furthered on the very last page of the graphic novel, where the rabbi uses this story (but changing his role to observer and not eater) as part of a Sabbath sermon; see Sfar 2005, 142. For discussion of this final scene, see Koltun-Fromm 2020, 164–167 (the panel is reproduced on 166).
66 In the movie, Harry is played by actor the James Caan. Though perhaps best known for his role as Sonny Corleone in *The Godfather* (1972), Caan grew up in a Jewish home, and his father was a wholesaler of kosher meat. See Haberman 2022, A22.
67 On several occasions, some specific legal issues involved with raising pigs in Israel are noted in passing; e.g., see Sthers 2019, 1, 27–28, 77, 95. We discuss these issues further in the pigs in modern Israel section later in this chapter.
68 Sthers 2019, 114.
69 Sthers 2019, 72. A brief history of Jews and pigs (including reference to the rabbinic pig idiom of *davar aḥer*) is offered in a letter to Harry by his friend Rabbi Moshe Cattan. See Sthers 2019, 63–64.
70 Sthers 2019, 123.
71 Of the numerous examples I could choose, see the brief overviews of Jewish twists on salami and sausage in Marks 2010, 520–521, 527–528. In general, Marks's encyclopedia is an excellent resource on Jewish food history.
72 Toaff 2011, 55–69; also see the brief note in G. Allen 2015, 102; and Siporin 1994, 279n12. Flora Cassen (2018, 36–37) notes Toaff's work as she carefully speculates on whether the sausage in the sixteenth-century pantry of the Jewish Nantua family contained pig.
73 See the "artichoke" entry in Marks 2010, 23–24; and the discussion of Roman-Jewish cuisine in Moyer-Nocchi and Rolandi 2019, 159–163. I have much more to say on the history of *carciofi alla giudia*, which I hope to explore in future research.

74 Quoted in Moyer-Nocchi 2015, 22, original emphasis (also quoted in Moyer-Nocchi and Rolandi 2019, 163).
75 The third dish mixes milk and meat. For a brief comment on the historical inaccuracies of Renata's claims, see Moyer-Nocchi 2015, 22.
76 These final two sentences reflect my own original argument, based on my reading of primary and secondary sources. I am not a specialist in this subject, so while I think I am right, I acknowledge that I might be proven wrong.
77 See Michelson 2022, 2n2 (also see Mampieri 2020, 370n78). Numerous news articles are available online. Rather than choose one particular source, I encourage readers to conduct their own search. For instance, a quick internet search for articles on "pig's head Roman synagogue" led me to multiple news articles (some of which involve pigs' heads left in other geographic and historical locations).
78 See Mampieri 2020, 370n78. While the slogan "Lazio fans don't eat pork" could also be viewed as anti-Muslim, it both immediately and subsequently was consistently connected with anti-Jewish slogans and iconography (e.g., Holocaust and Nazi symbols), making its primary intention abundantly clear.
79 Strictly speaking, this story is liminal: it relates events slightly before 1800 and in a city that is now part of Russia (a country I discuss in another section). Though I felt it worked best here, it does not affect my argument if the reader wishes to mentally assign this data to another section and/or chapter.
80 The journal's title in English would be "The Collector"; for documentation of this journal's beginnings, see, e.g., Mendes-Flohr and Reinharz 1995, 80–85. In Hebrew, the Jewish Enlightenment is referred to as the *Haskalah*, and Enlightenment thinkers are referred to as *Maskilim* (singular: *Maskil*).
81 As quoted in Efron 2001, 98. The connection between German pigs eating acorns and Germans to their land was used for antisemitic purposes in Nazi Germany; for discussion, see Saraiva 2018, 101. Today, acorn-fed pigs in Spain are used to produce some of the world's most desired (and expensive) ham; see Rogers 2012, 15.
82 In spring 2009, Gantt Gurley told me to take a look at this novel for pig references. Many years later, to my great benefit, I took that advice.
83 Goldschmidt 1852, 9.
84 See Goldschmidt 1852, 23.
85 Goldschmidt 1852, 24, original emphasis.
86 Goldschmidt 1852, 68.
87 The translation renders the word "Valhalla" as "balhalla," but for clarity, I chose to use the more popular English rendering.
88 This is obviously a very Christian argument, echoing Jesus's words in the New Testament. See Mark 7:14–23; and for discussion, see Rosenblum 2016b, 78–79.
89 Goldschmidt 1852, 68.
90 Goldschmidt 1852, 76–77. Jacob continues to struggle with his identity, and pig continues to be part of that proverbial struggle. For example, see Goldschmidt 1852, 93–94.
91 Since the video has been removed, I am relying on news stories (including screenshots) about the video and its reception. Scrabble mavens will probably note two things: (1) this hand would be worth at least sixty-nine points: nineteen points

for the letters, plus the fifty-point bingo bonus for using all tiles in your hand, which would then be added to whatever other points that are achieved based on the word's placement on the board; and (2) Scrabble hands have seven and not eight tiles, so (unless the player uses a tile on the board to complete the word) this would not be a legal word to play in the game.

92 As quoted in JTA and TOI Staff 2019.
93 Armanios and Ergene 2018, 247; Bilefsky 2016.
94 If you want to dig deeper into the history of Jews in this region, see Dubnow's classic work, which references Jews and the pig twice (1916, 30, 266).
95 Wex 2007, 86; Rothstein 2013, 138 (and for additional Yiddish idioms that feature both pigs and dogs, see 139, 141, 144n360). For further discussion of pig words and idioms in Yiddish, see Wex 2006, 72–74, 131, 175–176, 181–182; Goodman 2017, 85.
96 Here I have used different transliteration conventions. For Hebrew, I have used the one scholars in my field tend to use for biblical and rabbinic Hebrew, and for Yiddish, I have used one in line with the YIVO standards for transliterations. There are some dialectical differences in how Yiddish speakers pronounce certain words. For example, some pronounce *davar* as *duver* (see Wex 2007, 155).
97 There is evidence of Jewish tavern owners in Poland in the late sixteenth century raising pigs and feeding them the by-products of beer production, but this is small potatoes compared to the operations under discussion. See Dynner 2014, 65–66 (and the literary reference in the Yiddish short story by I. J. Singer [1938, 264]).
98 For example, see Fleischman 2020, which focuses on East Germany.
99 As quoted and translated in Estraikh 2018, 128.
100 See Estraikh 2018, 128.
101 Text and translation from Shternshis 2008, 94 (on this poem, also see Estraikh 2018, 128).
102 On this genre, see Shternshis 2006, 119–126 (pigs appear on 121).
103 For more information on the history of Jewish participation in pig-breeding collectives, see Estraikh 2018, 126–129; Shternshis 2006, 84–85, 160–161.
104 The tension between these differing practices is embodied in the pig in a Yiddish short story titled "Blood" by I. J. Singer (1938). In this story, a Jew is born to a Jewish mother, and as everyone seems to know, his biological father is not her Jewish husband but is Stepan, the pig-sticker's son. The son, born Shmarya Wolf but eventually nicknamed "Shmerele Pork-sausage," becomes first an apostate and then converts to Christianity and marries a Christian widow. Pig plays a prominent role in the story: first in his transgressions as he resists but then relents to eating pig (see 251–252, 255) and then when he eventually becomes "immensely fond of ham and sausage and beer" (259). His encounters with pig appear regularly throughout the story. For example, to demonstrate both how low he has sunk and how much he is manipulated by his wife, we learn, "Deliberately, the ex-widow made him kill pigs on the Sabbath, so that the squealing of the animals could be heard in the quiet of Jewish homes or pierced the ears of Jews returning, their prayer-shawls and prayer-books under their arms, from the synagogue" (264–265). I thank Sunny Yudkoff both for this reference and for lending me a copy of the story.

105 For example, a memoir about Kiev in the 1890s notes a Jew who would eat pig but "would nonetheless organize a prayer quorum in his house for the High Holy Days" (Meir 2007, 628).
106 Here I follow Irad Ben Isaak (2019, 63–64), who argues that Ravitch's omission of the pig is intentional and not coincidental.
107 Quoted in Hadda 1997, 360; I revisit Singer's pig signature in the conclusion. I thank Sunny Yudkoff for this reference and David Stromberg for sharing his image of the postcard with me. Importantly, while Hadda dates this to 1937, the postcard is postmarked June 12, 1939.
108 Estraikh 2018, 129 (reference on 137n64).
109 Quoted and translated by Estraikh 2018, 124 (reference on 136n47).
110 Jews in Germany ate gefilte fish at least since medieval times. For discussion, see Marks 2010, 219–223. More commonly, the inclusion of pig can serve to deidentify a food as "Jewish." For example, see the discussion of Hungarian cholent/sólet in Rac 2019, 242–244.
111 Shternshis 2015, 17.
112 See Shternshis 2015, 16–18; 2006, 1–2. Estraikh (2018, 131) quotes and interacts with Shternshis's work but notes, "in my own experience I never met such people."
113 Shternshis 2015, 18.
114 Even though the Ukrainian salo that Vladimir P. procures from friends visiting from Ukraine is probably not slaughtered by one of the special ritual slaughterers he remembers from his youth (I leave aside whether this was ever the case), it is notable that he still identifies the Ukrainian salo as "Jewish food"; and hence, the larger point that Shternshis makes would still hold in this case.
115 Barak-Erez 2007; see also the brief summary of this work in Barak-Erez 2017, 377–380—an essay that, given her appointment to the Supreme Court, required the inclusion of the following caveat: "This chapter reflects only the academic writings of the author, and not the official views of the Court" (2017, 365). In addition, there is at least one other book chapter by another scholar on this subject; see Ben-Porat 2013, 138–175.
116 Barak-Erez 2007, 3.
117 On food austerity in Israel at this time, see Rozin 2015 (on pig, see especially 74–77); and for food shortages prior to 1948 in British Mandate Palestine (with special attention to pig and camel meat), see Gilad 2022.
118 Quoted in Barak-Erez 2007, 88. For references to *Shmukler*, see 170nn33, 35; 173n91.
119 On this case, see Barak-Erez 2007, 97–105; 2017, 379–380. My summary here especially draws on Barak-Erez 2007, 97–98; 2017, 379–380.
120 Ironically, this has led to pig monopolies, as certain regions where pig-breeding is permitted have asserted control of the market, especially since the importation of nonkosher meat into Israel is legally prohibited. See Barak-Erez 2007, 103.
121 Barak-Erez notes briefly that these discussions focus on views of Israeli Jews toward the pig and not on the views of Israeli Arabs (a community that includes both Muslims and Christians); see 2007, 99–100, 109–110.
122 Barak-Erez 2007, 107.
123 Barak-Erez 2007, 113–114.

124 As quoted in Rubel 2010, 54. I omit the gloss of Torah as "(bible)." Given what we have learned previously about rabbinic claims that pigs were involved in Rome's destruction of the Second Temple, this is quite an inflammatory statement.
125 On Tiv Ta'am, see Ben-Porat 2013 (which also notes that this is about more than just Jewish identity); and on the first pig cookbook in Israel, see Yoskowitz 2010. A recent online article suggests that the popularity of the pig (and shrimp) is waning in Israeli cookbooks; see Leshem 2023. Time will tell whether this is a blip or an enduring trend, though I strongly believe that we have by no means seen the last of the pig in Israel.
126 Independence Day cookouts serve to frame *Praise the Lard* (2016), a documentary on the Israeli pig industry and the symbolism of the pig in Israel. I thank Shayna Weiss for bringing this documentary to my attention.
127 Avieli 2015, 150. Despite the city's secular identity, Tel Aviv actually has a richer and more complex porcine history than is commonly known. See Barak-Erez 2007, 46–48, 59–65, 69–70, 73–74, 79, 115.
128 Certainly this is the most controversial ham sandwich in Israeli history. To my knowledge, the three other competitors for the worldwide award for "most controversial Jewish ham sandwich" are (1) the Karl Marx Special, mentioned earlier; (2) the ham sandwich that Sandy Koufax was alleged to have eaten in a Minnesota hotel's elevator on the same week in 1965 when he refused to pitch in Game 1 of the World Series because the game fell on Yom Kippur (see Leavy 2003, 193, discussed in chapter 6); and (3) the ham sandwich that, according to urban legend, Mama Cass (born Ellen Naomi Cohen) allegedly died by choking on in 1974 (see McNeil 2020, which reports that the actual cause of Cass's death was a heart attack). I thank Molly Parr for reminding me about Mama Cass's ham sandwich. I leave aside the British politician Ed Miliband's pig sandwich, discussed earlier, because it was technically a bacon sandwich and not a ham sandwich.
129 There are numerous articles on this kerfuffle easily accessible online; e.g., Chabin 2015.
130 Kibbutzim: in addition to being discussed throughout Barak-Erez 2007, also see Yoskowitz 2008; and the documentary *Praise the Lard* (2016). It is worth taking a moment to dispel an urban legend: these kibbutzim do not raise pigs on platforms in order not to raise pigs *on* the land of Israel. (For an example of this urban legend in literary form, see Sthers 2019, 1, 77, 95.) The best explanation for this legend that I have found is Barak-Erez 2007, 31. I thank Jeffrey Yoskowitz, who reconfirmed for me in a personal communication that this is indeed an urban legend. Yom Kippur: see Rosner 2008, 92. I will discuss the phenomenon of eating pig on Yom Kippur further in chapter 6.
131 As quoted in Yoskowitz 2009.
132 While the concern about offending the Israeli public was paramount here, clearly the offense to Mexico and Mexicans was not considered in these deliberations. For another pandemic-related pig in Israel story (this time in regard to COVID-19 and wild boars in Haifa), see D. Williams 2020.
133 As quoted in Sales 2018.
134 Mishnah, *Bava Qamma* 7:7; discussed in chapter 2.

135 See Rosenthal 1991, 49.
136 Davis 1948, 18, as quoted in Diner 2018, 64 (with minor correction; and for background on which I draw, 63–64). Davis titles this story "The Bacon Incident."
137 His son does claim, "I don't think the [sic] Dad told the good woman the cause of the mishap" (Davis 1948, 18).
138 As quoted and translated in Estraikh 2018, 128.
139 See Kaplan 2018, 254–256.
140 Klein 2016, 87. For another South American example, see the report from 1770s Suriname that Jewish soldiers would eat pig without scruple (Schorsch 2004, 248–249).
141 Klein 2016, 89.
142 Klein 2016, 89 (in general, see 87–92, 120).

CHAPTER 6. "NO JEW EVER DIED REFUSING TO EAT SHRIMP"

1 Horowitz 2006, 108 (and, in general, 108–109). On the story of chicken in the United States more broadly, see Rude 2016.
2 One of the anonymous reviewers of an earlier draft of this book wondered how the Jewish market could have such an impact. As Horowitz notes (2006, 108), this was because Jewish consumers significantly contributed to the overall demand of the New York City chicken economy and New York City was the largest market for chickens in the United States; thus, "farmers in the Delmarva peninsula were the principal beneficiaries of this burgeoning demand for chicken." Over time, infrastructure built up in this region, and as broader demand in the United States grew, it became a major chicken supplier both domestically and globally.
3 The Pew poll is cited in Price 2020, 192.
4 For an excellent case study of similarity and difference, see the now classic Diner 2001.
5 We also have evidence of New York Jews who traveled elsewhere in the United States. For example, the Swedish traveler Peter Kalm noted in 1748 that, while New York Jews commonly did not eat pig, many did so when they traveled. See Marcus 1999, 83–84; Gurock 2009, 34.
6 Traditionally, these adults were required to be male. While some Jewish communities today will include all adults (male, female, nonbinary) in their counting of a minyan, many of these communities had less than ten adults regardless of gender, which is why I chose to word this sentence thusly.
7 To be sure, there is also evidence that many immigrant Jews in the nineteenth-century United States had no concern with eating pig and/or trading pigs. For example, see Steinberg and Prost 2011, 10–11.
8 Diner 2018, 62 (and, on pig and modern Jewish peddlers worldwide, see this Diner article generally).
9 As quoted in Rabin 2017, 81. For another contemporaneous account of a Jew in Hancock County, Georgia, refusing to eat pig, see Sarna and Mendelsohn 2011, 230.
10 As quoted in Schloff 1996, 96–97. Dukovna, who moved to his farm in 1905, goes on to say that his parents would get kosher meat when they could.
11 As quoted in Rabin 2017, 81–82 (also see Steinberg and Prost 2011, 15–16). Carvalho was not the only American Jewish immigrant who worked in the railroad industry

and encountered pig. Edward Rosewater rode on trains across the country as a telegraph operator. On his journeys, he "ate non-kosher food, including Alabama barbecue and pork rinds" (Rabin 2017, 1).

12 As quoted in Schloff 1996, 96. Thal goes on to admit that she no longer follows Jewish dietary laws but maintains certain other religious practices (such as observing Passover and Yom Kippur).

13 As quoted in Marcus 1996, 351. Sapinsky comments earlier that her "church" was really a synagogue in Louisville. She also continues on to note that they did not mix milk and meat. Though I do not focus on the latter dietary prohibition, that is another Jewish food regulation that is mentioned almost as often in these narratives as the abstention from pig.

14 For but a few of the myriad examples, see Ferris 2005, 72–73; Gurock 2009, 34, 49–50, 60; Sarna 2019, 9, 25; Schloff 1996, 83, 98; and for examples from Jewish peddlers both in the United States and across the globe, see Diner 2018. Some of these tales are clearly apocryphal, such as the story about a Jewish man named Rosenthal who lived in Bellevue, Iowa, and was reputed to have taught Ulysses S. Grant about the pork trade (see Sarna 2012, 64). Other stories have some basis in fact but have overtones that give pause as to what other elements might be behind certain assertions—for example, the claim that a Jewish man named Otto Mears launched his political career in Saguache, Colorado, in the 1870s by buying votes with free ham and bacon (see Uchill [1957] 2000, 59).

15 As quoted in Peck 1987, 106. I first found this reference in Diner 2018, 64.

16 As quoted in Uchill (1957) 2000, 206 (background for this paragraph can be found on 205–206, 226).

17 As we covered this topic previously in chapter 5, I will not devote significant attention here to the ways in which the pig taboo was used to mock Jews in the United States. Suffice it to say, it occurred (and continues to occur) often and does not add much to our discussion to delve too deeply into that muck. To cite one of the more colorful examples, at the turn of the twentieth century, there was a widespread belief that Jews were criminals, especially associated with arson. One contemporary cartoon features a stereotyped drawing of two Jews sharing the following joke: "What is the only thing our race hates more than pork?" The punch line: "asbestos" (Joselit 1983, 37).

18 Metzker 1971, 169, 170. I will cite direct quotations, but when I summarize details, I am drawing from 169–173.

19 Metzker 1971, 170.

20 Metzker 1971, 171. Left unresolved is how the rabbi would respond if, after he divests from the pig business, the man follows through on his intention to "endow liberally" the Orthodox shul (171). Would his porcine divestment, in essence, launder the money and make it kosher for synagogue use? Or, in the rabbi's opinion, will it forever be tainted?

21 Metzker 1971, 172.

22 This playful wording is adopted, with a slight tweak, from Jennifer 8. Lee's chapter on this topic. See Lee 2008, 89–106.

23 One reason for the popularity of this term might be that the article is most commonly cited in a republished format with a new title—"'Safe Treyf': New York Jews and Chinese Food"—that is available on multiple sites on the internet (search "safe treyf" in your preferred internet browser, and you will find it).
24 As noted in chapter 2, the pig becomes a metonym for all nonkosher food starting in the Rabbinic Period.
25 Tuchman and Levine 1993, 388, original emphasis.
26 Here I summarize and augment Tuchman and Levine 1993, 388–392.
27 For a brief overview of the development of this rabbinic prohibition, see Rosenblum 2020, 78–86.
28 Similarly, see D. Kraemer 2009, 144–145.
29 Coe 2009, 203. And for their full argument, see Tuchman and Levine 1993, 392–394.
30 Roth (1967) 1994, 90, original emphasis. Tuchman and Levine (1993, 391–392) reference this quote in their section on safe treyf, not cosmopolitanism; however, I argue that it fits more in the latter theme. Also see W. Allen 1971, 67; and for more literary remarks on Jews and Chinese food, see Coe 2009, 200–204.
31 Lee 2008, 96, where she also provocatively asserts (but does not empirically prove), "The average American Reform Jew is more likely to know how to use chopsticks than how to write the Hebrew alphabet."
32 For more information on the caterer of this event, see M. Weiss 2018. I thank Joe Weber for this reference.
33 Here we focus on Reform Judaism in the United States. However, it is worth noting that forty-two years earlier (in 1841) in Hamburg, Germany, a Jewish boys' school held a twenty-fifth-anniversary dinner that, with far less fanfare, served a meal that featured not only crabs and oysters but pig's head as well. See Joselit 1994, 174 (and on the *Terefah* Banquet, see 174–175).
34 Horowitz 2006, 47 (on Cincinnati more broadly, see 46–49). Also see J. L. Anderson 2019, 110–118; Mizelle 2011, 46–54. Cincinnati was not the only location in the United States that earned this nickname; Madison, Indiana, was also referred to as "Porkopolis." To learn more about Jews and the pig in Madison, Indiana, see Gurock 2009, 73–74.
35 As quoted in Mendelsohn 2016, 86.
36 For the full document, see Marcus 1996, 241–243 (this quote is on 242). Of course, many Reform Jews had been advocating in favor of disregarding all dietary laws, including the pig taboo. That position was also invoked in denominational polemics against Reform Judaism. For example, see Rabin 2017, 98.
37 See Leviticus 11:9–12; Deuteronomy 14:9–10.
38 Kurlansky 2007.
39 Sussman 2005, especially 35, 39, 49n28. Further, according to reports, the caterer for the *Terefah* Banquet felt that pig was taboo but that seafoods "were so good they had to be kosher" (Joselit 1994, 175).
40 See Balin 2011, 8 (and the relevant references on 15nn11–12). Wise is not the only American Jew to have owned a pig named Kosher. The popular author Michael Pollan reports that, as a child, his father gave him a pet pig named Kosher (2014, 62–65).

41 Sussman 2005, 38.
42 Sussman 2005, 44–45.
43 In general, see Marx de Salcedo 2015 (and on the role of pig in ancient warfare logistics, see especially 39–41).
44 In this chapter, I focus on Jews in the US military. Obviously, there is evidence that Jews fought (and continue to fight) in other nations' military efforts. For example, the Hapsburg Empire issued an edict on May 7, 1789, that, among other rulings, stated that Jews were subject to military conscription "and would serve in transportation divisions with provisions for kosher food and religious observance" (Sorkin 2019, 84; and for the broader context, see 82–85). On Jews in world militaries in general, see Penslar 2013 (who notes on p. 62 that, later on, "whether due to logistical difficulties or residual prejudice, the Hapsburg military was not as forthcoming about giving Jewish soldiers easy access to kosher meat"). I discussed pig in the Israeli military in chapter 5. Finally, for a recent evaluation of the evidence for Jewish dietary observance in the ancient Roman army, see Olshanetsky 2023.
45 As quoted in Rabin 2017, 80. Cohen was from Cincinnati; the connection between his hometown and pig is discussed earlier.
46 For additional references to pig and Jewish Union soldiers' interactions therewith, see Mendelsohn 2022, 8, 20–21, 143–145, 153, 156, 163, 168, 202.
47 As quoted in Mendelsohn 2022, 144 (for original citation, see 291n40).
48 Mendelsohn 2022, 144.
49 On the Evil Inclination, temptation, and the pig, see Rosenblum 2015.
50 Rabin 2017, 78. Rabin continues on to note that "although his wartime conditions were extreme, Kursheedt's wary consideration of pork without unreserved consumption or outright rejection was typical of the relationship of nineteenth-century American Jews to kosher food laws" (78). Rabin then expands on this point on 78–85.
51 For discussion of the general importance of pig during the Civil War, see J. L. Anderson 2019, 18–20, 78–82. For additional references, see Rosen 2021, 34, 103, 173, 199. And for the use of pig as part of antisemitic remarks against Jews engaging in Civil War–related business, see Sarna and Mendelsohn 2011, 366. Though Adam Mendelsohn was still working on another monograph about Confederate Jewish soldiers during the Civil War at the time of my writing this chapter, he confirmed for me in a personal communication that pig was a common, and often unremarkable, part of Jewish Confederate soldiers' diets. As for their Union brethren, pig was routinely eaten by soldiers, whether Jewish or Christian.
52 As quoted in Stahl 2017, 34. For further historical context, see Cooperman 2018 (with a focus on kosher food on 72–85).
53 Stahl 2017, 33.
54 Moore 2006, 57 (in general, see pp. 49–57). Also see Gurock 2009, 151–153.
55 In Philip Roth's novel *Portnoy's Complaint*, the main character reports that his cousins, their friends, and he used to chant a cheer that begins almost verbatim: "Ikey, Mikey, Jake, and Sam / We're the boys that eat no ham, / We play football, we play soccer— / And we keep matzohs in our locker! / Aye, aye, aye, Weequahic High!" ([1967] 1994, 56). The author Rich Cohen reports that in his youth, he attended Camp Menominee in Managua, Wisconsin—a Jewish camp with a Native American

name—where campers would chant, "Easy, Izzy, Jake, and Sam, we're the boys who eat no ham. Matzoh, matzoh, that's our cry; matzoh, matzoh, 'til we die. Yeah, Menominee!" (1999, 104).

56 As quoted in Moore 2006, 49. The phrase "GI Jew" is taken from the title of Moore's book. According to popular lore, "In the War of 1812 so much pork was supplied to American soldiers by a New York packer called 'Uncle Sam' Wilson that he came to personify the entire government and was portrayed by cartoonists as a giant figure in a tall hat under a banner that read 'Uncle Sam is feeding the Army'" (Rogers 2012, 72). While this lore may or may not be historically accurate, even the claim that it is adds yet another layer to our porcine story.

57 Eggs and pig product is viewed by many people as a quintessential American breakfast. For an example of this belief in a Jewish Egyptian memoir, see the discussion in Berg 2018, 73.

58 As quoted in Moore 2006, 54. For a fictional account of World War II–era American Jews interacting with nonkosher food in military mess halls, see P. Roth (1959) 1993, 172–173 (with ham specifically mentioned on 173).

59 Gorenstein's case is actually a bit more complicated. He reports that even though he tried to keep eating ham for Uncle Sam, even pretending that the Sunday pork chops were lamb chops, he could not get over his aversion to pork. Therefore, he stopped eating pig in the Army. See Moore 2006, 54–56.

60 Ironically, according to rabbinic law, the prohibition against mixing milk and meat only applies to meat that is either kosher or potentially kosher. Therefore, butter on a pork chop does not violate that prohibition (even though the pork itself is forbidden).

61 Moore 2006, 56–57.

62 As quoted in Stahl 2017, 133.

63 Gurock 2009, 152.

64 American Jews are not the only Americans who grapple with their religious identity in porcine terms. For example, the pig plays pivotal roles in an American Muslim novel; see Akhtar 2012, 3–5, 18, 68, 86, 216, 277.

65 Horn 2003, 88. Pig appears only one time also in a more recent book by the same author; see Horn 2021, 43.

66 Rakoff 2010, 81–96. While Rakoff was born and spent his formative years in Canada, he settled in the United States and eventually became a US citizen (without renouncing his Canadian citizenship). For this reason, I include his work in this chapter.

67 See Rakoff 2010, 85, 87–88. For more on the colorful history of Yom Kippur balls in the United States, see Portnoy 2018, 83–88.

68 Rakoff 2010, 84. I will resist the urge to correct his Latin because this is a joke and not a grammar lesson.

69 Rakoff 2010, 84. Similarly, the author Michael Chabon includes the following line in one of his novels: "the craving of a Jew for pork, in particular when it has been deep-fried, is a force greater than night or distance or a cold blast off the Gulf of Alaska" (2007, 14).

70 Rakoff 2010, 85.

71 Rakoff 2010, 87.
72 Rakoff 2010, 84. We discussed carbonara in chapter 5.
73 Rakoff 2010, 88, original emphasis.
74 Though Rakoff here refers to the popular explanation for this Jewish wedding practice, the history of the broken glass is much richer and more complex; see Lauterbach 1925.
75 Rakoff 2010, 89.
76 It is worth noting that, at the end of the essay, Rakoff admits that, for himself, eating pig is less about personal transgression. He contrasts himself with a friend of his, whom he claims eats pig "with gusto and frequency" because she "feels that she is getting back at her mother with each bite" (2010, 95).
77 Clips of this exchange are readily available online. This interchange is briefly discussed in Plaut 2012, 65.
78 Looking for belonging through Christmas rituals is also expressed in a 2003 episode of the popular television show *The O.C.* In season 1, episode 13, titled "The Best Chrismukkah Ever," the son of an intermarried couple combines elements of Christmas and Hanukkah to create this blended holiday. Eating Chinese food is only mentioned briefly in this episode but is identified as a Jewish practice. For discussion of this episode, including the assertion that this is the Ur-text for the term "Chrismukkah," see Mehta 2018, 136. Additional references to Jews and Chinese food (both on Christmas and in general) in humor (in print, stand-up, and television), can be found in Plaut 2012, 69–71. For the fascinating history of another Jewish Christmas Eve practice, known as "Nittel Nacht," which predates our present discussion, see Scharbach 2013.
79 See Lee 2008, 98–99; and for a longer discussion of American Jews eating Chinese food on Christmas, see Plaut 2012, 65–86. Of course, Jews are not the only Americans who visit Chinese restaurants on Christmas. Non-Jews visit for a variety of reasons, too. For example, there is a 1902 newspaper article about Bohemians who choose to eat Christmas dinner at Chinese restaurants (for discussion and reference, see Coe 2009, 169, 260n27); and, perhaps most famously, there is the unexpected Christmas family dinner scene in the now classic Christmas movie *A Christmas Story* (1983).
80 I refer throughout to the version quoted and discussed in Plaut 2012, 73–77 (reference to original citation on 186n36).
81 Plaut 2012, 74.
82 Plaut 2012, 74.
83 Plaut 2012, 74.
84 Plaut 2012, 75.
85 For an example of pigs in a poem, see "A woman and a girl feed pigs at sundown" (Grossman 2001, 53–55; which opens with a quote from Isaiah 65:3–4 and clearly references Psalm 137 throughout). On this poem, and for an additional pig poem reference, see Barak-Erez 2007, 22–23. While I have noted examples of both historical fiction and nonfiction throughout this book, I will add here a novella by Cynthia Ozick (1969). I thank Sunny Yudkoff for this reference. On Jews and pigs in a Pulitzer Prize–winning novel, see Chabon 2000, 585; and in American Jewish

detective stories, see L. Roth 2004, 89, 155, 220. For novels in the South, see, e.g., Mirvis 2000, 81, 111, 238; and in the East, Auslander 2006, 2, 7, 42, 59, 64, 119–120, 139, 169.

86 Spinner 2020.

87 Nor for that matter is the explicit Jewishness of Peppa Pig's family. The book is cleverly written in an ambiguous manner, as the family never concretely identifies as Jews but never denies that fact. (If it were Passover, this would be quite telling, but for Hanukkah, it works.)

88 Snyder 2010. This book contains no page numbers, so I will not cite them; but it is short, so the quotations are easily locatable by the interested reader. Further, all emphasis is in the original.

89 It is worth noting that Baxter has officially had his request to become kosher—that is, to convert to Judaism—rejected three times already. It is normative Jewish practice to deny a potential convert's request to convert three times before accepting. When he meets Rabbi Rosen, therefore, it is a kosher moment for conversion!

90 While I have chosen to focus on this particular genre, the pig plays a role in many other genres of Jewish memoirs, as well, for example, in memoirs of people who are born Jewish and discuss navigating life in a largely non-Jewish world (e.g., Altman 2016; Greene 2020, 13, 41, 46, 68, 112) and people who convert to Judaism (e.g., Twitty 2018, 68; 2022, 10, 122, 126, 230, 233, 247, 248–249). A whole series of brief pig-related memoirs—from Jews, Muslims, and others—can be found on Jeffrey Yoskowitz's website: *Pork Memoirs: Personal Stories about a Complicated Meat*, https://porkmemoirs.com.

91 In general, see Rubel 2010.

92 In general, see Cappell and Lang 2020.

93 Stein 2019. On the OTD narrative as a genre, with particular attention to gender, see Skinazi 2018, 30–74.

94 Stein 2019, 223. Additional references to pig can be found on 226 and 228.

95 Stein describes herself as eating pig on a subsequent Yom Kippur (see 2019, 228). For further reference to OTDers (and atheist Jews) eating pig on Yom Kippur, see Linfield 2019, 142; and for an example of the pig-eating Yom Kippur practices of nonbelieving Jews in pre–World War II Poland, see Orenstein 1997, 12.

96 Prosciutto is thinly sliced, dry-cured ham from Italy.

97 Feldman 2012, 232.

98 Feldman 2012, 232. Feldman has written a second memoir, in which pig rarely appears. See Feldman 2015, 110–111, and especially 113. The dramatic miniseries *Unorthodox* was released on Netflix in 2020.

99 Auslander 2008, 79. Interestingly, while the paperback version of Auslander's book initially had a red cover with various scenes in white outline, a subsequent edition featured a very different cover: a picture of a sitting pig, which is turning its head to its left seemingly to gaze at the reader.

100 Auslander 2008, 83–84.

101 Auslander 2008, 84–85.

102 Mann 2007, 12 (also see 36, where consuming pork sausage is described as a litmus test for transgression). Mann's story is set in London and Israel, not in the United

States. However, I include it here because it fits into the larger genre of OTD memoirs.

103 See Schantz et al. 1992. I thank Dr. Bennett Vogelman for this reference.

104 I have highlighted only a few examples. Additional references can be found in, e.g., Mann 2007, 12, 36, 79, 152; Vincent 2015, 144, 202. Scholarship by anthropologists and sociologists about those who went OTD, expressed doubt, or lived double lives also includes narratives of interactions with the pig. For example, see Davidman 2015, 22, 101, 149; Fader 2020, 56, 166; Newfield 2020, 104–108 (which includes some fascinating personal narratives), 151.

105 The presumption is that this is beef salami, but whether it is *kosher* beef salami is not explicitly mentioned.

106 I thank Tony Michels for bringing this show to my attention. For a little more context on why this show became "the highest-rated network show ever to be cancelled," see Dauber 2023, 151.

107 Pig is also used to mark the Jewishness of Prince John in the 1993 Mel Brooks comedy *Robin Hood: Men in Tights*. Jeremy Dauber summarizes the scene in question: "Faced with suckling pig, [Prince John's] immediate response is to yelp, '*Treyf!*' (that is, 'unkosher')" (2023, 145; on the movie in general, see 143–148).

108 I want to be clear here that I am denying neither the existence of nor the important lived experiences of Jews of color. However, I do not believe that this cinematic scene is engaging with that reality. Rather, the humor depends on the audience being surprised that one would think that Jules is Jewish. Also worthy of note is the complete absence of any discussion about whether Jules is Muslim (he never denies it, though he does not affirm it in any way either).

109 For another example, see the brief discussion in Meyers 2021, 105–106, of pig—in the form of bacon cheeseburger—in the movie *Wish I Was Here* (2014).

110 Season 3, episode 4. The title clearly is a play on the professional wrestling event known as "WrestleMania."

111 To offer one tacit example, in season 5, episode 5 (1993) of the sitcom *Seinfeld*, the main plot revolves around—as its title, "The Bris," implies—a Jewish circumcision. But a subplot involves Kramer encountering a "pig man" at the hospital. While humor unfolds, the connection between the pig and a Jewish circumcision ritual is never directly made. However, I would argue that their appearance in the same episode tacitly connects them to play on some of the notions discussed throughout this section.

112 *Onion* 1998.

113 I grew up hearing this joke from many friends and relatives. I take the wording of the punch line from the version that appears in Schnall 2017, 33.

114 See Diner 2018, 62.

115 "Selectively treyf": Kirshenblatt-Gimblett 1990, 80 (discussed in Joselit 1994, 172–173); "selective kashrut": Fishkoff 2010, 233.

116 On kosher style and the American Jewish deli (and all things deli in general), see Merwin 2015; Sax 2009; and more broadly, see D. Kraemer 2009, 139–145; R. Gross 2021, 156–188. Some common deli fare actually represents a decision to substitute for pig in order to make a dish potentially kosher. For example, the pig's blood and pork

from the eastern European sausages called kishke were routinely replaced with kosher alternatives and then incorporated into American Jewish delicatessen fare in their pig-free form. See G. Allen 2015, 59–60; Sax 2009, 22.

117 Joselit 1994, 173–174 (in general, see 171–177).
118 On nostalgia for food as an American Jewish religious practice, see R. Gross 2021, 156–188.
119 Even those who eschew pig are not above using the pig to make a statement about their religious culinary practice. Take for example the annual kosher barbecue contest held in Memphis, Tennessee. This allows for a fusion of southern and Jewish identities, which occurs not in a melting pot but in a smoker. And where does the pig play into this discussion? "The contest logo appears on T-shirts and team baseball caps and outlaws pork with its 'Pig Free' design—a circle with a slash mark across the face of a smiling pink pig" (Ferris 2005, 242; and on the contest more broadly, see 239–243).
120 Again, there are also Jews who are willing to eat pig without caveat. For example, the Council of Jewish Women in Portland, Oregon, published a cookbook in 1914 that included, without comment, a recipe for "Club House sandwiches" that, in addition to buttered white bread and "slices of chicken well seasoned," calls for "thin slices of crisp fried bacon" (as quoted in Wilson 2010, 79–80).
121 See R. Gross 2021, 180–181. I take the term "culinary apostasy" from Joselit 1994, 176.
122 Fishkoff 2010, 228.
123 An excellent overview of the history and mythology of that day can be found in Leavy 2003, 167–194.
124 Leavy 2003, 193. Another Jewish baseball player / pig story: the Hall of Fame first basemen Hank Greenberg (who sat out the September 10, 1934, World Series game that fell on Yom Kippur) regularly received antisemitic jeers at the ballpark. Among the many racial slurs rained down on him, "they shouted about Moses and pork chops" (Kurlansky 2011, 71).
125 See Marcus 1999, 83–84; Gurock 2009, 34. See note 5 above.
126 As quoted in Seligman 2020, 69 (reference on 249n18; for an additional pig reference, see 204).
127 For discussion, see Alvarez 2014; Jones 2017; Siporin 2015 (especially 64, 72); and for the issue in Europe (particularly in regard to Islam), see Armanios and Ergene 2018, 249–250.

CONCLUSION

1 As quoted in Gurvis 2021. Similar arguments were advanced by Islamic certification agencies.
2 I leave aside the history of debates about certifying pig gelatin as kosher. For an excellent survey of this issue, see Horowitz 2016, 47–74; and for similar issues with regard to halal foods, see Armanios and Ergene 2018, 169–173.
3 Joselit 1994, 193.
4 In regard to another modern food technology debate, the kosher status of lab-grown pig remains unresolved. For discussion, see Popper 2018 (which focuses on the Orthodox Union's role in this debate).

5 Gurock 2009, 240. Of the many other such kosher fake pig products, I will only note one more: the 2007 invention of Bacon Salt, which is certified as kosher. For discussion, see Fishkoff 2010, 229–230.
6 See chapter 6 for discussion of "safe treyf."
7 Solsman 2020.
8 Rosenblum 2019a.
9 The actual biblical text states, "the making of many books is without limit."
10 I thank one of the anonymous reviewers for suggesting that I make this point more explicit.
11 Mishnah, *Avot* 5:22.
12 Quoted in Hadda 1997, 360; I discussed Singer's pig signature in chapter 5. I again thank Sunny Yudkoff for this reference and David Stromberg for sharing his image of the postcard with me. Importantly, as noted earlier, while Hadda dates this to 1937, the postcard is postmarked June 12, 1939.
13 Shapiro and Rosenthal 2022.
14 Shapiro and Rosenthal 2022, A13 (noted again on A14).
15 From early on in this project, my editor, Jennifer Hammer, pushed me to answer why "some Orthodox Jews won't even draw a pig, or play with a pig toy figure or puzzle, even if the depiction is not related to food" (personal communication). I hope that, both here and throughout, I have answered her important question.
16 Price 2020, 191, referring to Schorsch 2018. I agree with Price's criticism here, which is also why my citations to Schorsch's problematic book are sparse throughout.
17 For the history of this advertising campaign, which started in 1986, see Essig 2015, 207–219.

REFERENCES

Ackerman, Diane. 2008. *The Zookeeper's Wife*. New York: Norton.
Ackerman-Lieberman, Phillip and Rakefet Zalashik, eds. 2013. *A Jew's Best Friend? The Image of the Dog throughout Jewish History*. Portland, OR: Sussex Academic Press.
Ainsztein, Reuben. 1964. "The Jewish Background of Karl Marx: His Mother Strongly Opposed Conversion." *Jewish Observer and Middle East Review*, October 23, 1964, 14–16.
Akhtar, Ayad. 2012. *American Dervish*. New York: Back Bay Books.
Allen, Gary. 2015. *Sausage: A Global History*. The Edible Series. London: Reaktion Books.
Allen, Woody. 1971. *Getting Even*. New York: Random House.
Altman, Elissa. 2016. *Treyf: My Life as an Unorthodox Outlaw*. New York: New American Library.
Alvarez, Lizette. 2014. "You Don't Have to Be Jewish to Love a Kosher Prison Meal." *New York Times*, January 21, 2014, A1.
Anderson, H. 1985. "4 Maccabees." In *Old Testament Pseudepigrapha*, ed. James H. Charlesworth, vol. 2, 531–564. New York: Doubleday.
Anderson, J. L. 2019. *Capitalist Pigs: Pigs, Pork, and Power in America*. Morgantown: West Virginia University Press.
Armanios, Febe, and Boğaç Ergene. 2018. *Halal Food: A History*. New York: Oxford University Press.
Auslander, Shalom. 2006. *Beware of God: Stories*. New York: Simon and Schuster.
———. 2008. *Foreskin's Lament: A Memoir*. New York: Riverhead Books.
Avieli, Nir. 2015. "Size Matters: Israeli Chefs Cooking Up a Nation." In *Jews and Their Foodways*, Studies in Contemporary Jewry, ed. Anat Herman, 142–159. New York: Oxford University Press.
Bailey, Christian. 2023. *German Jews in Love: A History*. Stanford Studies in Jewish History and Culture. Stanford, CA: Stanford University Press.
Bakhos, Carol. 2007. "Figuring (Out) Esau: The Rabbis and Their Others." *Journal of Jewish Studies* 58 (2): 250–262.
Balin, Carole B. 2011. "Making Every Forkful Count: Reform Jews, Kashrut, and Mindful Eating, 1840–2010." In *The Sacred Table: Creating a Jewish Food Ethic*, ed. Mary L. Zamore, 5–16. New York: CCAR.
Barak-Erez, Daphne. 2007. *Outlawed Pigs: Law, Religion, and Culture in Israel*. Madison: University of Wisconsin Press.
———. 2017. "What Does It Mean for a State to Be Jewish?" In *The Cambridge Companion to Judaism and Law*, ed. Christine Hayes, 365–385. New York: Cambridge University Press.

Baumgarten, Elisheva. 2007. *Mothers and Children: Jewish Family Life in Medieval Europe.* Princeton, NJ: Princeton University Press.

Ben Isaak, Irad. 2019. "'I Am a Vegetarian': The Vegetarianism of Melech Ravitch." In *Jewish Veganism and Vegetarianism: Studies and New Directions,* ed. Jacob Ari Labendz and Shmuly Yanklowitz, 49–66. Albany: SUNY Press.

Ben-Porat, Guy. 2013. *Between State and Synagogue: The Secularization of Contemporary Israel.* Cambridge Middle East Studies. New York: Cambridge University Press.

Bentley, Amy. 2014. *Inventing Baby Food: Taste, Health, and the Industrialization of the American Diet.* California Studies in Food and Culture. Berkeley: University of California Press.

Berg, Nancy E. 2018. "Jews among Muslims: Culinary Contexts." In *Global Jewish Foodways: A History,* ed. Hasia R. Diner and Simone Cinotto, 70–88. Lincoln: University of Nebraska Press.

Berkowitz, Beth A. 2018. *Animals and Animality in the Babylonian Talmud.* New York: Cambridge University Press.

Berlin, Adele, and Marc Zvi Brettler, eds. 2004. *The Jewish Study Bible.* New York: Oxford University Press.

Bilefsky, Dan. 2016. "Mandatory Pork: Menu Rule in Denmark Opens New Front in Immigration Debate." *New York Times,* January 21, 2016, A10.

Birnbaum, Pierre. 2013. *La République et le cochon.* Paris: Éditions du Seuil.

Blenkinsopp, Joseph. 2003. *Isaiah 56–66: A New Translation with Introduction and Commentary.* AB 19B. New York: Doubleday.

Boyarin, Adrienne Williams. 2021. *The Christian Jew and the Unmarked Jewess: The Polemics of Sameness in Medieval English Anti-Judaism.* The Middle Ages Series. Philadelphia: University of Pennsylvania Press.

Boyarin, Daniel. 1999. *Dying for God: Martyrdom and the Making of Christianity and Judaism.* Stanford, CA: Stanford University Press.

Bukey, Evan Burr. 2011. *Jews and Intermarriage in Nazi Austria.* New York: Cambridge University Press.

Bynum, Caroline Walker. 2020. *Dissimilar Similitudes: Devotional Objects in Late Medieval Europe.* New York: Zone Books.

Cappell, Ezra, and Jessica Lang, eds. 2020. *Off the Derech: Leaving Orthodox Judaism.* Albany: SUNY Press.

Cassen, Flora. 2018. "The Sausage in the Jews' Pantry: Food and Jewish-Christian Relations in Renaissance Italy." In *Global Jewish Foodways: A History,* ed. Hasia R. Diner and Simone Cinotto, 27–49. Lincoln: University of Nebraska Press.

Chabin, Michele. 2015. "Israel Soldier's Ham Sandwich Nearly Lands Him in Military Prison." *Religion News Service,* June 2, 2015. https://religionnews.com.

Chabon, Michael. 2000. *The Amazing Adventures of Kavalier & Clay.* New York: Picador.

———. 2007. *The Yiddish Policemen's Union.* New York: HarperCollins.

Coe, Andrew. 2009. *Chop Suey: A Cultural History of Chinese Food in the United States.* New York: Oxford University Press.

Cohen, Gerson D. 1967. "Esau as Symbol in Early Medieval Thought." In *Jewish Medieval and Renaissance Studies,* ed. A. Altmann, 19–48. Cambridge, MA: Harvard University Press.

Cohen, Rich. 1999. *Tough Jews: Father, Sons, and Gangster Dreams*. New York: Vintage Books.
Cohen, Shaye J. D. 2000. *The Beginnings of Jewishness: Boundaries, Varieties, Uncertainties*. Berkeley: University of California Press.
Colson, F. H., trans. 1939. *Philo: Volume VIII*. LCL 341. Cambridge, MA: Harvard University Press.
———, trans. (1941) 2001. *Philo: Volume IX*. LCL 363. Cambridge, MA: Harvard University Press.
———, trans. (1962) 2004. *Philo: The Embassy to Gaius*. LCL 379. Cambridge, MA: Harvard University Press.
Cooperman, Jessica. 2018. *Making Judaism Safe for America: World War I and the Origins of Religious Pluralism*. The Goldstein-Goren Series in American Jewish History. New York: New York University Press.
Darshan, Guy. 2022. "Pork Consumption as an Identity Marker in Ancient Israel: The Textual Evidence." *Journal for the Study of Judaism in the Persian, Hellenistic and Roman Period* 53:1–23.
Dauber, Jeremy. 2023. *Mel Brooks: Disobedient Jew*. Jewish Lives. New Haven, CT: Yale University Press.
Davidman, Lynn. 2015. *Becoming Un-Orthodox: Stories of Ex-Hasidic Jews*. New York: Oxford University Press.
Davis, Eliot R. 1948. *A Link with the Past*. Auckland, New Zealand: Unity.
Delman, Edward. 2015. "The Defining Image of the British Election: Parsing the Significance of Ed Miliband's Bacon Sandwich." *The Atlantic*, May 10, 2015. www.theatlantic.com.
Deutsch, Yaakov. 2012. *Judaism in Christian Eyes: Ethnographic Descriptions of Jews and Judaism in Early Modern Europe*. Translated by Avi Aronsky. New York: Oxford University Press.
Diemling, Maria. 2015. "About Bakers, Butchers, Geese and Pigs: Food and the Negotiating of Boundaries between Jews and Christians in Johann Jacob Schudt's 'Jüdische Merckwürdigkeiten.'" *Frankfurter Judaistische Beiträge* 40:115–138.
Diner, Hasia R. 2001. *Hungering for America: Italian, Irish, and Jewish Foodways in the Age of Migration*. Cambridge, MA: Harvard University Press.
———. 2018. "Global Jewish Peddling and the Matter of Food." In *Global Jewish Foodways: A History*, ed. Hasia R. Diner and Simone Cinotto, 50–69. Lincoln: University of Nebraska Press.
Dubnow, S. M. 1916. *History of the Jews in Russia and Poland: From the Earliest Times Until the Present Day*. Translated by I. Friedlander. Vol. 1. Philadelphia: Jewish Publication Society of America.
Dunne, J., E. Biddulph, P. Manix, T. Gillard, H. Whelton, S. Teague, C. Champness, et al. 2021. "Finding Oxford's Medieval Jewry Using Organic Residue Analysis, Faunal Records and Historical Documents." *Archaeological and Anthropological Sciences* 13:48.
Dynner, Glenn. 2014. *Yankel's Tavern: Jews, Liquor, and Life in the Kingdom of Poland*. New York: Oxford University Press.
Efron, John M. 2001. *Medicine and the German Jews: A History*. New Haven, CT: Yale University Press.

Ehrman, Bart D. 2003. *The Apostolic Fathers, II.* LCL 25. Cambridge, MA: Harvard University Press.

Elliott, J. K. 2005. *The Apocryphal New Testament: A Collection of Apocryphal Christian Literature in an English Translation Based on M. R. James.* New York: Oxford University Press.

Endelman, Todd M. 1999. *The Jews of Georgian England, 1714–1830: Tradition and Change in a Liberal Society.* Ann Arbor: University of Michigan Press.

Essig, Mark. 2015. *Lesser Beasts: A Snout-to-Tail History of the Humble Pig.* New York: Basic Books.

Estraikh, Gennady. 2018. "Soviet Jewish Foodways: Transformation through Detabooization." In *Global Jewish Foodways: A History*, ed. Hasia R. Diner and Simone Cinotto, 115–138. Lincoln: University of Nebraska Press.

Fabre-Vassas, Claudine. 1997. *The Singular Beast: Jews, Christians, and the Pig.* Translated by Carol Volk. New York: Columbia University Press.

Fader, Ayala. 2020. *Hidden Heretics: Jewish Doubt in the Digital Age.* Princeton, NJ: Princeton University Press.

Feldman, Deborah. 2012. *Unorthodox: The Scandalous Rejection of My Hasidic Roots.* New York: Simon and Schuster.

———. 2015. *Exodus: A Memoir.* New York: Plume.

Felsenstein, Frank. 1995. *Anti-Semitic Stereotypes: A Paradigm of Otherness in English Popular Culture, 1660–1830.* Baltimore: Johns Hopkins University Press.

Fermaglich, Kirsten. 2018. *A Rosenberg by Any Other Name: A History of Jewish Name Changing in America.* New York: New York University Press.

Ferris, Marcie Cohen. 2005. *Matzah Ball Gumbo: Culinary Tales of the Jewish South.* Chapel Hill: University of North Carolina Press.

Fishkoff, Sue. 2010. *Kosher Nation: Why More and More of America's Food Answers to a Higher Authority.* New York: Schocken Books.

Fleischman, Thomas. 2020. *Communist Pigs: An Animal History of East Germany's Rise and Fall.* Seattle: University of Washington Press.

Foer, Jonathan Safran. 2010. *Eating Animals.* New York: Back Bay Books.

Fox, Michael V. 2009. *Proverbs 10–31: A New Translation with Introduction and Commentary.* AB 18B. New Haven, CT: Yale University Press.

Freidenreich, David M. 2022. *Jewish Muslims: How Christians Imagined Islam as the Enemy.* Oakland: University of California Press.

Geller, Jay. 2018. *Bestiarium Judicum: Unnatural Histories of the Jews.* New York: Fordham University Press.

Gilad, Efrat. 2022. "Camel Controversies and Pork Politics in British Mandate Palestine." *Global Food History*, August 1, 2022. https://doi.org/10.1080/20549547.2022.2106074.

Golden, Mark. 1988. "Male Chauvinists and Pigs." *Echos du Monde Classique: Classical Views* 32 (7): 1–12.

Goldschmidt, M. 1852. *The Jew of Denmark: A Tale.* Translated by A. S. Bushby. London: Routledge.

Goldstein, David B. 2014. "Jews, Scots, and Pigs in 'The Merchant of Venice.'" *Studies in English Literature, 1500–1900*, 54 (2): 315–348.

———. 2017. *Eating and Ethics in Shakespeare's England*. New York: Cambridge University Press.

Goodman, Allegra. 2017. *The Family Markowitz*. New York: Dial.

Grantham, Billy. 1996. "A Zooarchaeological Model for the Study of Ethnic Complexity at Sepphoris." PhD diss., Northwestern University.

Greene, Matt. 2020. *Jew(ish): A Primer, a Memoir, a Manual, a Plea*. Seattle: Little A.

Gross, Aaron S. 2015. *The Question of the Animal and Religion: Theoretical Stakes, Practical Implications*. New York: Columbia University Press.

Gross, Rachel B. 2021. *Beyond the Synagogue: Jewish Nostalgia as Religious Practice*. New York: New York University Press.

Grossman, Allen. 2001. *How to Do Things with Tears*. New York: New Directions Books.

Grottanelli, Cristiano. 2004. "Avoiding Pork: Egyptians and Jews in Greek and Latin Texts." In *Food and Identity in the Ancient World*, ed. Cristiano Grottanelli and Lucio Milano, 59–93. Padua, Italy: S.A.R.G.O.N. Editrice e Libreria.

Gurock, Jeffrey S. 2009. *Orthodox Jews in America*. The Modern Jewish Experience. Bloomington: Indiana University Press.

Gurvis, Jacob. 2021. "Impossible Pork Is Here—but the Plant-Based Meat Won't Be Certified as Kosher." *Jewish Telegraphic Agency*, September 27, 2021. www.jta.org.

Haberman, Clyde. 2022. "James Caan, Hot-Tempered Sonny of 'The Godfather,' Is Dead at 82." *New York Times*, July 7, 2022, A22.

Hadda, Janet. 1997. "Isaac Bashevis Singer in New York." *Judaism: A Quarterly Journal of Jewish Life and Thought* 46 (3): 346–363.

Har-Peled, Misgav. 2013. "The Dialogical Beast: The Identification of Rome with the Pig in Early Rabbinic Literature." PhD diss., Johns Hopkins University.

———. 2016. "The Pig Libel: A Ritual Crime Legend from the Era of the Spanish Expulsion of the Jews (15th–16th Centuries)." *Revue des Études Juives* 175 (1–2): 107–133.

Harris, Eve. 2013. *The Marrying of Chani Kaufman*. New York: Black Cat.

Harris, Marvin. 1998. *Good to Eat: Riddles of Food and Culture*. Long Grove, IL: Waveland.

Hart, Mitchell B. 2007. *The Healthy Jew: The Symbiosis of Judaism and Modern Medicine*. New York: Cambridge University Press.

Hayes, Christine. 2015. *What's Divine about Divine Law? Early Perspectives*. Princeton, NJ: Princeton University Press.

Hesse, Brian, and Paula Wapnish. 1997. "Can Pig Remains Be Used for Ethnic Diagnosis in the Ancient Near East?" In *The Archaeology of Israel: Constructing the Past, Interpreting the Present*, ed. N. A. Silberman and D. Small, 238–270. Sheffield, UK: Sheffield Academic Press.

Honigman, Sylvie. 2021. *Tales of High Priests and Taxes: The Books of the Maccabees and the Judean Rebellion against Antiochus IV*. Oakland: University of California Press.

Horn, Dara. 2003. *In the Image*. New York: Norton.

———. 2021. *People Love Dead Jews: Reports from a Haunted Present*. New York: Norton.

Horowitz, Roger. 2006. *Putting Meat on the American Table: Taste, Technology, Transformation*. Baltimore: Johns Hopkins University Press.

———. 2016. *Kosher USA: How Coke Became Kosher and Other Tales of Modern Food*. New York: Columbia University Press.

Jones, Michael Owen. 2017. "Pig Tales: Assumptions, Beliefs, and Perceptions Regarding Pork Bans Real and Rumored." *Western Folklore* 76 (4): 379–414.

Joselit, Jenna Weissman. 1983. *Our Gang: Jewish Crime and the New York Jewish Community, 1900–1940*. The Modern Jewish Experience. Bloomington: Indiana University Press.

———. 1994. *The Wonders of America: Reinventing Jewish Culture, 1880–1950*. New York: Hill and Wang.

JTA and TOI Staff. 2019. "Norway's State Broadcaster Airs 'Jewish Swine' Cartoon." *Times of Israel*, July 19, 2019. www.timesofisrael.com.

Jung, Courtney. 2015. *Lactivism: How Feminists and Fundamentalists, Hippies and Yuppies, and Physicians and Politicians Made Breastfeeding Big Business and Bad Policy*. New York: Basic Books.

Kaplan, Marion. 1991. *The Making of the Jewish Middle Class: Women, Family, and Identity in Imperial Germany*. Studies in Jewish History. New York: Oxford University Press.

———. 2018. "From the Comfort of Home to Exile: German Jews and Their Foodways." In *Global Jewish Foodways: A History*, ed. Hasia R. Diner and Simone Cinotto, 239–265. Lincoln: University of Nebraska Press.

Kirshenblatt-Gimblett, Barbara. 1990. "Kitchen Judaism." In *Getting Comfortable in New York: The American Jewish Home, 1880–1950*, ed. Susan Braunstein and Jenna Weissman Joselit, 75–101. New York: Jewish Museum.

Kisch, Guido. 1949. *Jewry-Law in Medieval Germany: Laws and Court Decisions concerning Jews*. New York: American Academy of Jewish Research.

———. 1970. *The Jews in Medieval Germany: A Study of Their Legal and Social Status*. 2nd ed. New York: Ktav.

Klein, Misha. 2016. *Kosher Feijoada and Other Paradoxes of Jewish Life in São Paulo*. Gainesville: University Press of Florida.

Koltun-Fromm, Ken. 2020. *Drawing on Religion: Reading and the Moral Imagination in Comics and Graphic Novels*. University Park: Pennsylvania State University Press.

Kornblut, Anne E. 2006. "Volatile Mix: Campaigning and Religions." *New York Times*, September 22, 2006. www.nytimes.com.

Kraemer, David C. 2009. *Jewish Eating and Identity through the Ages*. New York: Routledge.

Kraemer, Joel L. 2008. *Maimonides: The Life and World of One of Civilization's Greatest Minds*. New York: Doubleday.

Kraemer, Ross Shepard. 2012. *Unreliable Witnesses: Religion, Gender, and History in the Greco-Roman Mediterranean*. New York: Oxford University Press.

Kreiner, Jamie. 2020. *Legions of Pigs in the Early Medieval West*. New Haven, CT: Yale University Press.

Kritzler, Edward. 2008. *Jewish Pirates of the Caribbean: How a Generation of Swashbuckling Jews Carved Out an Empire in the New World in Their Quest for Treasure, Religious Freedom—and Revenge*. New York: Anchor Books.

Kulp-Hill, Kathleen. 2000. *Songs of Holy Mary of Alfonso the Wise*. Medieval and Renaissance Texts and Studies. Tempe: Arizona Center for Medieval and Renaissance Studies.

Kurlansky, Mark. 2007. *The Big Oyster: History on the Half Shell*. New York: Random House.

———. 2011. *Hank Greenberg: The Hero Who Didn't Want to Be One*. Jewish Lives. New Haven, CT: Yale University Press.

Lauterbach, Jacob Z. 1925. "The Ceremony of Breaking Glass at Weddings." *Hebrew Union College Annual* 2:351–380.

Leavy, Jane. 2003. *Sandy Koufax: A Lefty's Legacy*. New York: Perennial.

Lee, Jennifer 8. 2008. *The Fortune Cookie Chronicles: Adventures in the World of Chinese Food*. New York: Twelve Books.

Leibman, Laura Arnold. 2013. *Messianism, Secrecy and Mysticism: A New Interpretation of Early American Jewish Life*. Chicago: Vallentine Mitchell.

Leshem, Eitan. 2023. "Farewell, Shrimp and Pork: Israel Really Is Becoming More Kosher." *Haaretz*, April 20, 2023. www.haaretz.com.

Levine, Amy-Jill, and Marx Zvi Brettler, eds. 2011. *The Jewish Annotated New Testament*. New York: Oxford University Press.

Lev-Tov, Justin. 2003. "'Upon What Meat Doth This Our Caesar Feed . . . ?': A Dietary Perspective on Hellenistic and Roman Influence in Palestine." In *Zeichen Aus Text und Stein: Studien auf dem Weg zu einer Archäologie des Neuen Testaments*, ed. Stefan Algier and Jürgen Zangenberg, 420–446. Tübingen: Mohr Siebeck.

Liberles, Robert. 2012. *Jews Welcome Coffee: Tradition and Innovation in Early Modern Germany*. Waltham, MA: Brandeis University Press.

Lincoln, Bruce. 2014. *Discourse and the Construction of Society: Comparative Studies in Myth, Ritual, and Classification*. 2nd ed. New York: Oxford University Press.

Linfield, Susie. 2019. *The Lion's Den: Zionism and the Left from Hannah Arendt to Noam Chomsky*. New Haven, CT: Yale University Press.

Lipton, Sara. 2014. *Dark Mirror: The Medieval Origins of Anti-Jewish Iconography*. New York: Metropolitan Books.

Liss, David. 2004a. *The Coffee Trader*. New York: Ballantine Books.

———. 2004b. *A Conspiracy of Paper*. New York: Ballantine Books.

———. 2014. *The Day of Atonement*. New York: Random House.

Loewen, Harry. 2015. *Ink against the Devil: Luther and His Opponents*. Waterloo, ON: Wilfrid Laurier University Press.

Maciejko, Paweł. 2011. *The Mixed Multitude: Jacob Frank and the Frankist Movement, 1755–1816*. Jewish Culture and Contexts. Philadelphia: University of Pennsylvania Press.

Magness, Jodi. 2019. *Masada: From Jewish Revolt to Modern Myth*. Princeton, NJ: Princeton University Press.

Mampieri, Martina. 2020. "When the Rabbi's Soul Entered a Pig: Melchiorre Palontrotti and His *Giudiata* against the Jews of Rome." *Jewish History* 33 (3–4): 351–375.

Mann, Reva. 2007. *The Rabbi's Daughter: A Memoir*. New York: Dial.

Marcus, Jacob Rader, ed. 1996. *The Jew in the American World: A Source Book*. Detroit: Wayne State University Press.

———, ed. 1999. *The Jew in the Medieval World: A Source Book: 315–1791*. Rev. ed. Cincinnati, OH: Hebrew Union College Press.

Marcus, Jacob Rader, and Marc Saperstein, eds. 2015. *The Jews in Christian Europe: A Source Book, 315–1791*. Cincinnati, OH: Hebrew Union College Press / University of Pittsburg Press.

Marks, Gil. 2010. *Encyclopedia of Jewish Food*. Hoboken, NJ: Wiley.

Marx de Salcedo, Anastacia. 2015. *Combat-Ready Kitchen: How the U.S. Military Shapes the Way You Eat*. New York: Current.

McGowan, Andrew. 2021. "Animal Acts: Diet and Law in the Acts of the Apostles and Early Christian Practice." In *Animals and the Law in Antiquity*, ed. Saul M. Olyan and Jordan D. Rosenblum, 105–119. Providence, RI: Brown Judaic Studies.

McNeil, Liz. 2020. "Mama Cass of Hit '60s Band Mamas & the Papas Did Not Die from a Ham Sandwich: What Really Happened." *People*, July 29, 2020. https://people.com.

Mehta, Samira K. 2018. *Beyond Chrismukkah: The Christian-Jewish Interfaith Family in the United States*. Chapel Hill: University of North Carolina Press.

Meir, Natan. 2007. "From Pork to *Kapores*: Transformation in Religious Practice among the Jews of Late Imperial Kiev." *Jewish Quarterly Review* 97 (4): 616–645.

Mendelsohn, Adam D. 2016. *The Rag Race: How Jews Sewed Their Way to Success in America and the British Empire*. The Goldstein-Goren Series in American Jewish History. New York: New York University Press.

———. 2022. *Jewish Soldiers in the Civil War: The Union Army*. New York: New York University Press.

Mendes-Flohr, Paul, and Yehuda Reinharz, eds. 1995. *The Jew in the Modern World: A Documentary History*. 2nd ed. New York: Oxford University Press.

Mermelstein, Ari. 2022. "What Did It Feel Like to Be a Jew? The Kosher Food Laws and Emotional Norms among Ancient Jews." *Journal for the Study of Judaism in the Persian, Hellenistic and Roman Period* 53:344–376.

Merwin, Ted. 2015. *Pastrami on Rye: An Overstuffed History of the Jewish Deli*. New York: New York University Press.

Metzker, Isaac, ed. 1971. *A Bintel Brief: Sixty Years of Letters from the Lower East Side to the "Jewish Daily Forward."* New York: Schocken Books.

Meyers, Helene. 2021. *Movie-Made Jews: An American Tradition*. New Brunswick, NJ: Rutgers University Press.

Michelson, Emily. 2022. *Catholic Spectacle and Rome's Jews: Early Modern Conversion and Resistance*. Princeton, NJ: Princeton University Press.

Milgrom, Genie. 2019. *Recipes of My 15 Grandmothers: Unique Recipes and Stories from the Times of the Crypto-Jews during the Spanish Inquisition*. New York: Gefen.

Milgrom, Jacob. 1991. *Leviticus 1–16: A New Translation with Introduction and Commentary*. AB 3. New York: Doubleday.

Mirvis, Tova. 2000. *The Ladies Auxiliary*. New York: Ballantine Books.

Mizelle, Brett. 2011. *Pig*. Animal. London: Reaktion Books.

Mokhtarian, Jason Sion. 2022. *Medicine in the Talmud: Natural and Supernatural Therapies between Magic and Science*. Oakland: University of California Press.

Moore, Deborah Dash. 2006. *GI Jews: How World War II Changed a Generation*. Cambridge, MA: Harvard University Press.

Moore, Stephen D., and Janice Capel Anderson. 1998. "Taking It like a Man: Masculinity in 4 Maccabees." *Journal of Biblical Literature* 117 (2): 249–273.

Morris, Mary. 2019. *Gateway to the Moon*. New York: Anchor Books.

Moss, Candida. 2014. *The Myth of Persecution: How Early Christians Invented a Story of Martyrdom*. New York: HarperOne.

Moyer-Nocchi, Karima. 2015. *Chewing the Fat: An Oral History of Italian Foodways from Fascism to Dolce Vita*. Perrysburg, OH: Medea.

Moyer-Nocchi, Karima, with Giancarlo Rolandi. 2019. *The Eternal Table: A Cultural History of Food in Rome*. Big City Food Biography Series. Lanham, MD: Roman and Littlefield.

Neis, Rafael Rachel. 2023. *When a Human Gives Birth to a Raven: Rabbis and the Reproduction of Species*. Oakland: University of California Press.

Newfield, Schneur Zalman. 2020. *Degrees of Separation: Identity Formation While Leaving Ultra-Orthodox Judaism*. Philadelphia: Temple University Press.

Nirenberg, David. 2014. *Anti-Judaism: The Western Tradition*. New York: Norton.

Olshanetsky, Haggai. 2023. "Keeping Kosher: The Ability of Jewish Soldiers to Keep the Dietary Laws as a Case Study for the Integration of Minorities in the Roman Army." *Jewish Quarterly Review* 113 (1): 59–82.

Olyan, Saul M. 2000. *Rites and Rank: Hierarchy in the Biblical Representations of Cult*. Princeton, NJ: Princeton University Press.

———. 2008. *Disability in the Hebrew Bible: Interpreting Mental and Physical Differences*. New York: Cambridge University Press.

———. 2017. *Friendship in the Hebrew Bible*. New Haven, CT: Yale University Press.

Onion. 1998. "Jewish Elders Lift 6,000-Year Ham Ban." September 30, 1998. www.theonion.com.

Orenstein, Henry. 1997. *I Shall Live: Surviving the Holocaust against All Odds*. New York: Beaufort Books.

Orwell, George. (1933) 2021. *Down and Out in Paris and London*. New York: Harcourt.

Ozick, Cynthia. 1969. *Envy; or, Yiddish in America—A Novella*. *Commentary*, November 1, 1969.

Panayi, Panikos. 2022. *Fish and Chip: A Takeaway History*. London: Reaktion Books.

Pareles, Mo. 2019. "Already/Never: Jewish-Porcine Conversion in the Middle English Children of the Oven Miracle." *Philological Quarterly* 98 (3): 221–242.

Patton, Pamela A. 2012. *Art of Estrangement: Redefining Jews in Reconquest Spain*. University Park: Pennsylvania State University Press.

Peck, Abraham J. 1987. "That Other 'Peculiar Institution': Jews and Judaism in the Nineteenth Century South." *Modern Judaism* 7 (1): 99–114.

Penniman, John David. 2017. *Raised on Christian Milk: Food and the Formation of the Soul in Early Christianity*. New Haven, CT: Yale University Press.

Penslar, Derek J. 2013. *Jews and the Military: A History*. Princeton, NJ: Princeton University Press.

Pines, Shlomo, trans. 1963. *The Guide of the Perplexed*. By Maimonides. Vol. 2. Chicago: University of Chicago Press.

Plaut, Joshua Eli. 2012. *A Kosher Christmas: 'Tis the Season to Be Jewish*. New Brunswick, NJ: Rutgers University Press.

Pollan, Michael. 2014. *Cooked: A Natural History of Transformation*. New York: Penguin Books.

Popper, Nathaniel. 2018. "Meat Labs Pursue a Once-Impossible Goal: Kosher Bacon." *New York Times*, October 1, 2018, B1.

Portnoy, Eddy. 2018. *Bad Rabbi: And Other Strange but True Stories from the Yiddish Press*. Stanford Studies in Jewish History and Culture. Stanford, CA: Stanford University Press.

Preuss, Julius. (1978) 2004. *Biblical and Talmudic Medicine*. Translated and edited by Fred Rosner. Lanham, MD: Rowman and Littlefield.

Price, Max D. 2020. *Evolution of a Taboo: Pigs and People in the Ancient Near East*. New York: Oxford University Press.

Rabin, Shari. 2017. *Jews on the Frontier: Religion and Mobility in Nineteenth-Century America*. New York: New York University Press.

Rac, Katalin Franciska. 2019. "How Shabbat Cholent Became a Secular Hungarian Favorite." In *Feasting and Fasting: The History and Ethics of Jewish Food*, ed. Aaron S. Gross, Jody Myers, and Jordan D. Rosenblum, 235–250. New York: New York University Press.

Rajak, Tessa. 2000. "Dying for the Law: The Martyr's Portrait in Jewish-Greek Literature." In *The Jewish Dialogue with Greece and Rome: Studies in Cultural and Social Interaction*, 99–133. Boston: Brill.

Rakoff, David. 2010. *Half Empty*. New York: Anchor Books.

Ray, Jonathan, ed. 2013. *The Jew in Medieval Iberia: 1100–1500*. Jews in Space and Time. Boston: Academic Studies.

Rhyder, Julia. 2023. "The Jewish Pig Prohibition from Leviticus to the Maccabees." *Journal of Biblical Literature* 142 (2): 221–241.

Rogers, Katharine M. 2012. *Pork: A Global History*. The Edible Series. London: Reaktion Books.

Rosen, Robert N. 2021. *The Jewish Confederates*. Columbia: University of South Carolina Press.

Rosenblum, Jordan D. 2010a. *Food and Identity in Early Rabbinic Judaism*. New York: Cambridge University Press.

———. 2010b. "From Their Bread to Their Bed: Commensality, Intermarriage, and Idolatry in Tannaitic Literature." *Journal of Jewish Studies* 61 (1): 18–29.

———. 2010c. "'Why Do You Refuse to Eat Pork?': Jews, Food, and Identity in Roman Palestine." *Jewish Quarterly Review* 100 (1): 95–110.

———. 2015. "The Night Rabbi Aqiba Slept with Two Women." In *A Very Reliable Witness: Essays in Honor of Ross Kraemer*, ed. Nathaniel P. DesRosiers, Shira Lander, Jacqueline Pastis, and Daniel C. Ullucci, 67–75. Providence, RI: Brown Judaic Studies.

———. 2016a. "'Blessings of the Breasts': Breastfeeding in Rabbinic Literature." *Hebrew Union College Annual* 87:147–179.

———. 2016b. *The Jewish Dietary Laws in the Ancient World*. New York: Cambridge University Press.

———. 2017. "Dining in(to) the World to Come." In *Olam ha-zeh v'olam ha-ba: This World and the World to Come in Jewish Belief and Practice*, ed. Leonard Greenspoon, 105–114. West Lafayette, IN: Purdue University Press.

———. 2018. "The Unwashed Masses: Handwashing as a Ritual of Social Distinction in Rabbinic Judaism." *Historia Religionum* 10:79–90.

———. 2019a. "A Brief History of Jews and Garlic." In *Feasting and Fasting: The History and Ethics of Jewish Food*, ed. Aaron S. Gross, Jody Myers, and Jordan D. Rosenblum, 147–156. New York: New York University Press.

———. 2019b. "The Swine Suicides: On the Appearance and Disappearance of Pork-Related Jewish Martyrdom in Antiquity." *Journal of Religious Competition in Antiquity* 1:37–47.

———. 2020. *Rabbinic Drinking: What Beverages Teach Us about Rabbinic Literature*. Oakland: University of California Press.

Rosenthal, Odeda. 1991. *Not Strictly Kosher: Pioneer Jews in New Zealand*. 2nd ed. Wainscott, NY: Starchand.

Rosner, Abbie. 2008. "An Interview with Erez Komarovsky, Erez Breads, Israel." *Gastronomica* 8 (4): 91–94.

Roth, Cecil. 1992. *A History of the Marranos*. 5th ed. New York: Sepher-Hermon.

Roth, Laurence. 2004. *Inspecting Jews: American Jewish Detective Stories*. New Brunswick, NJ: Rutgers University Press.

Roth, Paul. 2014. Cartoon. *New Yorker*, July 7–14, 2014, 49.

Roth, Philip. (1959) 1993. *"Goodbye, Columbus" and Five Short Stories*. New York: Vintage Books.

———. (1967) 1994. *Portnoy's Complaint*. New York: Vintage Books.

Rothstein, Robert A. 2013. "'If a Jew Has a Dog . . .': Dogs in Yiddish Proverbs." In *A Jew's Best Friend? The Image of the Dog throughout Jewish History*, ed. Phillip Ackerman-Lieberman and Rakefet Zalashik, 135–146. Portland, OR: Sussex Academic Press.

Rowling, J. K. 1999. *Harry Potter and the Sorcerer's Stone*. New York: Scholastic Inc.

Rozin, Irit. 2015. "Craving Meat during Israel's Austerity Period, 1947–1953." In *Jews and Their Foodways*, Studies in Contemporary Jewry, ed. Anat Herman, 65–88. New York: Oxford University Press.

Ruane, Nicole J. 2015. "Pigs, Purity, and Patrilineality: The Multiparty of Swine and Its Problems for Biblical Ritual and Gender Construction." *Journal of Biblical Literature* 134 (3): 489–504.

Rubel, Nora L. 2010. *Doubting the Devout: The Ultra-Orthodox in the Jewish American Imagination*. New York: Columbia University Press.

Rubens, Alfred. 1954. *A Jewish Iconography*. London: Jewish Museum.

Rubenstein, Jeffrey L. 2018. "The Role of Disgust in Rabbinic Ethics." In *Strength to Strength: Essays in Honor of Shaye J. D. Cohen*, ed. Michael L. Satlow, 421–436. Providence, RI: Brown Judaic Studies.

Rubin, Aaron D. 2017. "Judeo-Italian." In *Handbook of Jewish Languages: Revised and Updated Edition*, ed. Lily Kahn and Aaron D. Rubin, 298–365. Boston: Brill.

Rude, Emelyn. 2016. *Tastes like Chicken: A History of America's Favorite Bird*. New York: Pegasus Books.

Safrai, Ze'ev. 2014. *The Economy of Roman Palestine*. New York: Routledge.

Sales, Ben. 2018. "A Political Cartoon Costs an Israeli Artist His Job." *Jewish Telegraphic Agency*, July 25, 2018. www.jta.org.

Saraiva, Tiago. 2018. *Fascist Pigs: Technoscientific Organisms and the History of Fascism*. Inside Technology. Cambridge, MA: MIT Press.

Sarna, Jonathan D. 1982. "The Pork on the Fork: A Nineteenth Century Anti-Jewish Ditty." *Jewish Social Studies* 44 (2): 169–172.

———. 2012. *When General Grant Expelled the Jews*. New York: Nextbook Schocken.

———. 2019. *American Judaism: A History*. 2nd ed. New Haven, CT: Yale University Press.

Sarna, Jonathan D., and Adam Mendelsohn, ed. 2011. *Jews and the Civil War: A Reader*. New York: New York University Press.

Satlow, Michael L. 2006. *Creating Judaism: History, Tradition, Practice*. New York: Columbia University Press.

———. 2013. "Jew or Judean?" In *"The One Who Sows Bountifully": Essays in Honor of Stanley K. Stowers*, ed. Caroline Johnson Hodge, Saul M. Olyan, Daniel Ullucci, and Emma Wasserman, 165–175. Providence, RI: Brown Judaic Studies.

Sax, David. 2009. *Save the Deli: In Search of Perfect Pastrami, Crusty Rye, and the Heart of Jewish Delicatessen*. Boston: Houghton Mifflin Harcourt.

Schäfer, Peter. 1998. *Judeophobia: Attitudes toward the Jews in the Ancient World*. Cambridge, MA: Harvard University Press.

Schantz, Peter M., et al. 1992. "Neurocysticercosis in an Orthodox Jewish Community in New York City." *New England Journal of Medicine* 327:692–695.

Scharbach, Rebecca. 2013. "The Ghosts in the Privy: On the Origins of Nittel Nacht and Modes of Cultural Exchange." *Jewish Studies Quarterly* 20 (4): 340–373.

Schiebinger, Londa. 2004. *Nature's Body: Gender in the Making of Modern Science*. 2nd ed. New Brunswick, NJ: Rutgers University Press.

Schloff, Linda Mack. 1996. *"And Prairie Dogs Weren't Kosher": Jewish Women in the Upper Midwest since 1855*. St. Paul: Minnesota Historical Society Press.

Schnall, Etan. 2017. "Kosher for Passover Teeth?!" *Pesach-Yom Haatzmaut 5777* (Rabbi Isaac Elchanan Theological Seminary, The Benjamin and Rose Berger CJF Torah To-Go Series), 33–38. https://shiurim.yutorah.net.

Schofer, Jonathan Wyn. 2005. *The Making of a Sage: A Study in Rabbinic Ethics*. Madison: University of Wisconsin Press.

Scholem, Gershom. 2016. *Sabbatai Ṣevi: The Mystical Messiah, 1626–1676*. Bollingen Series XCIII. Princeton, NJ: Princeton University Press.

Schorsch, Jonathan. 2004. *Jews and Blacks in the Early Modern World*. New York: Cambridge University Press.

———. 2018. *The Food Movement, Culture, and Religion: A Tale of Pigs, Christians, Jews, and Politics*. Cham, Switzerland: Palgrave Macmillan.

Schwartz, Seth. 2014. *The Ancient Jews from Alexander to Muhammad*. Key Themes in Ancient History. New York: Cambridge University Press.

Seligman, Scott D. 2020. *The Great Kosher Meat War of 1902: Immigrant Housewives and the Riots That Shook New York City*. Lincoln, NE: Potomac Books.

Sfar, Joann. 2005. *The Rabbi's Cat*. Translated by Alexis Siegel and Anjali Singh. New York: Pantheon Books.

Shachar, Isaiah. 1974. *The Judensau: A Medieval Anti-Jewish Motif and Its History*. London: Warburg Institute.

———. 1975. "The Emergence of the Modern Pictorial Stereotype of 'the Jews' in England." In *Studies in the Cultural Life of the Jews in England*, ed. Dov Noy and Issachar Ben-Ami, 331–365. Folklore Research Center Studies 5. Jerusalem: Magnes.

Shakespeare, William. 2003. *The Merchant of Venice*. Edited by M. M. Mahood. Cambridge: Cambridge University Press.

Shapiro, Eliza, and Brian M. Rosenthal. 2022. "Failing Schools, Public Funds: Hasidic Students in New York State Are Deprived of Basic Skills." *New York Times*, September 11, 2022, A1, 12–15.

Shapiro, James. 1996. *Shakespeare and the Jews*. New York: Columbia University Press.

———. 2000. "Shakespur and the Jewbill." In *Shakespeare and Race*, ed. Catherine M. S. Alexander and Stanley Wells, 124–138. New York: Cambridge University Press.

Shils, Edward, ed. 1991. *Remembering the University of Chicago: Teachers, Scientists, and Scholars*. Chicago: University of Chicago Press.

Shternshis, Anna. 2006. *Soviet and Kosher: Jewish Popular Culture in the Soviet Union, 1923–1939*. Bloomington: Indiana University Press.

———. 2008. "May Day, Tractors, and Piglets: Yiddish Songs for Little Communists." In *The Art of Being Jewish in Modern Times*, ed. Barbara Kirshenblatt-Gimblett and Jonathan Carp, 83–97. Philadelphia: University of Pennsylvania Press.

———. 2015. "Salo on Challah: Soviet Jews' Experience of Food in the 1920s–1950s." In *Jews and Their Foodways*, Studies in Contemporary Jewry, ed. Anat Herman, 10–27. New York: Oxford University Press.

Simkovich, Malka Z. 2018. "Esau the Ancestor of Rome." TheTorah.com. www.thetorah.com.

———. 2019. "Why Is Rome Likened to a Boar." TheTorah.com. www.thetorah.com.

Singer, I. J. 1938. *The River Breaks Up*. Translated by Maurice Samuel. New York: Knopf.

Siporin, Steve. 1994. "From Kashrut to Cucina Ebraica: The Recasting of Italian Jewish Foodways." *Journal of American Folklore* 107 (424): 268–281.

———. 2015. "The Kosher Con Game: Who's Keeping Kosher in Prison?" *Western Folklore* 74 (1): 58–79.

Skinazi, Karen E. H. 2018. *Women of Valor: Orthodox Jewish Troll Fighters, Crime Writers, and Rock Stars in Contemporary Literature and Culture*. New Brunswick, NJ: Rutgers University Press.

Snyder, Laurel. 2010. *Baxter, the Pig Who Wanted to Be Kosher*. Berkeley, CA: Tricycle.

Solomons, Natasha. 2011. *Mr. Rosenblum Dreams in English*. New York: Back Bay Books.

Solsman, Joan E. 2020. "Impossible Burger's Biggest Eaters Aren't the People You Think: Vegetarians, Vegans, Even Kosher and Halal Eaters Closed Out of Pork and Cheeseburgers Before—We're Not the Ones Making New Fake Meat Go Viral." *CNET*, January 16, 2020. www.cnet.com.

Sorkin, David. 2019. *Jewish Emancipation: A History across Five Centuries*. Princeton, NJ: Princeton University Press.

Spiegelman, Art. 1986. *Maus I: A Survivor's Tale: My Father Bleeds History*. New York: Pantheon Books.

———. 1991. *Maus II: A Survivor's Tale: And Here My Troubles Began*. New York: Pantheon Books.

Spinner, Cala. 2020. *Peppa Pig: Happy Hanukkah!* New York: Scholastic.

Stahl, Ronit Y. 2017. *Enlisting Faith: How the Military Chaplaincy Shaped Religion and State in Modern America*. Cambridge, MA: Harvard University Press.

Stallybrass, Peter, and Allon White. 1986. *The Politics and Poetics of Transgression*. Ithaca, NY: Cornell University Press.

Steel, Karl. 2011. *How to Make a Human: Animals and Violence in the Middle Ages*. Interventions: New Studies in Medieval Culture. Columbus: Ohio State University.

Stein, Abby Chava. 2019. *Becoming Eve: My Journey from Ultra-Orthodox Rabbi to Transgender Woman*. New York: Seal.

Steinberg, Ellen F., and Jack H. Prost. 2011. *From the Jewish Heartland: Two Centuries of Midwest Foodways*. Urbana: University of Illinois Press.

Stern, Menahem, ed. (1974) 1998. *Greek and Latin Authors on Jews and Judaism*. 3 vols. Jerusalem: Israel Academy of Sciences and Humanities.

Stern, Sacha. 1994. *Jewish Identity in Early Rabbinic Writings*. Arbeiten zur Geschichte des antiken Judentums und des Urchristentums. New York: Brill.

Sternberg, Claudia. 2015. "From Pig Farmer to Infidel: Diasporic Infertility and Transethnic Kinship in Contemporary British Jewish Cinema." In *Hidden in Plain Sight: Jews and Jewishness in British Film, Television, and Popular Culture*, ed. Nathan Abrams, 181–204. Evanston, IL: Northwestern University Press.

Sthers, Amanda. 2019. *Holy Lands: A Novel*. New York: Bloomsbury.

Stow, Kenneth. 2001. *Theater of Acculturation: The Roman Ghetto in the 16th Century*. Seattle: University of Washington Press.

Sussman, Lance J. 2005. "The Myth of the Trefa Banquet: American Culinary Culture and the Radicalization of Food Policy in American Reform Judaism." *American Jewish Archives Journal* 57 (1–2): 29–52.

Teplitsky, Joshua. 2022. "Imagined Immunities: Medieval Myths and Modern Histories of Jews and the Black Death." *AJS Review* 46 (2): 320–346.

Teter, Magda. 2020. *Blood Libel: On the Trail of an Antisemitic Myth*. Cambridge, MA: Harvard University Press.

Thomson, R. W., James Howard-Johnston, and Tim Greenwood. 1999. *The Armenian History Attributed to Seabees: Parts 1 and 2*. Translated Texts for Historians 31. Liverpool: Liverpool University Press.

Toaff, Ariel. 2011. *Mangiare alla giudia: Cucine ebraiche dal Rinascimento all'età moderna*. Biblioteca storica. Bologna: Società editrice il Mulino.

Tokarczuk, Olga. 2022. *The Books of Jacob; or, A Fantastic Journey across Seven Borders, Five Languages, and Three Major Religions, Not Counting the Minor Sects. Told by the Dead, Supplemented by the Author, Drawing from a Range of Books, and Aided by Imagination, the Which Being the Greatest Natural Gift of Any Person. That the Wise Might Have It for a Record, That My Compatriots Reflect, Laypersons Gain Some Understanding, and Melancholy Souls Obtain Some Slight Enjoyment*. Translated by Jennifer Croft. New York: Riverhead Books.

Trachtenberg, Joshua. 1983. *The Devil and the Jews: The Medieval Conception of the Jew and Its Relation to Modern Anti-Semitism*. 2nd ed. Philadelphia: Jewish Publication Society.

Tseëlon, Efrat. 2001. "Reflections on Mask and Carnival." In *Masquerade and Identities: Essays on Gender, Sexuality and Marginality*, ed. Efrat Tseëlon, 18–37. New York: Routledge.

Tuchman, Gaye, and Harry Gene Levine. 1993. "New York Jews and Chinese Food: The Social Construction of an Ethnic Pattern." *Journal of Contemporary Ethnography* 22 (3): 382–407.

Twitty, Michael W. 2018. *The Cooking Gene: A Journey through African American Culinary History in the Old South*. New York: Amistad Books.

———. 2022. *Koshersoul: The Faith and Food Journey of an African American Jew*. New York: Amistad Books.

Uchill, Ida Libert. (1957) 2000. *Pioneers, Peddlers and Tsadikim: The Story of Jews in Colorado*. Boulder: University Press of Colorado.

Vincent, Leah. 2015. *Cut Me Loose: Sin and Salvation after My Ultra-Orthodox Girlhood*. New York: Penguin Books.

Vuong, Lily C. 2019. *The Protevangelium of James*. Early Christian Apocrypha 7. Eugene, OR: Cascade Books.

Wallenbrock, Nicole Beth. 2015. "Almost but Not Quite Eating Pork: Culinary Nationalism and Islamic Difference in Millennial French Comedies." *Performing Islam* 4 (2): 107–127.

Weiss, Brad. 2016. *Real Pigs: Shifting Values in the Field of Local Pork*. Durham, NC: Duke University Press.

Weiss, Marshall. 2018. "A Mystery of U.S. Jewish History with Dayton Ties." *Dayton Jewish Observer*, August 23, 2018. https://daytonjewishobserver.org.

Wertheimer, Elaine. 2009. "Converso 'Voices' in Fifteenth- and Sixteenth-Century Spanish Literature." In *The Conversos and Moriscos in Late Medieval Spain and Beyond*, ed. Kevin Ingram, vol. 1, 97–119. Boston: Brill.

Wex, Michael. 2006. *Born to Kvetch: Yiddish Language and Culture in All of Its Moods*. New York: Harper Perennial.

———. 2007. *Just Say Nu: Yiddish for Every Occasion (When English Just Won't Do)*. New York: St. Martin's.

Wiedl, Birgit. 2010. "Laughing at the Beast: The *Judensau*: Anti-Jewish Propaganda and Humor from the Middle Ages to the Early Modern Period." In *Laughter in the Middle Ages and Early Modern Times: Epistemology of a Fundamental Human Behavior, Its Meaning, and Consequences*, ed. Albrecht Classen, 325–364. New York: De Gruyter.

Williams, Dan. 2020. "Beware the Boar: Wild Pigs Patrol Israeli City Under Coronavirus Closure." *Reuters*, April 17, 2020. www.reuters.com.

Williams, Jillian. 2019. *Food and Religious Identities in Spain, 1400–1600*. Religious Cultures in the Early Modern World. New York: Routledge.

Wilson, Bee. 2010. *Sandwich: A Global History*. The Edible Series. London: Reaktion Books.

Yoskowitz, Jeffrey. 2008. "On Israel's Only Jewish-Run Pig Farm, It's the Swine That Brings Home the Bacon." *Forward*, April 24, 2008. https://forward.com.

———. 2009. "As Israel Ignores Swine Flu Reality, Global Risk." *The Atlantic*, April 29, 2009. www.theatlantic.com.

———. 2010. "In Israel, a Pork Cookbook Challenges a Taboo." *New York Times*, September 29, 2010, D2.

Zalashik, Rakefet. 2018. "Appetite and Hunger: Discourses and Perceptions of Food among Eastern European Jews in the Interwar Years." In *Global Jewish Foodways:*

A History, ed. Hasia R. Diner and Simone Cinotto, 161–180. Lincoln: University of Nebraska Press.

Zias, Joseph. 1998. "Whose Bones? Were There Really Jewish Defenders? Did Yadin Deliberately Obfuscate?" *Biblical Archaeology Review* 24 (6): 40–45, 64–65.

———. 2000. "Human Skeletal Remains from the Southern Cave at Masada and the Question of Ethnicity." In *The Dead Sea Scrolls Fifty Years after Their Discovery: Proceedings of the Jerusalem Congress*, ed. Lawrence H. Schiffman, Emanuel Tov, and James C. VanderKam, 732–739. Jerusalem: Israel Exploration Society.

INDEX

Page numbers in italics indicate Figures.

abominable things, 8, 190n27
Abraham, 67
"The Adventure of Silver Blaze," 198n48
Aeneas, 45
Age of Discovery (Renaissance), 83
Agrippa II (King), 20, 21
Aḥer (Other), 29, 58, 79, 108, 181
aikias anekestous (desperate ill-usage), 31
Albom, Mitch, 172
Allen, George, 1–2
Allen, Woody, 167
Almoz, Motti, 136
Alonso, Hernando, 205n82
Alvy Singer (fictional character), 167
Amazing Adventures of Kavalier & Clay (Chabon), 189n3
Animal Farm (Orwell), 109, 136
animality, of pig, 4–5
Animals and Animality in the Babylonian Talmud (Berkowitz), 4
Annabelle Rosenmerck (fictional character), 120
"Anna Vanna" (Kvitko), 127–28
Annie Hall, 167
another thing (*davar aḥer*), 37, 39, 127, 196n19, 206n89
Antiochus Epiphanes, 24–27, 29, 30, 194n50
antiquity (*vestustas*), 64
antisemitism, 63, 103; in France, 116–17; in Germany, 115; The Jew's Bill and, 94; in Medieval Period, 59, 83; in *The Merchant of Venice*, 85; in Modern Period England, 108; of Nazis, 215n39; in Norway, 125–26; pig and, 156–62; on plague, 213n8; toward Greenberg, 230n124. *See also Judensau*
Apion, 192n17
Apocryphal Childhood of Christ, 67
Apology (Plato), 194n54
Aqiba (Rabbi), 46–48, 180
Aronson, Menshevik Grigori, 128
Aryan women, 215n38
Asaph, 10
Augustine of Hippo, 64, 201n21
Augustus, 21
Auslander, Shalom, 164–65, 228n99
Avodah Zarah (Talmudic tractate on idolatry), 39

Babylonians, 15, 35
Babylonian Talmud, 38, 39; Daniel and, 200n85; Hanukkah in, 193n43; Jewish Oath and, 68–69; on pig dirtiness, 55; pig raising in, 200n86; Rome in, 198n51; Vespasian and Titus in, 197n41
bacon, 92–93; beef frye and, 176; buying votes with, 223n4; with chicken, 89–90; deliciousness of, 22; with *matzah*, 171; in military, 154; on Yom Kippur, 162–66
bacon bits, 176–77
Bacon Salt, 231n5
Bag Bag, Ben, 178
baptism, 64, 76, 92, 93
Barak-Erez, Daphne, 132–35, 190n19, 220n121

bardaian (infidel), 117
Bar Kokhba Revolt, 42, 51–52
Bar Mitzvah, 124
Barr Labs, 1
Bassanio (fictional character), 84–86
Baxter, the Pig Who Wanted to Be Kosher, 160–62, 228n89
beard, 72, 92–93, 209n47; sex and, 212n6
Becoming Eve (Stein), 162–63
beef: fake, 175
beef frye, 175, 176, 177
beef salami, 229n105
behemah (quadrupeds), 6, 17
Belasco, Aby, 108–9, 213n13
ben Abuyah, Elisha, 79
Ben Isaak, Irad, 220n106
ben Moses, Isaac, 78–79
Berenice, 20
Berkowitz, Beth A., 4
Bernays, Martha, 215n35
Bernie Steinberg (fictional character), 166–67
Bernstein, Eduard, 115–16
Bethel (House of God), 41
Bible: *Judensau* and, 73–74; in *The Merchant of Venice*, 85. See also Hebrew Bible; New Testament; Old Testament
The Big Lebowski, 173
The Big Oyster (Kurlansky), 151
birds, 199n78
Blake, William, 106, 108
"Blood" (Singer, I. J.), 219n104
bloodletting, 38, 39
bones, of pig, 11–12, 202n31
Bonner, Thomas, 90–91, *91*
Brazil, 138–39
breast milk, 75–78
Brian Chadwick (fictional character), 109–10
Bridget Loves Bernie, 166–67
Bridget Theresa Mary Colleen Fitzgerald (fictional character), 166–67
"A Brief History of Jews and Garlic" (Rosenblum), 178
"The Bris," 229n111

Broderick, Matthew, 168
Brooks, Mel, 229n107
Bynum, Caroline Walker, 70

Caan, James, 217n66
Calvert, William, 96–97
camel (*gamal*), 6, 7, 12, 15; in Israel, 220n117
Canaan, 41
Candide (Voltaire), 89–90
cannibalism, 202n29, 213n12
carciofi alla giudia (Jewish artichoke), 121, 217n73
Caribbean, 138
Carnival, 86–87
Carvalho, Solomon Nunes, 143, 222n11
Cassen, Flora, 207n19, 217n72
Catholicism, 204n72; conversion to, 64, 76–77; sex and, 172
Celsus Philosophus, 19
Chabon, Michael, 189n3, 226n69
Chani Kaufman (fictional character), 110–11
chicken, 55; bacon with, 89–90; in United States, 143–44, 222nn1–2
children's blocks, 12–14, *13*
Chinese food: on Christmas, 149, 158–60, 227nn78–79; kosher style with, 171; in United States, 146–50, 158–60
Christianity: baptism in, 64, 76, 92, 93; in Early Modern Period, 83–103; Easter in, 97–99; forced conversion to, 90–91, *91*; in Germany, 111–21; Inquisition of, 75–78; in Israel, 132; Jewish Oath and, 68–70, *69*; *Judensau* and, 74; lamb and, 124; martyrdom in, 194n48; in Medieval Period, 59–67, 75–78, 81–82; *The Merchant of Venice* and, 84–86; metaphor in, 62–65; pig and, 59–69, 75–78, 81–82, 108, 204n72, 211n84; pig blood and, 206n91; pig raising and, 216n40; in Rome, 57–80; wet nurses and, 78–79. See also Catholicism
Christmas, Chinese food on, 149, 158–60, 227nn78–79
A Christmas Story, 227n79

Chrysostom, John, 201n20
chuleta (pork chop), 205n82
Cicero, 193n29
Cincinnati (Porkopolis), 150, 224n34
circumcision, 17, 20, 210n55; Christianity and, 64; on *Seinfeld*, 229n111
Civil War, 152–54, 225n51
Classical Rabbinic Period, 195n2; censoring in, 179; euphemisms for pig in, 37–40; martyrdom in, 46–51; pig in, 2, 35–58, 45; pig raising in, 55–57; pretending to eat pork in, 49–54; Rome in, 40–46; Second Temple destruction and, 40–46; swine stigmas in, 55–57; Talmud in, 37, 38; wet nurses in, 79
cleft/split hooves, 6, 42
Coe, Andrew, 148
Coen brothers, 173
Cohen, Ellen Naomi (Mama Cass), 220n128
Cohen, Nathan, 152–53
Cohen, Rich, 225n55
Columbus, Christopher, 204n64
comedy, 20–21
consecrated meat, 51
The Conversion of Nathan (Bonner), 90–91, *91*
Converso, 75–78, 205n78, 205n82
Corcos the Elder, Tranquillo, 86–89, 122
corruption, 40, 57
Council of Nicaea, 98
crabs, 150, 177, 224n33
Cruikshank, George, 106–8, *107*
cud chewing, 6–7, 42, 43
culinary nationalism, 117–18, 216n52
Cyrus (King), 15

Daniel, 200n85
Dante, 203n60
"Dark Meat" (Rakoff), 156–58
Dauber, Jeremy, 229n107
davar aḥer (another thing), 37, 39, 127, 196n19, 206n89
David Rosenmerck (fictional character), 120

Day of Atonement. *See* Yom Kippur
de gustibus non est disputandum (there is no accounting for taste), 37
dehumanization, 195n64; in Medieval Period, 65–70, 67, 69
Denmark, 124–25, 126
derekh (path), 162–66. *See also* off the *derekh*
desperate ill-usage (*aikias anekestous*), 31
Deuteronomy: 14, 189n13; 14:6, 190n15; 14:7, 190n16, 191n40; 14:8, 6–7, 67, 194n54; 14:12, 10, 191n40; 14:16, 191n40
devil, 106; Jesus and, 96–97; in *The Merchant of Venice*, 85–86
Diner, Hasia R., 143
Diodorus the Sicilian, 24–25
dogs, 200n88; on Sabbath, 56; in Yiddish, 219n95
Dokovna, Joe, 143
Dolgopolski, Tsodek, 127, 138
Dominican Republic, 138
donkey, 108, 199n78
Down and Out in Paris and London (Orwell), 109
Downcast eyes, 20
Doyle, Arthur Conan, 46
Dreyfus, Alfred (Dreyfus Affair), 116

eagle (*nesher*), 10, 190n36
Early Modern Period: Christianity in, 83–103; forced ingestion in, 89–93, *91*; funeral in, 86–89; *The Merchant of Venice* in, 84–86; messianic leaders in, 99–102; mockery in, 83–103; pig in, 83–103; transgressive eating in, 83–84
Earth and seed, 19
Easter, 189n5; ham at, 209n43; Passover and, 98–99, 111; pig and, 97–99
Ecclesiastes: 7:12, 54; 12:12, 178
Edgeworth, Maria, 213n12
Edom, 41–43
Egelson, Louis, 154
eggs: for Easter, 111, 189n5; in New Zealand, 137; in United States, 226n57
Eleazar, 26–27, 30, 49, 50

England: the Enlightenment in, 93–97, 95; in Modern Period, 105–11, 107
Enlightenment: in England, 93–97, 95; Jewish, 123
Epictetus, 18
epilepsy, 18
Epistle of Barnabas, 63
"*Erev* Christmas," 159
Erotianus, 18
Esau, 40–43
Euchel, Isaac, 123
"The Everlasting Gospel" (Blake), 106
exorcism, by Jesus, 61–62
Ezekiel 25:17, 168

Fabre-Vassas, Claudine, 66–67, 87, 214n28
Fabricius, Laurentius, 73–74
Factor, Lori, 159
fake pig, 175–77, 230n4, 231n5
fastidio et orrore (nausea and horror), 64
feijoada, 138–39
Feldman, Deborah, 164, 228n98
Felsenstein, Frank, 93, 212n6
Fishkoff, Sue, 171–72
Flaccus, 30–31
flexitarian, 171
Foer, Jonathan Safran, 115
forced ingestion, 17, 24–32, 27; in Early Modern Period, 89–93, 91; in Modern Period England, 108; by women, 30–32
Fox, Michael V., 9
France: Easter in, 97–99; in Modern Period, 116–21; Muslims in, 214n21
Frank, Jacob, 99–102
French Revolution, 83
Freud, Sigmund, 113, 215n35
Frost, Robert, 162
funeral, in Early Modern Period, 86–89

Gaius, 22–23
gamal. See camel
gammon, 106, 212n7
garlic, 178
gefilte fish, 220n110
Geller, Jay, 112, 203n50

Genack, Menachem, 175–76
Genesis: 25, 40–41; 27:22, 42
Genesis Rabbah 65:1, 43
Gentiles, 61, 109–10; *kashrut* for, 157
Germany: Christianity in, 111–21; gefilte fish in, 220n110; *Judensau* in, 70–75, 73, 203n53; in Modern Period, 111–21; pig in, 216n42, 218n81
Getz, Meir Yehuda, 135
Gideon, Sampson, 96–97
GI Jew, 155–56, 226n56
giudata, 86–89
goats, 15, 40, 70, 76, 202n39
The Godfather, 217n66
Goldschmidt, Meir Aron, 124–25
Goldstein, David B., 85–86, 207n3
Gorenstein, Artie, 155, 226n59
Grant, Ulysses S., 223n4
greed: breast milk and, 80; in *Judensau*, 70–71, 74; pig as symbol of, 40, 57; Shachar on, 202n42
Greenberg, Hank, 230n124
Gross, Aaron, 189n9
Grottanelli, Cristiano, 18–19
The Guide for the Perplexed (Maimonides), 204n69
Gurock, Jeffrey, 176–77

H1N1 (swine flu), 136, 196n12
Haas, Aaron, 143
Hadrian, 42, 51–52
Haggadah, 214n29
halakhah (rabbinic law), 162, 217n61
halal: Impossible Pork and, 175; Islam and, 126
Halton, Patrick, 108–9
Halversen, Charlo, 126
ham: buying votes with, 223n4; at Easter, 209n43; in Israel, 220n128; Marx, K., and, 220n128; in New Zealand, 137; from Spain, 218n81; in United States, 152–56, 153; in United States popular culture, 166–70
ha-Meassef, 123
hand washing, 52–53

Hanukkah, 24; in Babylonian Talmud, 193n43
Hanway, Jonas, 94
Hapsburg Empire, 225n44
hares, 6, 7, 15
Har-Peled, Misgav, 197n23
Harrington (Edgeworth), 213n12
Harris, Marvin, 199n80
Harry Rosenmerck (fictional character), 120–21
Hasidic Jews: censoring by, 179–80; OTD, 163–64
ḥazir (pig), 48, 127
ḥazor (turn), 48
Hebrew Bible, 6–10, 138, 190n19; metaphor in, 190n36; transgressive eating in, 100
Herod the Great, 21
Herzl, Theodor, 113
"he shall live by them," 49, 50, 51, 53, 54
Heuer, Herman, 155–56
Hillel Sandwich, 214n29
Himmler, Heinrich, 113–14
Hogan, Hulk, 169
Hogan, Nick, 169
Hogan Knows Best, 169
Holocaust, 114–15, 122–23, 215n39; refugees from, 138
Holy Lands (Sthers), 119–21, 213n18, 216n53
homoerotic intercourse, 39
Horn, Dara, 156
horned cap (*pileum cornutum*), 71
Horowitz, Roger, 141, 222n2
House of God (*Bethel*), 41
Hunan Pig, 159

ideological persuasion, 30
IDF. *See* Israel Defense Forces
idolatry, 8, 208n33; martyrdom and, 49, 50; Talmud on, 39
Impossible Pork, 175–77
Inferno (Dante), 203n60
infidel (*bardaian*), 117
Inquisition, 75–78
intermarriage, 39, 166–67
In the Image (Horn), 156

Irish: potatoes and, 108–9; in United States, 146
Iron Age, 5
Isaac, 41
Isaiah (individual), 8
Isaiah 40:31, 190n36
Islamic Golden Age, 200n1
Islam/Muslims, 168, 198n62, 216n42; in France, 117, 214n21; halal and, 126, 175; lamb and, 124; superhero of, 216n58
Israel, 41, 42; camel in, 220n117; ham in, 220n128; kibbutzim in, 136, 221n130; in Modern Period, 132–37; Nazis and, 215n39; pig in, 190n32, 220n121, 221n143; pig raising in, 137, 217n67; shrimp in, 221n135
Israel Defense Forces (IDF), 136
Israelites, 6, 15–16; pig raising by, 200n84
Italy: in Modern Period, 121–23; syphilis in, 205n76. *See also* Rome
Iuramentum Iudaeorum (Jewish Oath), 68–70, 69

Jack Rosenblum (fictional character), 110
Jackson, Samuel L., 168
Jacob, 41–42, 218n90
Jesus, 60–62, 66–67, 67, 85, 202n39; devil and, 96–97; Easter and, 97–99
Jewish artichoke (*carciofi alla giudia*), 121, 217n73
Jewish Daily Forward, 145
"Jewish Elders Lift 6,000-Year Ham Ban," 169–70
Jewish Emancipation, 93–97, 95, 209n49
Jewish Enlightenment, 123
The Jewish Naturalization Act (The Jew's Bill), 93–97, 95
Jewish Oath (*Iuramentum Iudaeorum*), 68–70, 69
Jewish Question, in World War II, 113–15, 114
Jewish Revolution, 45–46
Jewish sausage, 205n85
Jewish Swine (*Saujud*), 113, 125–26
Jewish Welfare Board, 154

The Jew of Malta (Marlowe), 207n4
Jews. *See specific topics*
The Jew's Bill (The Jewish Naturalization Act), 93–97, *95*
En Jøde (Goldschmidt), 124–25
John 1:14, 202n28
Jonathan's robbers, 94, 210n62
Jones, Joseph, 108
Joseph of Rohatyn, 100–101
Josephus, 192n17
Judeans, 6
Judensau, 95–96; in Germany, 203n53; in Medieval Period, 70–75, *73*; in Modern Period, 112–13
The Judensau (Shachar), 102–3
Judith Geller (fictional character), 214n20
Jules (fictional character), 168, 193n24, 229n108
Juvenal, 20–21

Kagan, Elena, 158
Kalm, Peter, 222n5
Kamala Khan (fictional character), 216n58
kashrut, 132, 157; beef frye and, 176; situational, 143, 170–72
Katz, Avi, 136–37
khazar, 127
khazeyrim-yid (pigs-Jew), 128
kibbutzim, 136, 221n130
kishke, 229n116
Klein, Misha, 139
Klinkowstein, M., 144–45
Koller, Carl, 113
Koltun-Fromm, Ken, 118
kosher, 42, 61, 68; beef salami as, 229n105; from conversion to Judaism, 228n89; at delicatessens, 229n116; in Early Modern Period mockery, 88–89; fake pig as, 230n4, 231n5; Impossible Pork and, 175–76; lamb as, 44; meat riots, 173; in Medieval Period, 68; metaphor of, 197n36; in military, 225n44; milk and, 101, 226n60; in Soviet Russia, 126–31, *129*, *130*; at *Terefah* Banquet, 224n39; in United States, 142–52, 160–62; in The World To Come, 181, 208n33. *See also* nonkosher

"Koshermania," 169
kosher style, 170–72
Koufax, Sandy, 172, 173, 175, 220n128
Kraemer, Ross, 31
Kramer (fictional character), 229n111
Kreiner, Jamie, 4, 45, 62, 64–65, 81–82
Kurlansky, Mark, 151
Kursheedt, Edwin, 154, 225n50
Kvitko, Leyb, 127–28

lamb, 124, 226n59; as kosher, 44
Landsberger, Benno, 216n42
Last Supper, 98
leavened bread, on Passover, 100, 211n77
Legion, 61–62, 85
Legio X Fretensis (Tenth Legion), 45
Leon Geller (fictional character), 109–10
Leon the Pig Farmer, 109–10, 169, 213n18, 214nn19–20
Lepra, 19
leprosy (*tzara'at*), 196n13
Lev, Aryeh, 155–56
Levi, Joseph C., 153–54
Levine, Harry Gene, 146–50, 224n30
Leviticus: 11, 189n13; 11:3, 190n15; 11:4, 191n40; 11:4-6, 190n16; 11:7, 42, 67, 164, 194n54; 11:13, 10, 191n40; 11:17, 191n40; 11:29, 190n27; 18:5, 49
Leviticus Rabbah 13:5, 42–43
Lincoln, Bruce, 30, 217n64
Liss, David, 204n72
Litzman, Yaakov, 136
Luke 15:11-32, 201n5
Luther, Martin, 72–73

Maccabee, Judah, 41–42
1 Maccabees: 1:47, 194n50; 1:62-63, 27, 194n50
2 Maccabees 6:18-7:42, 26
4 Maccabees, 49; 5-18, 26; 13:2, 28
Macrobius, 21
Maimonides, 204n69

Mama Cass (Ellen Naomi Cohen), 220n128
Mampieri, Martina, 89, 207n15
Mann, Reva, 165, 228n102
Manoah (Rabbi), 87–88
Marcus, Bruce, 159
Markish, Peretz, 129
Marlowe, Christopher, 207n4
Marranos, 75–78, 205n76
marriage, 39, 166–67
The Marrying of Chani Kaufman (Solomon), 110–11
martyrdom: in Christianity, 194n48; in Classical Rabbinic Period, 46–51; in Second Temple Period, 17, 24–32, 27
Marx, Henrietta, 111–12, 115
Marx, Karl, 111–12, 115, 211n81; ham and, 220n128
Matthew 7:6, 201n5
matzah, 144, 214n28; bacon with, 171; Marx and, 211n81; on Passover, 214n29
mazal, 88, 208n32
Mears, Otto, 223n4
Medieval Period: antisemitism in, 59, 83; Christianity in, 59–67, 75–78, 81–82; dehumanization in, 65–70, 67, 69; *Judensau* in, 70–75, 73, 95–96; kosher in, 68; mockery in, 59–82; pig in, 59–82
Meir (Rabbi), 53–54
Meldola, Leah, 108
Mendelsohn, Adam, 225n51
The Merchant of Venice (Shakespeare), 84–86, 207n3, 207n10, 207n12, 209n51
messianic leaders, in Early Modern Period, 99–102
metaphor: in Christianity, 62–65; in Hebrew Bible, 190n36; of kosher, 197n36; pig as, 7–10
Mexico, 136, 205n82, 221n143
mice, 8, 190n27
Michaelis, Johann, 211n84
Michelson, Emily, 89
Milgrom, Genie, 205n82
Miliband, Ed, 213n17

military: kosher in, 225n44; of Rome, 45, 201n13; of United States, 152–56, *153*, 225n44, 225n51, 226n56, 226n58
milk, 101, 226n60
Mills, Lawrence M., 62
Mishnah, 55–56, 101; on pig raising, 137; *Yoma 8:5*, 198n64
mockery, 20–21; in Early Modern Period, 83–103; in Medieval Period, 59–82
Modern Period: England in, 105–11, *107*; France in, 116–21; Germany in, 111–21; Israel in, 132–37; Italy in, 121–23; *Judensau in*, 112–13; New Zealand in, 137–38; pig in, 105–39, 141–73; Scandinavia in, 123–26; United States in, 141–73
Monique Duchene (fictional character), 120–21
Montoro, Antón de, 76–77, 204nn72–73
Moore, Deborah Dash, 154–55
morning after pill (Plan B emergency contraception), 1
Moses, 36, 63, 68, 144
Moss, Candida, 194n48, 195n64
mourning, 56–57
Mr. Rosenblum Dreams in English (Solomon), 110
Mt. Sinai, 36
Mud and shit, 19–20
murder, 49, 50
"Museum of Horrors" (*Musée des Horreurs*), 116
Muslims. *See* Islam

National Pork Producers Council, 181
nausea and horror (*fastidio et orrore*), 64
Nazis, 113–14, *114*; Israel and, 215n39
nesher (eagle), 10
Netanyahu, Benjamin, 137
New Testament, 66, 85, 201n5; Blake on, 106; Gospels of, 60, 61
New Yorker, 22, 23
New Zealand, 137–38
Nirenberg, David, 63
"Nittel Nacht," 227n78

nonkosher, 32, 36–37, 38; France in, 116–21; pregnancy and, 51; Rabbi Aqiba and, 48; rabbinic law on, 217n61; shrimp as, 156–62; in United States, 146–62, 153
Norway, 125–26
N R K, 125–26

The O.C., 227n78
off the *derekh* (OTD), 162–66, 229n104; on Yom Kippur, 228n95
Old Testament, 64, 67, 68, 201n21; plague in, 213n8
Olyan, Saul, 196n14
The Onion, 169–70
oppression, 40, 57, 137
Oral Torah, 36
Orthodox Jews, 170; in military, 154; OTD, 162–66; pig and, 231n15
Orwell, George, 109, 136
OTD. *See* off the *derekh*
Other (Aḥer), 29, 58, 79, 108, 181
Outlawed Pigs (Barak-Erez), 132–35
owl (*yanshuf*), 12
oysters, 151, 170, 224n33
Ozick, Cynthia, 227n85

Palestine, 17, 191n7; in Classical Rabbinic Period, 36
Pallontrotti, Melchior, 87–89
Passover: Christianity and, 64; Easter and, 98–99, 111; *Haggadah* on, 214n29; leavened bread on, 100, 211n77; *matzah* on, 214n29; in Modern Period England, 108; observing of, 223n2; Sabbatians and, 100; transgressive eating on, 100; in United States, 144
Pastrizio, Giovanni, 87–88
path (*derekh*), 162–66
Paul, 61
Paul III (Pope), 72–73
Paulita, Tia, 205n82
"pearls before swine," 201n5
Peppa Pig (fictional character), 160, 228n87
Persians, 15
Petronius, 20

Philo of Alexandria, 22–23, 30–32, 193n38, 195n69
Phoenicians, 19
pig: animality of, 4–5; antisemitism and, 156–62; bones of, 11–12, 202n31; in Brazil, 138–39; breast milk of, 78–79; breeding of, 127–28, 220n120; censoring of, 179–81; Christianity and, 59–69, 75–78, 81–82, 108, 204n72, 211n84; in Classical Rabbinic Period, 2, 35–58, 45; comedy on, 20–21; deliciousness of, 22–23, 23; as dirty, 19–20, 55, 61–62, 70, 195n6, 199n80; in Early Modern Period, 83–103; Easter and, 97–99; in England, 105–11, 107; euphemisms for, 37–40; eyes of, 20; fake products of, 175–77, 230n4, 231n5; forced ingestion of, 17, 24–32, 27; in France, 116–21; at funeral, 86–89; in Germany, 111–21, 216n42, 218n81; in Hebrew Bible, 6–10; in Israel, 132–37, 190n32, 220n121, 221n143; in Italy, 121–23; meanings of, 4; in Medieval Period, 59–82; as metaphor, 7–10; in Modern Period, 105–39, 141–73; in New Zealand, 137–38; Orthodox Jews and, 231n15; as other white meat, 181; plague and, 38, 213n8; pretending to eat, 49–54; real and perceived, 5–6; rectum of, 70–75, 73; Rome and, 40–62; in Scandinavia, 123–26; in Second Temple Period, 15–34; skin ailments and, 19, 38, 192n20, 196nn13–15; in soil, 19; in Soviet Russia, 126–31, 129, 130; in Spain, 218n81; in Ukraine, 131, 220n114; in United States, 141–73; 222n5, 223n7; weaponization of, 43–46, 123; worship of, 20
pig blood, 8, 24; Christianity and, 206n91; dipping finger in, 54
Pig Faced Lady (fictional character), 106–8, 107, 180
piggulim (unclean things), 8
pig raising, 55–57, 109–10, 120–21; in Babylonian Talmud, 200n86; by Christians, 216n40; in Israel, 137, 217n67; by Israelites, 200n84; in Poland, 219n97

pigs-Jew (*khazeyrim-yid*), 128
the pig speaks for itself (*sus ipso loquitur*), 19
pileum cornutum (horned cap), 71
Pittsburg Platform, 150, 156
plague, 196n12; antisemitism on, 213n8; in Old Testament, 213n8; pig and, 38, 213n8
Plan B emergency contraception (morning after pill), 1
Plato, 194n54
Plutarch, 18–20, 192nn16–20, 193n29
Poland: Catholicism in, 101–2; pig raising in, 219n97
Pollan, Michael, 224n40
pork chop (*chuleta*), 205n82
Porkopolis (Cincinnati), 150, 224n34
pork tapeworm (*Taenia solium*), 165–66
pork terrorism, 81–82
"Pork — the Other White Meat," 181
Porphyry, 19
Portnoy's Complaint (Roth), 225n55
potatoes, Irish and, 108–9
poultry: in United States, 141. *See also* chicken
Praise the Lard, 221n130
pregnancy, 50–51, 198n64, 199n67
prestidigitation, 54, 199n77
Price, Max, 43, 81, 180, 191n38, 202n23
Prince John (fictional character), 229n107
Proverbs, 9
Psalms, 10; 137:4, 191n2
Pulp Fiction, 167–68, 193n24, 229n108

quadrupeds (*behemah*), 6, 17

rabbinic Judaism, 36
rabbinic law (*halakhah*), 162, 217n61
Rabbis. *See* Classical Rabbinic Period
The Rabbi's Cat (Sfar), 117–19
Rabin, Shari, 154, 225n50
Rajak, Tessa, 25, 30
Rakoff, David, 156–58, 226n66, 227n76
rape, 31
Rashi, 39, 56

Rathenau, Walther, 113, 215n38
Ravitch, Melech, 128, 130, 178, 220n106
Rav Papa, 37
Rebekah, 41
Recceswinth (King), 64
Reform Judaism, 216n43; situational kashrut and, 170–71; in United States, 150–56, 223n33, 224n31
Renaissance (Age of Discovery), 83
Revelation of Torah, 36
Richson, Charles, 213n8
"Rivers of Babylon," 191n2
Robin Hood, 229n107
rock badger, 6, 7, 32, 162, 190n16
Rome: in Babylonian Talmud, 198n51; Christianity in, 57–80; in Early Modern Period, 83–103; military of, 45, 201n13; pig and, 40–62; women of, 46–48. *See also* Second Temple
Rosen (Rabbi), 161
Rosewater, Edward, 222n1
Roth, Philip, 148, 225n55
Rothschild, Henri, 116

Sabbath: dogs on, 56; *feijoada* on, 139; Freud and, 215n35; observance of, 17, 20; Shabbat dinner on, 160–62; transgressive eating on, 101; in United States, 144–45
Sabbatians, 100–102; Israel and, 135
sacrificial system, 15
safe treyf, 146–49, 177, 224n30
Sapinsky, Ruth, 143–44, 223n3
Sarkozy, Nicolas, 117
satirists, 20–22, 33–34, 193n29
Satlow, Michael L., 189n4
Saujud (Jewish Swine), 113, 125–26
scabies, 19
Scandinavia, 123–26
Schäfer, Peter, 18, 194n44
Schandbild, 70
Scholem, Gershom, 99
Schrödinger's pig, 148
Schudt, Johann Jacob, 196n19
Schumer, Charles, 158

Schwarz, Leon, 144
Scrabble, 125–26, 218n91
Second Temple, destruction of, 40–46, 56, 158, 221n124
Second Temple Period: Christianity in, 60–61; martyrdom in, 17, 24–32, 27; non-Jews in, 17–21; pig in, 15–34; pretending to eat pork in, 49
Seinfeld, 229n111
Seleucid, 25
self-control, 29; of Rabbi Aqiba, 47
semiotics, 16–17, 29
Sermon on the Mount, 61
sex: beard and, 212n6; Catholics and, 172; homoerotic intercourse, 39; martyrdom and, 49, 50; during mourning period, 56–57; Rabbi Aqiba and, 46–48; as "that thing," 196n18
Sfar, Joann, 117–19
Shabbat dinner, 160–62
Shachar, Isaiah, 71, 94, 95–96, 102–3, 113; on greed, 202n42
Shakespeare, William, 83, 84–86, 103, 106, 207n3, 207n10, 207n12, 209n51
Sherlock Holmes (fictional character), 46
Shmarya Wolf (fictional character), 219n104
Shmuel (fictional character), 168–69
shrimp: in Israel, 221n135; as nonkosher, 156–62
Shternshis, Anna, 129, 131
shul, 145
Shulamis (fictional character), 111
Shylock (fictional character), 84–86, 96, 207n3, 207n12
"The Signifying Swine," 16–17, 21, 29, 32, 33, 191n4; Christianity and, 64
Simon of Trent, 205n80
Singer, I. J., 219n104
Singer, Isaac Bashevis, 128, 130, 178
situational kashrut, 143, 170–72
skin ailments, 19, 38, 192n20, 196nn13–15
Smith, Jonathan Z., 189n4
soccer, in Italy, 123

Solodkin v. Municipality of Beth Shemesh, 133–34, 190n32
Solomon, Natasha, 110–11
Sonny Corleone (fictional character), 217n66
Soviet Russia, 126–31, 129, 130
Spain, 204nn64–65; ham from, 218n81; pig in, 218n81
Spiegelman, Art, 215n39
Stahl, Ronit, 154
State of Israel v. Shmukler, 133
Stein, Abby Chava, 162–63, 228n95
Steinfeld, Paul, 155
Sthers, Amanda, 119–21, 213n18, 216n53
Suitors to the Pig Laced Lady (Cruikshank), 106–8, *107*
sus ipso loquitur (the pig speaks for itself), 19
Sussman (Rabbi), 151
Sutherland, John, 213n8
swine flu (H1N1), 136, 196n12
swine stigmas, in Classical Rabbinic Period, 55–57
syphilis, in Italy, 205n76

Tacitus, 19
Taenia solium (pork tapeworm), 165–66
Talmud: in Classical Rabbinic Period, 37, 38; on idolatry, 39; *Judensau* and, 73–74. See also Babylonian Talmud
Talmudic tractate on idolatry (*Avodah Zarah*), 39
Tarantino, Quentin, 167–68
Tenth Legion (Legio X Fretensis), 45
Terefah Banquet, 150, 151, 156; kosher at, 224n39
Thal, Sarah, 143, 144
there is no accounting for taste (*de gustibus non est disputandum*), 37
Titus, 44–45, 197n41, 198n42
Toaff, Ariel, 217n72
To Dust, 168–69, 213n18
Tokarczuk, Olga, 99, 212n85
Torah: Bag Bag on, 178; Jewish Oath and, 68–70, *69*; women and, 135

transgressive eating: in Early Modern Period, 83–84; on Passover, 100; Rakoff on, 227n76; by Sabbatians, 100–102
Travolta, John, 168
treyf (nonkosher), 146–50. *See also* safe treyf
Tuchman, Gaye, 146–50, 224n30
turn (*ḥazor*), 48
Turow, Scott, 172
tzara'at (leprosy), 196n13
Tzvi, Shabbatai, 99–102

Ukraine, 131, 220n114
Ullucci, Daniel, 194n54
unclean things (*piggulim*), 8
United States: chicken in, 143–44, 222nn1–2; Chinese food in, 146–50, 158–60; eggs in, 226n57; ham in, 152–56, 153; Jewish literature in, 156––162; kosher in, 142–52, 160–62; military of, 152–56, 153, 225n44, 225n51, 226n56, 226n58; in Modern Period, 141–73; nonkosher in, 146–62, 153; pig in, 141–73, 222n5, 223n7; popular culture in, 166–70; poultry in, 141; Reform Judaism in, 150–56, 223n33, 224n31
urine, 203n50
usury, 203n60

Vespasian, 43–45, 45, 197n41, 198n42
vestustas (antiquity), 64
Vincent (fictional character), 168
Visigoths, 64
Voltaire, 89–90
Vox Populi, Vox Dei, or the Jew Act Repealed, 96–97

Wallenbrock, Nicole Beth, 118, 214n21
Waters, Roger, 215n39

Weissman-Joselit, Jenna, 171, 176
Wertheimer, Elaine, 204n73
wet nurses, 78–79
Wilson, "Uncle Sam," 226n56
Wise, Isaac Meyer, 151, 224n40
"A woman and a girl feed pigs at sundown," 227n85
women, 9; Aryan, 215n38; censoring of, 179–81; forced ingestion by, 30–32; genitalia of, 196n20; in Israel, 135; in kosher meat riots, 173; pregnancy of, 50–51, 198n64, 199n67; Rabbi Aqiba and, 46–48; Torah and, 135; weaker mind of, 29; as wet nurses, 78–79
The World To Come, 88; kosher in, 181, 208n33
World War I, 154
World War II: in Italy, 121–22; Jewish Question in, 113–15, *114*; United States military in, 154–56, 226n58
Written Torah. *See* Hebrew Bible

xenophobic laws, 25, 194n46

yanshuf (owl), 12
Yiddish, 178, 219n96; dogs in, 219n95; in Soviet Russia, 126–31, *129*, *130*; in United States, 145
Yishai, Eli, 190n32
Yoma 8:5, 198n64
Yom Kippur (Day of Atonement), 50; bacon on, 162–66; Greenberg and, 230n124; in Israel, 136; Koufax and, 220n128; observing of, 223n2; OTD on, 228n95; pregnancy at, 198n64; in United States, 144, 156–57, 162–66

ABOUT THE AUTHOR

JORDAN D. ROSENBLUM is the Belzer Professor of Classical Judaism and Director of the Mosse/Weinstein Center for Jewish Studies at the University of Wisconsin–Madison. He is the author of *Rabbinic Drinking: What Beverages Teach Us about Rabbinic Literature*; *The Jewish Dietary Laws in the Ancient World*; and *Food and Identity in Early Rabbinic Judaism*, as well as the coeditor of four volumes, including *Feasting and Fasting: The History and Ethics of Jewish Food* (published by New York University Press) and *Animals and the Law in Antiquity*.

www.ingramcontent.com/pod-product-compliance
Lightning Source LLC
Chambersburg PA
CBHW031145020426
42333CB00013B/517